Dear Bishop !

Memoirs of the author concerning
The HISTORY of the BLUE ARMY

by
John M. Haffert

AMI International Press
Washington, N.J. (USA) 07882

NIHIL OBSTAT: Rev. Msgr. William E. Maguire, S.T.D.

Having been advised by competent authority that this book contains no teaching contrary to the Faith and Morals as taught by the Church, I approve its publication according to the Decree of the Sacred Congregation for the Doctrine of the Faith. This approval does not necessarily indicate any promotion or advocacy of the theological or devotional content of the work.

IMPRIMATUR: Most Rev. John C. Reiss, J.C.D.
Bishop of Trenton
October 7, 1981

This Book Dedicated To
The Most Rev. George W. Ahr, S.T.D.,
Seventh Bishop of Trenton
— and to —
The Most Rev. John P. Venancio, D.D.,
Second Bishop of Leiria - Fatima
and
Former International President,
The Blue Army of Our Lady of the Rosary of Fatima

Above: The Most Rev. John P. Venancio, D.D. (left), and the
Most Rev. George W. Ahr, S.T.D. (right), at the dedication and
blessing of the Holy House, U.S.A. on August 22, 1973. At the
time of the dedication, Bishop Venancio was the Ordinary of the
Diocese of Leiria-Fatima and International President of the Blue
Army, and Bishop Ahr was the Ordinary of the Diocese of
Trenton.

TABLE OF CONTENTS

iv

phere of holiness comes to our National Center; 8) Shrine at our National Center proposed; 9) Bishop decides it should be built now

PREFACE

On July 14, 1978, my Bishop, the Most Rev. George W. Ahr, gave me a personal mandate to record my recollections concerning the history of the Blue Army.

Three weeks before Christmas, 1980, I had the occasion to visit Bishop Ahr. I apologized that his letter of July 14, 1978, *was still pinned to the wall directly over my desk,* but said that I would "get around to it."

Since His Excellency knew of the special difficulties I had encountered at that time, I felt sure he would say something like: "Well, I know you have been under strain and will do it when you have time." But instead, to my surprise, His Excellency looked at me seriously and said:

"It is important that you write this story. The Blue Army is important to the Church."

Perhaps looking for an additional excuse, I added: "I have difficulty remembering."

The Bishop said (and as it proved, correctly!): *"You will remember one thing...and that will remind you of another."*

Two days later I pulled the plugs to my office telephones and began to work. I began by writing a note to the retired Bishop of Fatima, the Most Rev. John P. Venancio, telling him what I have said above, and asking his blessings and prayers. (I had always felt that in the Blue Army we had *two* Bishops "in charge": our local Bishop and the Bishop of Fatima.) It was a month before Bishop Venancio was able to answer:

"I am very pleased that you are writing (as only you can do!) the marvelous history of the Blue Army. I rejoice that

Bishop Ahr is of the same opinion and gave you a mandate to do so already two and a half years ago! And I ask myself: Where is your obedience? His Excellency was your Bishop and always your great friend. So, to the work! You have a gift for writing. And the Blue Army—and still more Our Lady of Fatima—merits this effort on your part."

Bishop Venancio sent this letter from Portugal on January 13, 1981. And by that time (only three weeks after I had begun), I was able to reply *that I had already finished!*

Writing under obedience (after more than two and a half years of hesitation and procrastination), I felt that I was not writing "alone." Not only was I strengthened by the virtue of obedience, but also *by the community of prayer and love of millions who have responded to the requests of Our Lady of Fatima* (through the Blue Army) to bring about the fulfillment of Her great promise—the conversion of Russia and the triumph of Her Immaculate Heart in the world.

Many of those involved (like Msgr. Colgan, Bishop da Silva, Cardinal Tisserant, and many others!) are now in Heaven with our Queen, Our Lady of Victory, Help of All Christians. Their "aura" pervades these pages.

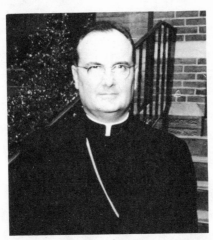

Above: The Most Rev. George W. Ahr, S.T.D., on the steps of St. Mary's Church in Plainfield, N.J., in 1953, when His Excellency spoke on "Mary, My Hope" at a Blue Army national convention. (See p. 149.)

Chapter One

---

1) Blessed Nuno relic opens door - 2) The Bishop and the Secret - 3) The Blue Army Pledge is written - 4) First Saturdays - 5) Lucia herself - 6) Frightening responsibility

Below: Most Rev. Jose Correia da Silva, first Bishop of Fatima, with Lucia...as the author saw them in 1946.

SISTER LUCIA
AND THE PLEDGE

"You may promulgate this as coming from me."
— *Most Rev. Jose Correia da Silva,*
first Bishop of Fatima

I n 1946 I had been referred to the Bishop of Fatima as "a prominent American Catholic" by a Carmelite in Lisbon who knew the Bishop well. As a result the Bishop invited me to come to Portugal with permission to interview Sr. Lucia, sole survivor of the three children who had seen Our Lady of Fatima.

I was not entirely unfamiliar with the country since I had already written and had published the first English biography of the national hero of Portugal, Blessed Nuno, to whom the Bishop of Fatima was particularly devoted.

On the day that I arrived at the Bishop's palace in Leiria, His Excellency had just been given an important relic of Blessed Nuno by the Marquesa de Cadaval, a Portuguese noblewoman who was a blood descendant of the Blessed. It was a fortuitous and, for me, most important coincidence.

Because it is so significant, I feel a few words of explanation are in order.

To understand how rare a major relic of Blessed Nuno would be, one must realize that he was not only beatified (and undoubtedly will one day be canonized), but he was considered, as we have said, a *major* national hero in Portuguese history. He was, in a sense, the "George Washington" of Portugal.

One can imagine how great would be the value of a major relic of George Washington, if this were a Catholic nation and George Washington had been beatified. Indeed, one can imagine the value of *anything* which belonged to George Washington, let alone an important

1

first class relic, kept in his own family for some 600 years!

The Bishop of Fatima had a particular devotion to Blessed Nuno for good reason. As I had explained in *The Peacemaker*,[1] Blessed Nuno was the "precursor of Fatima." He was the third Count of Ourem, which is the district of Fatima. It was just at the foot of the mountain of Fatima that Blessed Nuno had fought "the great battle"—commemorated by one of the most magnificent monuments in Portugal (and perhaps in all Europe) which determined the future course of the Portuguese nation.

This monument was built by Blessed Nuno and King John I of Portugal in thanksgiving to Our Lady for the victory, and in it were housed hundreds of Dominican monks to pray the Rosary, both in thanksgiving for the victory and for the future of Portugal. And so important is this monument that within it today is Portugal's Tomb of the Unknown Soldier from the First World War.

Before the apparitions of Our Lady of Fatima, this diocese, which includes Batalha and Fatima, had been without a Bishop. After the apparitions of Our Lady, the Holy See appointed Bishop Jose Alva Correia da Silva, who became known then as the "first Bishop of Fatima." And the new Bishop was given to understand that one of his major duties was to evaluate the Miracle of Fatima.

For seven years, prior to the apparitions of Our Lady, Portugal had been under an atheistic rule. Her clergy had been persecuted. Bishop da Silva had suffered in this persecution and as a result was partially crippled and could walk only with great difficulty. (Indeed, in his later years he could not walk at all.)

When I met this saintly man, it became apparent that my Carmelite friend in Lisbon had given me a great build-up as the author of the only English biography of Blessed Nuno, because the Bishop repeated over and over—still filled with the joy of the coincidence: "And to think, this very day that you come, I have been given this precious relic of Blessed Nuno!"

2 At the Bishop's house, I sat at the table on his right, with the four Canons. During that first dinner, Canon Jose Galamba de Oliveira, who was the "go between" with Lucia for the diocese and the Canonical Commission of Investigation, turned to me when the Bishop had left the room momentarily and asked: *"Why don't you ask the Bishop to open the Secret?"*

Endeavoring not to show my ignorance concerning Fatima—which at that time was almost complete—I simply looked at him without expression. He continued: "The Bishop can open the Secret. He does not have to wait until 1960."

Just then the Bishop returned and there was a long moment of awkward silence. The other Canons were obviously also interested in seeing whether or not I would broach the subject to the Bishop—the subject on which apparently he had silenced them on more than one previous occasion and on which Canon Oliveira was now taking advantage of a newcomer to again broach the question.

I finally broke the silence by saying to the Bishop that I understood there was a Secret still to be opened and was there some reason why the Bishop did not wish to open it.

His Excellency looked up with what to me was an unexpected degree of firmness.

As I look back on this, I can well realize why the Bishop did not want to open that Secret!

What a burden he had endured in those early years of evaluating Fatima! What a responsibility! Here was a message foretelling that another and a worse war was to begin in the reign of Pius XI. Here was a prediction that when an unknown light would be seen (over Europe)[2], it was a sign that God was about to chastise the world for its sins! Here was a message that error was to spread from an atheistic Russia *throughout the entire world*—and at that time Russia seemed virtually the least likely nation to become a threatening world power.

It was enough to be faced with the responsibility of determining whether or not the Miracle of the Sun *had been truly a miracle,* and that all of these extraordinary and unbelievable messages from heaven were autehentic. But to be confronted with the contents of the first parts of the Secret of Fatima and *with the responsibility of making them known to the Pope and the world*—it was enough to daunt the heart of the stoutest ecclesiastic.

The next day I left for Porto, the northern city of Portugal, where Lucia was a nun in the Dorothean Convent on the outskirts of the city. The Bishop had given me a letter indicating that she was to receive me as though he, himself, were also present. The Mother Superior needed no further prompting and even made a gesture of leaving us alone in the parlor. When I saw that she was about to leave, I remonstrated and said: "But Mother, are you not going to remain?"

I had planned to sit on the edge of a small settee. Before the Superior had come in, I had placed an arm chair right next to the settee so that I would be very close to Lucia during the interview. When Lucia saw that the Superior was going to remain, she came over, picked up the arm-chair (and I was amazed at how easily she handled it, for it was quite heavy), and carried it to a position facing the settee.

I immediately thought, with some disappointment, that she had decided that she was not going to sit so close to that layman from America.

But then just as easily and with just as much naturalness she picked up a simple chair and set it down where the armchair had been. She had merely moved the better chair in place for the Mother Superior.

The interview which followed lasted, to the best of my memory, for almost four hours. But it seemed timeless. I felt I had only just sat down when I found myself rising in farewell.

When one reads of other interviews with Lucia, especially the one she had in Pontevedra with another layman of whom she speaks critically in her Memoirs, perhaps it would be important to point out in this "history" that I had two special advantages:

1) I had had previous experience, over a period of years, with a similar privileged person and I knew that she would consider herself merely an instrument of God, perhaps less worthy than many others might have been, and she would not only dislike being treated as someone "special," but would positively resent it.

2) I was almost completely preoccupied with my sincere interest in finding out exactly what was necessary in order to obtain the conversion of Russia.

Apparently it was not only my own ignorance I was showing, but the ignorance of many others (because they were surprised when they heard this) when I opened the conversation by saying:

"Of course, Sister, I know that it is the Rosary which is the first and most important request of Our Lady of Fatima, but what are the other things we must do in order to obtain the conversion of Russia?"

She immediately answered: "But the Rosary is not the most important request."

And she went on to explain that the essential request of Our Lady of Fatima was conveyed to the children in the very first question Our Lady put to them when She said:

"Will you be willing to accept whatever God will send you and to offer it up for the conversion of sinners and in reparation for the offenses committed against the Immaculate Heart of Mary?"

Over and over again during those precious hours I was in her company, she emphasized that it is the fulfillment of one's daily duty, according to one's state in life (and the sanctification of this effort in reparation for our sins and for the conversion of sinners) which is the primary condition for the turning back of the tide of evil which threatens today's world, and which will also bring us the great favor of the conversion of Russia and an era of peace "for mankind."

But she also stressed that the Rosary is indeed important, because it is one of Our Lady's *principal aids* given to us *to facilitate the sanctification of our daily duty.*

In the Mysteries of the Rosary, we have not only a synthesis of the principal mysteries of the life of Christ, but we have the inspiration to overcome every possible temptation. (Indeed, many years later I wrote a book called *Sex and the Mysteries,* with 450 separate and different thoughts from the Mysteries of the Rosary just on the one subject of purity according to one's state in life.)

We talked about the Scapular and of consecration to the Immaculate Heart of Mary, and of the importance of this as an additional aid to the sanctification of daily duty.

I had with me a few yards of brown wool which I had carried first to England where, almost 700 years before, Our Lady had given the Scapular to St. Simon Stock. I had also taken it to various Marian shrines and had touched it to places of Our Lady's apparitions. Finally, during a private audience with Pius XII, I had asked the Pope to bless it, explaining that it was to be used for scapulars for persons who were helping in our apostolate. And the Pope actually took the cloth *into his hands*, held it for a moment, and then returned it to me, saying with a smile: *"It is all blessed."*

I wanted Lucia also to touch this cloth, but I did not want to offend her by indicating that this was my purpose. So when I asked her about the apparition of Our Lady of Mt. Carmel with the Scapular, I took the cloth from my briefcase, held it out to her and said: "Sister, was Our Lady clothed in a color like this?"

She was reflecting intently about the vision and about her answers, and almost without thinking she took the cloth in her hands, and then, as she was answering, placed it in her lap. She held it there during much of the rest of the interview, occasionally reaching down and picking bits of lint that glistened on its surface.

The pledge, as I wrote it down during the course of this interview, contained the following conditions: Pray the Rosary daily; Wear the Scapular as a sign of consecration to the Immaculate Heart; Offer up the sacrifices demanded by daily duty, extending our Morning Offering through the day.

Several things about it bothered me. But before I mention them, perhaps I ought to recall—just because of their interest—at least two other events of this interview:

4   We had completed the pledge, and she was satisfied. "Yes," she said, "these are the basic things which must be done in order to obtain the conversion of Russia." Yet she had not mentioned the Five First Saturdays.

When I called this to her attention, she replied that the Five First Saturdays were important because they were the occasion of *renewing our purpose,* of strengthening our resolve and our motives once a month and thus being able to do better in the month that followed in fulfilling these basic requests of Our Lady which centered on the sanctification of daily duty.

And when one reflects upon it, this is indeed the effect of the five conditions of the First Saturdays:

We are asked *to go to confession* on the first Saturday of the month whether we have committed mortal sins or not, and thus carefully to examine what we have done in the past month, and to resolve to do better and to mend our lives. We are asked also on this particular day not only *to pray the Rosary,* as we must do every day but, in addition, *to spend 15 minutes "with Our Lady" meditating upon the Mysteries*—thus practicing that essential element of the life of Christ to sanctify our own lives. And finally, we are reminded of the importance of reparation for the offenses committed against the Immaculate Heart of Mary and of offering up our daily sacrifices in reparation. All of the First Saturday conditions (*Confession, Communion, Rosary and the 15-minute meditation*) *are to be offered in the spirit of reparation* for the offenses committed against the Immaculate Heart of Mary.

And, of course, we know that in reply to a question from Lucia, Our Lord Himself explained that the reason for the *five* Saturdays was because He wants reparation made for the denial of Our Lady's Immaculate Conception, of Her divine maternity, of Her perpetual virginity, depriving children of devotion to Her, and dishonor to Her images.

While I was concentrating on the conditions of Our Lady 5 for the conversion of Russia and world peace, it happened that I asked two personal questions which gave a trenchant insight into Lucia herself and into her personal experiences with Our Lady.

It will be remembered that the children were imprisoned by the atheist authorities on August 13, 1917, just as they were about to go to the Cova da Iria for their meeting with Our Lady. After two days of interrogation, they were threatened with death in boiling oil if they refused to reveal the secret. The atheists, of course, fully expected to break down the children's resistance with this horrifying threat, thus giving the authorities every reason to proclaim that the little visionaries were either unworthy of having seen a vision from heaven or had never seen it, since by their own admission they would have betrayed the trust which heaven had strictly charged them to keep.

Jacinta and Francisco consoled each other in the prison because Our Lady had said that She would come soon and take them to heaven. They were convinced that now, after a few brief, agonizing moments of pain in a vat of boiling oil, they would be united with Our Lady in heaven.

But what did Lucia think?

During that second apparition, on June 13, just two months before, when the children had asked Our Lady if She would take them back to heaven with Her, She had said She would come soon for Francisco and Jacinta, but then added:

"However, Lucia, you are to learn to read and write. Through you, God wishes to establish in the world devotion to my Immaculate Heart."

So Lucia was to remain! Indeed, we know from her Memoirs that when Our Lady spoke these words she said she felt as though a knife were plunged at that moment into her heart—so great was her sense of grief—to think that she was going to be left alone without Francisco and Jacinta, besides being unable to go back to heaven with Our Lady.

And what did she think these two months later when *all three* were told flatly that they would be boiled alive in a vat of oil if they did not reveal the secret?

They had been given two hours—there, with criminals, in an evil-smelling prison—to make up their minds.

Lucia's answer amazed me—and since it was not included in her Memoirs, I am so pleased that I was inspired to ask it. She said quietly:

"When they took me out, I thought Francisco and Jacinta were already dead. And at that moment I thought that perhaps I had misunderstood Our Lady, and that I, too, was about to die."

Oh, the mystery of Our Lady's relationship with these three innocent children! What lessons for all of us!

That same day that they were freed from the prison (August 15), Our Lady appeared to them at Valinhos. How often I have stood on that spot and thought of the awesome statement Our Lady made to them on that day!

She said that because of what these atheists had done to them "the Miracle in October will not be as great."

We so often think that we are secure because of the promise of Our Lady that Russia will be converted—but each day that the conversion is delayed—each day that their evil is perpetrated throughout the world—the great rewards that God intends for us all *are diminished!*

And we are responsible—because it rests within our own grasp to shorten those days!

And then Our Lady said something which in depth seems more terrible, especially in view of the fact that these three children had that very day been willing to be cast into vats of boiling oil for Her.

Instead of reaching down and taking seven-year-old Jacinta into Her arms, or reaching to touch the shoulder of little Francisco, or perhaps reaching to caress the upturned face of Lucia, who had suffered so much in those few months since the first apparition—Our Lady spoke these soul-shattering words: *"Continue to make sacrifices! So many souls are lost because there is no one to pray and make sacrifices for them!"*

Just think—She wanted these children (who were so ready to do what She wished) to continue with their great sacrifices because *there is no one...*!

And the great lament of Our Lady: *"So many souls are lost...because there is no one to pray and to make sacrifices for them."* 6

Is it any wonder, Your Excellency, that I have never taken time out to write a "history"—or to do so many other things—when I have been constantly haunted by these words of Our Lady and of the crying need of securing more and more pledges, of building up more and more Blue Army cells in which dedicated souls—imitating that first cell of three children—would pray the Rosary together, contemplate the flood of evil in the world, and firmly resolve that they at least will do what they can to pray and make sacrifices so that fewer souls will be lost?

But I remember when you told us in the late 1970's to go ahead with the building of the Shrine of the Immaculate Heart of Mary in Washington, N.J., that my own thought was contrary. I thought we should spend that money to put Fatima on television, to publish more books and pamphlets, to proclaim the message of Our Lady. But inspired as you always have been by the Holy Spirit, you knew that the Shrine would be a greater declaration than any book, more lasting in its effect upon the nation than any television program, more effective in proclaiming Her message than anything else we could possibly have done.

And I pray that the sacrifice entailed in writing this little "history" may fill many souls with the urgency of responding to the requests of our dearest Mother who contemplates with grieving eyes the innumerable souls being lost in our sin-drenched world and the awful ruin towards which we are catapulting ourselves, and who pleads "with an indescribable sadness and tenderness," as Sr. Lucia expressed it, for the cooperation of, perhaps only a few, to open the floodgates of grace and mercy and so turn back the tide of evil.

FOOTNOTES

1. **The Peacemaker**, AMI Press. Actually I could not be considered the real author of this book. Fr. Gabriel Pausback, Assistant General of the Carmelites to whom I had been co-worker in the Scapular Apostolate in New York as I became to Msgr. Colgan in the Blue Army, had translated the work

from an Italian book and then, when he had to return to Rome after the war, gave the material to me. I simply "rewrote it."

2. The "Great Sign" was seen on the night of January 25-26, 1938, two months before Hitler invaded Austria — in the reign of Pope Pius XI. In a letter in 1941 to her Bishop, Lucia said that if scientists were to investigate the "aurora borealis" of January 25-26, 1938, they would discover that it could not have been a borealis.

Below: The Most Rev. Jerome J. Hastrich, D.D., President of the Blue Army in the United States.

After reading this "history" of the founding of the Blue Army, Bishop Hastrich said:

"We have to try our best to picture the Blue Army existing without our aid, when we are no longer here. This is a real challenge: To create an organization that will last beyond a person's life. It is a challenge that we must meet."

Chapter Two

Monsignor Harold Colgan speaking at a Blue Army meeting in Cleveland on September 11, 1954.

DIFFICULT BEGINNING

There will be an explosion for Our Lady!"
— *Fr. Daniel A. Lord, S.J.*

Many years ago, when Bishop Cletus Benjamin was made the Secretary to Cardinal Dougherty of Philadelphia, all his friends sent him condolences. They thought the Cardinal was "pretty tough."

Certainly this wonderful Archbishop of Philadelphia, who perhaps did more for Catholic education than any single Bishop in history, was a man inflexibly dedicated to duty. He used to get up very early in the morning (I'm afraid to state the hour for fear that some might consider it an exaggeration), make an hour of preparation before his Mass and arrive at his office every day promptly at eight o'clock.

One day a famous Catholic author had an interview with the Cardinal and asked permission to write his biography. Bishop Benjamin told me some years later that the Cardinal was not exactly abrupt, but it was one of the shortest interviews imaginable. His Eminence simply said:

"I have done nothing but my duty. Go and write the story of someone who has done *more* than his duty."

I am sure that this would have been just about the same answer a writer would have received who had approached *you* (addressed to Bishop Ahr) with his suggestion of writing *your* story.

And I am full of misgivings about writing of my role in the Blue Army because I have done *less* than my duty. While I might write of some of the things I have done, together with humble accomplishments of others, like Msgr. Colgan, I tremble at the thought of those things I have not done.

14

Not long after he had retired as pastor of St. Mary's Church in Plainfield, N.J., Msgr. Colgan suddenly said to me one day: "John, what do you really think of me?"

He looked at me intently with those wonderful, clear blue eyes of his. And I think I was a little more surprised by the serious way he awaited my answer than by the suddenness and somewhat strangeness of the question itself.

I wish I could remember exactly what I said. It would be the right way to begin this book because the story of the Blue Army (under the *title* of "Blue Army") began with Msgr. Colgan.

Do you remember the time that you were present and he gave that wonderful homily on the Immaculate Heart of Mary? It was a magnificent sermon and he said to you afterwards: "I guess you were surprised."

The gist of what I said to him in answer to his strange question was that I knew he often did and said things which put himself in a humble light, but that he was capable of doing even extraordinary things. Father Daniel Lord, S.J., who for many years was the leader of the Sodality of Our Lady in the United States and developed the "Schools of Catholic Action" from coast to coast, considered Msgr. Colgan one of the finest Marian priests in the United States. And, in God's Providence, Fr. Lord played an important part in my own decision to form a sort of "spiritual partnership" with Msgr. Colgan for the work of the Blue Army.

I was in a state of semi-retirement at the time, intending to no longer be actively involved in apostolate leadership after having left the Scapular Apostolate in New York in July of 1948.

I had moved out to a fairly remote farm in the northwestern part of the state of New Jersey with only one major piece of "unfinished business" from my previous apostolate. It was the Pilgrim Virgin statue which the Bishop of Fatima had blessed and confided to me for quiet (and, if necessary, secret) transfer to Russia, while two identical statues were traveling publicly from Fatima, one eastward and one westward around the world.

I had met Msgr. Colgan while lecturing in his parish during my previous apostolate and was much impressed both by him and his parishioners. They filled his ample auditorium to capacity and listened eagerly to the talk I gave on the Message of Fatima. Many in the audience

were wearing little blue ribbons and Msgr. Colgan
explained that he had asked everyone there who had made
a commitment to respond to the Message of Fatima to
wear something blue as outward evidence of that commitment. He said that in that parish they would be "the Blue
Army of Our Lady against the Red Army."

Your Excellency will remember that I had prepared an
oratory on the farm where the Pilgrim Virgin statue would
be kept until it might go to Russia. And as the months
passed, the presence of this wonderful image of Our Lady
became ever more meaningful, more personal. I wanted to
have Mass in the oratory, but of course, only privately.
And I invited Msgr. Colgan.

He was so touched by the atmosphere of "presence"
conveyed by the Pilgrim Virgin statue that he asked to
come back and bring some of the Sisters from his school.

On his third or fourth visit, Marie Hart, a parishioner
who had been most active in developing the blue ribbon
campaign in the parish, suggested that I should work with
Msgr. Colgan to develop the Apostolate along the lines
that I had previously developed the Scapular Apostolate.

Your Excellency knows that I have always looked to
"authority" for an indication of God's Will. And in the
field of the Marian apostolate in the United States at that
time, I saw Fr. Daniel Lord as a man of authority. Indeed,
I knew that he had thought, when I left the Scapular Apostolate in New York, that I might come to work with him in
the "Queen's Work."

Shortly after Marie Hart's suggestion I happened to run
into Fr. Lord in New York. It was a *very* rare "coincidence." I did not go into the city at that time more than
perhaps once a year. Also Fr. Lord, whose center was in
St. Louis, could not have been in New York very often.
And when one considers the immensity of the city and the
number of restaurants, and even the number of tables in
that restaurant, the "odds" against my seeing Fr. Lord
that day were astronomical.

Yet I "just happened" to pass a restaurant where Fr.
Lord was sitting alone at a table window. At once, *with a
feeling of confidence that what he would tell me would be
an indication of Our Lady's direction,* I went into the
restaurant, hardly took time to apologize for the intrusion,
and asked:

"Father, what would you think if I were to ask you

whether it might be fitting for me to join forces with Fr. Harold Colgan to promote the Message of Fatima?''

Fr. Lord (whom I considered the greatest Marian apostle of our time), looked up and answered with one single sentence: *"If you do, there will be an explosion for Our Lady."*

I was so stunned by the emphatic certainty of his reply that I was momentarily unable to speak. Still somewhat dazed by his words, I thanked him for his judgment, wished him well and left.

I resolved at once to write the Bishop of Trenton and ask permission to begin SOUL Magazine and a publishing house primarily to promote the Fatima Message. And your predecessor, Bishop Griffin, replied with a most positive and generous letter of permission.

The Bishop knew of my previous work with the Scapular Apostolate in New York, and perhaps a word of summary here would be important for those who may not have read my previous book titled *The Brother and I.**

As Your Excellency will remember, I had been teaching in St. Albert's College in Middletown, N.Y. (a Preparatory Seminary of the Carmelites) while completing work for a doctorate in philosophy at Fordham University where my previous scholastic work had been accepted on the level of a master's. At the same time I wrote my first book, to which Archbishop Sheen wrote the preface. It was a Catholic Book Club selection and not long after that the General of the Carmelite Order invited me to head the Scapular Apostolate in New York City, which, within the next eight years, became one of the most important Marian apostolates in our nation.

2

As director of this apostolate I was invited to Fatima in 1946 with permission to speak to Sister Lucia, sole survivor of the three children who saw Our Lady of Fatima.

I had the intention of writing a book about the Miracle of Fatima, but after my meeting with Lucia, I became so filled with the sense of urgency of the Message of Fatima that I used the power of the Scapular Apostolate (there were 163,000 copies of the magazine and organized centers of the apostolate throughout the nation) to promote

* First published in 1942 under the title **From A Morning Prayer**. It is the writer's autobiography up to the early years of the Blue Army. 1971, AMI Press, Washington, N.J., 212 pp.

signatures to the "pledge" which I had drawn up during my interview with Lucia *based on the essential conditions required by Our Lady for the conversion of Russia and world peace.*

In July of 1948, I retired at Cardinal Spellman's 3 suggestion. By then well over a million pledges had been signed. Many were from St. Mary's Parish in Plainfield, N.J., where those who signed the pledge were wearing that little blue ribbon—a sign of their commitment—a sign that at least in that one parish they wanted to stand up and be counted as "the Blue Army of Our Lady against the Red Army of atheistic Communism."

In addition to Marie Hart—the zealous parishioner mentioned previously—there was a curate in Msgr. Colgan's parish who had been responsible for introducing Msgr. Colgan himself to the Message of Fatima. He was Fr. Francis E. Byrne.

So it seemed that there were various forces and personalities at work, developing in both Msgr. Colgan and myself the idea of working together to promote what we had previously called a "March of Pledges" as a *"Blue Army of Our Lady of Fatima."* And we added not only the idea of wearing something blue as an outward sign of the pledge, but also of taking the names of all those who signed the pledge to Fatima and burying them beneath the tree under which the children used to wait for the coming of Our Lady on the 13th of each month from May to October in 1917.

At this time, Your Excellency was director of the major seminary of the Archdiocese of Newark, in Darlington, New Jersey. I had lectured in the seminary, I believe, in 1947. Subsequently I was a speaker at a large auditorium in Newark, and Your Excellency had been chosen to introduce me. (Incidentally, I shall never forget the warmth and kindness of that introduction—so undeserved and yet so encouraging.)

I did not know how Bishop Griffin would react to the unexpected opposition from New York (that is, unexpected by him, but not so much by myself). But meanwhile, I had another very, very important ally: Archbishop Thomas Boland.

You knew him well. You knew he was—like yourself and Cardinal Dougherty—a man dedicated to duty, of great purity of soul, simple, childlike, with a total devotion to Our Lady. He, too, had heard me lecture, and he also held Msgr. Colgan in high esteem. But, as yet, I was unaware of how important his support would prove to be.

This was a time of exceptional shock. I was not yet over the trauma of having left the Scapular Apostolate in New York, which had been compounded by the even greater shock some ten years before when I had left one Carmelite seminary and obtained a position as lay teacher in another.

Twice within ten years, when it seemed that the path of my future lay clear before me, a great iron gate had clanged shut across it.

4   And so, in 1950, I found myself in semi-retirement, able to write books because I had a settlement from the Scapular Press (which had been founded by my father), and had sold a large piece of property which had increased six times in value since its purchase years before. But now, convinced that it was God's Will that I join with Msgr. Colgan and continue the March of Pledges as "The Blue Army of Our Lady of Fatima," I risked everything to launch SOUL Magazine and AMI Press.

And yet, *each day* I almost trembled as I opened the mail, half expecting a letter from the Bishop of Trenton saying that he "thought it better" that this work should not continue....

Then suddenly—only months after it had all begun—Bishop Griffin died. The days that followed were full of suspense. Who would be the next Bishop? Would he be favorable to this work which was strongly opposed by the Cardinal Archbishop of New York, then the most influential prelate in America?

Knowing Cardinal Spellman's residence on Madison Avenue was called "the American Vatican," I thought it almost certain that the new Bishop of Trenton would be someone chosen by him personally, or at least appointed only with his approval. I did not know that this depended more on the Metropolitan of New Jersey.

What joy I felt when it was announced that *you* (who had so recently introduced me in one of the major lecture forums in Newark) *had been appointed the new Bishop!*

I suspect you knew, from the very beginning, that you need only have said that my work should not continue and the Apostolate would have been instantly terminated. And I must confess that it was not until eight years later that I finally became convinced that, despite the increasing burden that the Blue Army was heaping upon the diocese because of its nationwide scope, you would never have closed its doors.

My conviction sprang from that decisive event in the late 1950's when you literally saved the life of our Apostolate. At that time, we had a television program in New York every Saturday night, and were developing a distribution of the program which was later to be seen on about 100 stations throughout the nation. We had some 40 employees at the farm, now known as the *Ave Maria Institute,* and while I was on one of my trips to Portugal (we were completing the International Center at Fatima at the time), the Steel Workers' Union tried to organize the employees of the Institute.

What a problem this posed not only for us, but for the diocese, and perhaps for the Church.

Apparently our Institute was seen as vulnerable because there was no priest in residence, all of the workers were lay persons, it was not "diocesan" (even though it was under diocesan authority), and it was a Catholic non-profit organization.

As far as I know, it would have been the first such Catholic organization to be organized, and although we believed in social justice and in the right of labor to be organized, we had reason to believe that Communists were behind this—because of our program for the "conversion of Russia." Under the circumstances it was deemed better to close the Institute and to use other facilities for the Apostolate.

The Trustees voted unanimously in favor of this. And I shall never forget the day that Msgr. Colgan, myself, and one or two of the Trustees came to your office to tell you the decision!

I felt you would be relieved, and I imagined you thinking: "Well, thank heaven this headache will be over. Thank goodness they've decided to sidestep this highly controversial problem which this diocese could certainly do without!" But then you asked:

"What are you going to do with the mail?"

We explained that we were going to ask a religious community to receive it and process it for us. You then asked:

5

"And what about the magazine?"

We stated that we would continue the magazine, but would have it published elsewhere through another publishing house. And then you asked:

"But what will happen to the good name of the Blue Army if its National Center is closed?"

We sat in stunned silence. Not one of us had even thought that far. All our attention had been directed towards removing the above difficulty. And then Your Excellency said:

"I think you should see it through."

Your words acted on us like an incantation. The assurance of your support fired us with sudden determination, steeled us with resolution. And from that day on, conscious that you were fully behind us, we have grown like the proverbial mustard seed.

As it transpired, our employees voted *not* to join the union after all. Shortly after that, Mr. Frank McGowan, a famous time and motion expert, volunteered his services and came to the Institute for several weeks to help us perfect our own organization. Shortly thereafter, we were operating more efficiently, more effectively, and with more satisfied personnel than ever before. It was like a rainbow after a storm, like the rising glory of the sun after the darkest night....

Yet opposition and problems and more opposition have been our lot from the very beginning. How could it be otherwise? Satan was there the day that Our Lady announced that his program to extend the errors of militant atheism throughout the world would be crushed by Her—that She would convert Russia and bring an era of peace to mankind.

Satan was there when he heard Our Lady explain the conditions for the conversion of Russia. And he was there when Lucia participated in the formulation of the pledge containing these requests, and when the Bishop of Fatima told me: "You may promulgate this (pledge) as coming from me."

Confronted by his implacable fury and surrounded by the great wave of evil sweeping through the world, the Blue Army might easily have foundered, but mighty forces were being raised up by Our Lady to sustain it. Your Excellency will remember the joy we experienced when Pope Pius XII endorsed Fatima so emphatically, blessed the

Blue Army, and gave us Cardinal Tisserant, the Dean of the College of Cardinals, as a sort of "protector," and actually named him as his own Papal Legate for the blessing of our International Center at Fatima in 1956. And the joy and consolation when Pope Paul VI decided to go to Fatima on May 13, 1967; and the decision taken only a few months later by the Bishop of Fatima to become the International President of the Blue Army which he then actively began to promote personally, undertaking extensive journeys around the world.

One cannot help but recall all those devoted priests who helped us in so many ways through the hard years of our Apostolate. It would seem unfair to single out individual names, but I feel impelled to record the dedicated and unstinted assistance given us by Msgr. Kmiec, Msgr. Maguire and Msgr. Margerum and recall the many thousands of manuscript pages they helped to evaluate with such selfless zeal. Over the years, Msgr. Kmiec, who was your secretary and devoted aide, became a liasion with us, bringing compassion for all our trials, wise counsel and generous, unflagging assistance in every need. To these priests in particular, the Blue Army owes an incalculable debt of gratitude. 6

Below: Father Daniel Lord, S.J. and Monsignor Colgan among their beloved youth.

Chapter Three

1) What is the Blue Army? - 2) Blue Army Cell imitates children of Fatima - 3) First Saturday and Catechism - 4) The Rules - 5) Problems with mentioning "Russia" - 6) Battle is real - 7) Relation of Blue Army to similar apostolates - 8) Victory certain - 9) Special relation of Blue Army to Legion of Mary - 10) Blue Army is "the Fatima Apostolate".

Below: Blue Army banners of different nations in procession at Fatima.

TO THE READER

"The Blue Army of Our Lady of Fatima calls to each and all, great and small, rich and poor, cultured and ignorant." — *The Bishop of Fatima*

Does it seem a little confusing (this is addressed to you, the reader) to be sort of "looking over the shoulder" at a letter written to my Bishop?

When I began to write this "letter" it was my intention to later rewrite it as a "history" of the Blue Army rather than a series of personal reminiscences.

However, Francis Johnston, excellent English writer and author of *Fatima: The Great Sign*, wrote after receiving an advance copy: "I read through the night. I couldn't put it down."

Of course, being interested in Fatima, he was interested in personal recollections recorded in the following pages about some of the major Fatima events of our times, such as the Egypt-Israel "Peace Flight" on Passover Day, the "uprising" in Poland, the "miracle" of the termite-ridden convent of the First Saturday apparitions in Spain, the crowning of the Pilgrim Virgin statue in Moscow, the apparition of Our Lady of Fatima as reported in Vietnam, the hesitation and finally the consent of Pope Paul VI to participate in a simultaneous coronation of statues of Our Lady of Fatima in more than fifty countries, and so many more "almost incredible" events associated with or brought about by the Blue Army.

But I was surprised to find that Francis Johnston was not alone in finding the "letter" interesting. The Very Rev. Canon Galamba de Oliveira (who is mentioned in Lucia's Memoirs and who is himself an important and integral part of the "Fatima history") felt that some of my earlier "recollections" should also be included. (However this was perhaps done adequately in the book *The Brother and I.*) [1]

One chapter...which I wrote mostly because remembering it was to relive the excitement...concerns a sailing adventure in the famous Devil's Triangle. I was quite sure it would be eliminated in the final editing and was surprised that the Rev. Dr. Joaquin M. Alonso, editor of *Ephemerides Mariologicae* and official documentarian of Fatima, thought it was the most interesting chapter of the entire "letter"!

So in the end I decided to leave the "letter" pretty much as it is, and leave it to some more objective person... like Francis Johnston or Fr. Alonso himself...to do *a real history* of the Blue Army.

However, I interrupt to address you, the reader, since all the rest of the book is addressed to the Most Rev. George W. Ahr, my Bishop of thirty years. *And in the event that you may be someone who does not even know what the Blue Army is, let me explain:*

1   In simple terms the Blue Army is essentially an extension of the *Apostleship of Prayer* throughout the day. It is a response to those very first words of Our Lady to the children of Fatima: *"Will you be willing to accept whatever God will send you and to offer it up in reparation for sin and for the conversion of sinners?"*

Even the original Morning Offering used in the Apostleship of Prayer is an almost perfect response to the requests of Our Lady of Fatima—offering all that we are, have and do through the Immaculate Heart of Mary and in union with the Sacrifice of the Mass throughout the world.

To this Morning Offering, in keeping with the Message of Fatima, the Blue Army adds two elements: A *practiced* consecration to the Immaculate Heart of Mary implemented by the Scapular devotion; Meditative prayer implemented by the Rosary.

That, in a nutshell, is what the Blue Army is all about: the Morning Offering extended through the day with the help of the Scapular and Rosary devotions.

However, this opens the door to a whole new life, both for the individual who practices it and for the world (because of the promise of world peace when enough persons are responding).

While the first and primary purpose of the Blue Army is this extension of the Morning Offering through the day by means of the proper use of the Scapular and the Rosary, the Blue Army has two additional goals:

1) To cause those fulfilling the pledge *to deepen their response in association with others* (the Blue Army cell);

2) To encourage and to organize militant members *who will spread this message throughout the world* so as to hasten the fulfillment of the prophecy of Padre Pio: "Russia will be converted when there is a Blue Army member for every Communist"...and after the conversion of Russia, to aid in the triumph of Her Immaculate Heart in the entire world.

The children of Fatima practiced and lived the message and thus became the model of the Blue Army cell: two or three meeting at regular intervals to discuss the message, to pray together, and to help each other to fulfill the marvelous program of sanctity given by Our Lady of Fatima to the three children, and through them to us.

The Blue Army in its basic and simplest form is really like the opening of the door of the human heart to the heart of Mary, and through the heart of Mary to an intimate union with the Sacred Heart of Jesus in the Eucharist.

This process, although necessarily simple, can seem complex in its explanation. But to keep it simple, imagine this picture:

Our Lady, crowned as Queen, showing forth Her thorn-encircled heart, and reaching out to you with the Rosary and the Scapular. Lines of light flowing from the Scapular and the Rosary frame the question: *"Will you be willing to accept whatever God will send you...?"* Now add to the picture yourself accepting the Scapular and the Rosary as signs of your "Yes!"

Completing the picture, the same rays of light carry you (through the fulfillment of daily duty) to the great light of the final vision of Fatima[2], containing mysteries of the Trinity, Calvary, Eucharist, and with the Immaculate Heart of Mary.

Historically, we can look back on the first quarter century of this Apostolate and see it from two completely different viewpoints: As an Apostolate of Holiness (which is essentially what I have described above); and as a propaganda effort.

As this "letter" to my Bishop reveals, I personally have been involved primarily in the second part, but I had years of special spiritual preparation which are described in my earlier book, *The Brother and I*. And it is to be hoped that the reader *will not think*, because of this particular "letter" to my Bishop, *that the element of propaganda* ("action" of the Blue Army in making known the Message of Fatima in the world) *is by any means its primary objective.*

This is above all a silent army, an army of prayer and sacrifice, an army on its knees. The propaganda effort is merely to make known to the world the great miracle of Fatima so that more people will respond to Our Lady's appeal for prayer and penance.

Before concluding this effort to explain the Blue Army's nature and goals in simple terms, I should emphasize two other practices which, though not absolutely essential, are important for all Blue Army members: the First Saturday devotion and Catechetics.

3 The First Saturdays are of primary concern for all members of the Blue Army not only because of the promise made by Our Lady to all who complete this devotion,[3] but *because the First Saturdays are a primary tool for opening the Fatima door of holiness to persons who would otherwise never enter this sacred and happy portal.* They are also an occasion for all of us to purify our intentions once a month, to make a Eucharistic act of reparation for the offenses committed against the Immaculate Heart of Mary, to prepare ourselves for a more effective practice of the Rosary devotion and to strengthen a renewal of purpose for another four weeks in the extension of our Morning Offering throughout the day.

And finally, even though Our Lady did not specifically mention "catechism" at Fatima, She showed Herself to be the perfect catechist in Her instructions to the children, and in two subsequently reported apparitions of Our Lady of Fatima (one in Bogota, and one in Vietnam), Our Lady is said to have mentioned the importance of teaching children how to pray the Rosary, and at the same time the importance of teaching catechism. And this has become an important element in the Blue Army, especially through its youth apostolate, the Blue Army Cadets.

Certainly the best evaluation of the Blue Army ever written is the one issued by the Bishop of Fatima while he was International President of this Apostolate. It appears as the first appendix to this book.

The actual *organization* is based on canonical statutes, first drawn up at the direction of the first Bishop of Fatima, which were approved *ad experimentum* by the Holy See in 1956. Final approval was long delayed because of the revision of Canon Law after Vatican II, and as it was not clear as to whether the Blue Army should be considered a lay apostolate or a sort of pious union.

The statutes describe two levels of membership: **4** 1) Those who simply sign the pledge (commitment to the Morning Offering, Scapular and Rosary); 2) Those who, in addition to making the pledge, are organized into prayer cells and promotional groups.

Only the latter are "organized," and they are quite a small percentage of the total number who have signed the pledge...*now over twenty-five million in more than one hundred countries.*

On the parish level, the pastor has the last word. Organization or promotion *among* parishes requires permission of the Bishop. And from the diocesan leaders who are recognized by their Bishops a *National Council* is formed which elects its officers and its executive committee. The latter is responsible for the operation of the National Center (which in the United States is in Washington, NJ).

On the international level, three officers from each National Council form the International Council, and they elect their own officers and their own Executive Committee. The latter is responsible for the operation of the International Center in Fatima and the subsidiary International Secretariat in Switzerland.

Much conflict has arisen over the years, as will become **5** evident as one reads this "letter." Some is due to the fact that Communist Russia has considered the Blue Army to be the most important deterrent in the world, at the present time, to the success of its world revolution. (This is so extraordinary, and so important, that Appendix II to this book is the verbatim translation of an article from Russia's atheistic magazine *Science and Religion* of October, 1967, in which Hitler, the Cold War, and the Blue Army are stated as the three principal reasons why Russia's atheistic revolution has not yet gained the whole world.)

We presume that millions of dollars have been spent to slur the name of the Blue Army. Some evidence of this will appear during the course of this "history," although few words are wasted on it. Such opposition, even when subtle (like the book in France which claimed that the Blue Army was financed by Archbiship Lefebvre) or blatant, like published claims in Portugal and Spain that the Blue Army is a branch of the CIA, is understandable.

What is less understandable (and in the early years of the Apostolate, caused me great amazement) is the number of personality conflicts and opposition *within the Apostolate itself.*

But little by little we came to realize that *there is a mortal conflict taking place in the world today* between Our Lady and Satan—between his seed and Hers.

As will appear later in this "history," one of the main objections over the years to the Blue Army has been against the name itself: Blue *Army.* And yet how well the Apostolate is named an "army"!

6   We are really engaged in a battle—and the greatest and most important battle in the history of man. It is as though in the middle of the 20th century God permitted all the power of Satan to be unleashed upon the world in the wake of the promise of Our Lady, His Mother and our Queen, that She would bring about the conversion of Russia and an era of peace to mankind—that Her Immaculate Heart would triumph and that an era of peace would come to the entire world!

What more fitting title could be given to the response to this coming of Our Lady with the promise of Her triumph than the title of being "Her" army?

It is interesting that the militant atheists of Russia understood this more readily and more completely than the believers, and attributed to the Blue Army the power of being a major deterrent to the success of worldwide militant atheism (next to Hitler and the Cold War).

In this regard it is also interesting to note that at least three other Marian apostolates of modern times have a name signifying "army." Perhaps as a further aid to understanding the Blue Army it might be helpful to distinguish it from these other apostolates: *The Army of Mary, the Militia of the Immaculate,* and *the Legion of Mary.*

The Army of Mary was founded in Canada and has one basic and essential condition of membership: Consecration to Our Lady.

The Militia of the Immaculate was founded by Blessed Maximilian Kolbe without any specific conditions of membership. Its essential purpose is *to know* Our Lady, and *to make Her known* as the instrument of God for bringing about the triumph of Jesus in the world.

The Legion of Mary is an active parish apostolate which canvasses parishes to bring souls to Jesus through Mary.

The Blue Army is the fulfillment of the Message of Fatima.

All four of these apostolates represent various *degrees* of militant service to Our Lady to hasten the triumph of Her Immaculate Heart in the world, to bring about Her victory over evil, to be Her "heel" to crush the head of the serpent in today's world. **7**

One thing all of these apostolates have in common is the same ascetic basis: True Devotion to the Blessed Virgin, as explained by St. Louis Grignon de Montfort.

Not one *excludes* the others. The Most Rev. John Venancio, while Bishop of Fatima and International President of the Blue Army, wrote: "Far from there being any reason for competition among these apostolates, there is an overwhelmingly compelling need and fittingness for each to cooperate with the other in every possible way."

A major step was taken in this direction in the United States on December 8, 1945, when the leaders of all the principal Marian apostolates met at the National Shrine of the Immaculate Conception in Washington, D.C., to form a "Marian Federation." Fr. Daniel Lord on that occasion said:

"It is almost staggering to think of the great apostolic power that we could wield in the United States, and subsequently in the world, by uniting our strength in common objectives promoting together all the devotion which Mary through the centuries has given us. We have here, in this meeting, an opportunity such as we may not have again for a generation." [4] **8**

But of course everyone knows what happened to the Marian apostolates and the Marian devotions in the postconciliar period, and now another generation—in a new flourishing of the Marian Age, must look to Our Lady of Victories and unite themselves in the flames of the love of Her Immaculate Heart in order to bring about the triumph of that same heart as promised to us at Fatima.

Would it be fitting for me, having been involved in the Blue Army so intimately, to dare to make an evaluation of the four major Marian apostolates?

9 Were I to do so, I would put the Legion of Mary at the top of the ladder of apostleship, and the Blue Army next (and indeed the Blue Army, as an apostolate of holiness, is very similar to the auxiliary of the Legion of Mary). Next I would put the Militia of the Immaculate, because to know Mary—and especially to know Her to the degree that Blessed Maximilian Kolbe came to know Her—is to be consumed with a desire to make Her known to all the world.

I personally have always experienced a very great warmth on the higher levels of the apostolates. Some of the warmest memories I have, looking back over the years, are of my relationship with such leaders as Fr. Lord, Fr. Skelly of the Miraculous Medal Association, Fr. Peyton, Frank Duff and Fr. Balic of the Marian Academy.

Fr. Lord, when I asked him whether I should consider associating myself with Msgr. Colgan in an apostolate, answered without hesitation that if I did so there would be "an explosion for Our Lady."

And can we imagine the power that would be formed if the leaders of all the apostolates met—at least on the occasions of the Marian Congresses promoted by the Pontifical Marian Academy—to study ways in which they could cooperate to bring about the triumph of Mary's Heart in the world?

I know that I have been deeply impressed, and often motivated, by that vision of St. John Bosco in which he saw the Church going through a terrible tempest after a great council, and at which he saw the Holy Father guiding the bark of Peter through the great waves which threatened to engulf it at every moment until he brought it between two pillars, one of devotion to Mary and the other of devotion to the Eucharist. And at that moment, as lines flew forth to those two pillars, the storm subsided—and we may presume that this was the moment of the great victory which Our Lady promised in the twentieth century which will be even greater than the victory of Lepanto for the preservation of the Christian world and for the triumph of Christ's Church.

And finally, should not *every* Catholic make the Act of Consecration to Our Lady, and is this not the very first step to any degree of service in Her army?

Concerning the latter, we need but read the encyclical of Paul VI, *Signum Magnum,* issued on May 13, 1967, the day the Pope went to Fatima "as a humble pilgrim to pray for peace in the Church and in the world."

Back in the late 1940's, just when the Blue Army was founded and members of the Legion learned that Our Lady had appeared at Fatima holding the Scapular out of the sky, and that Lucia said that *"the Rosary and Scapular are inseparable,"* Frank Duff was asked to add the Scapular as a condition of membership in the Legion of Mary.

The holy founder of the Legion agonized over repeated petitions (from different parts of the world) concerning this. He confided to us that he did not feel that under any circumstances he should change the original "handbook" of the Legion.

(I have often wondered whether or not Our Lady Herself did not—at least in his heart—dictate that glorious manual of holiness and action.)

But then the Blue Army was founded, and Frank Duff encouraged members of the Legion to join the Blue Army, and indeed some of the greatest leaders in our Apostolate in the world have come from the ranks of the Legion—and perhaps, in so doing, became more effective Legionnaires as well.

Each apostolate has its own points of emphasis.

Oh, would that there were more Niepokalanows—Cities of the Immaculate—scattered over the world! I have always considered it a special gift from Blessed Maximilian—in addition to the crowning of the Pilgrim Virgin in his Niepokalanow outside of Warsaw in 1971—that Br. Juventyn, who had been imprisoned with Blessed Maximilian, chose to have his famous book *I Knew Blessed Maximilian* published by the Blue Army, with a chapter explaining the Blue Army as something that he knew would be dear to Blessed Maximilian and a movement which all the "Cities of the Immaculate" would promote in order to speed the triumph of Mary's Immaculate Heart as promised at Fatima. Indeed, some of the greatest support for the Blue Army in the United States came from America's own Niepokalanow, the publisher of IMMACU-LATA, and especially through that gifted and dedicated Franciscan, Br. Francis Mary, O.F.M. Conv.

Perhaps the best way to look on each and all of the various apostolates of Our Lady in the Church would be as various regiments, various "special services" in Her overall army which St. Grignon de Montfort prophesied would be raised up in the latter days to join with Our Lady and Queen in the conquest of Satan and his legions of evil.

In conclusion:

10   The Blue Army is a response to the Message of Fatima—both in its simplest form as an extension of the Morning Offering through the day, and in its far more complex form as a complete program of being born into intimate union with the Eucharistic Heart of Jesus through living our consecration to the Immaculate Heart of Mary.

In the course of the past thirty years I have written three books which to me express this spirituality in simple terms. One book is about the Scapular (*Sign of Her Heart*), another is about the Rosary (*Sex and the Mysteries*), and the third is about the Eucharist (*The World's Greatest Secret*).

Not even all the hundreds of pages of all three books can completely describe the richness of the scope of the Blue Army apostolate as it affects the sanctity of the individual member.

We need only remember that first vision of Fatima—that exclamation of the children as they were engulfed in the light streaming from the Immaculate Heart of Mary—to know that when the latter devotion is established in the world, men will fall to their knees and exclaim as did the children of Fatima: *"Oh Most Holy Trinity, I adore You! My God, my God, I love You in the Most Blessed Sacrament!"*

It is to be hoped that other writers, like Francis Johnston and Fr. Joaquin Alonso, may do more objective books both about the Blue Army history and about its spirituality.

Meanwhile, in obedience to the mandate of my Bishop, I will continue with my reminiscences, knowing full well as you "look over my shoulder" that the Bishop had you in mind when he asked me to write, and I also had you in mind when I obeyed.

FOOTNOTES

1.   This book, written in the early 1940's, was largely autobiographical. When the Blue Army began, I felt that it would be advantageous to publish a new edition, showing how the early stages in the Scapular Apostolate led largely to fulfillment in the Blue Army. The original title of this book, when first published, was **From A Morning Prayer**. (AMI Press, 1971, 212 pp.)

2. The vision to Lucia of June 12-13, 1929, described in her Memoirs in these words:

    I had sought and obtained permission from my superiors and confessor to make a Holy Hour from eleven o'clock until midnight, every Thursday to Friday night. Being alone one night, I knelt near the altar rails in the middle of the chapel and, prostrate, I prayed the prayers of the Angel. Feeling tired, I then stood up and continued to say the prayers with my arms in the form of a cross. The only light was that of the sanctuary lamp. Suddenly the whole chapel was illumined by a supernatural light, and above the altar appeared a cross of light, reaching to the ceiling. In a brighter light on the upper part of the cross, could be seen the face of a man and his body as far as the waist; upon his breast was a dove of light; nailed to the cross was the body of another man. A little below the waist, I could see a chalice and a large host suspended in the air, on to which drops of blood were falling from the face of Jesus Crucified and from the wound in his side. These drops ran down on to the host and fell into the chalice. Beneath the right arm of the cross was Our Lady and in her hand was her Immaculate Heart. (It was Our Lady of Fatima, with her Immaculate Heart in her left hand, without sword or roses, but with a crown of thorns and flames.) Under the left arm of the cross, large letters, as if of crystal clear water which ran down upon the altar, formed these words: "Grace and Mercy."

    I understood that it was the Mystery of the Most Holy Trinity which was shown to me, and I received lights about this mystery which I am not permitted to reveal.

    Our Lady then said to me:

    "The moment has come in which God asks the Holy Father, in union with all the Bishops of the world, to make the consecration of Russia to my Immaculate Heart, promising to save it by this means. There are so many souls whom the Justice of God condemns for sins committed against me, that I have come to ask reparation: sacrifice yourself for this intention and pray."

3. The actual promise as given in Lucia's Memoirs, for the First Saturdays, says:

    "You at least promise to console me and say that I promise to assist at the hour of death, with the graces necessary for salvation, all those who, on the first Saturday of five consecutive months, shall confess, receive Holy Communion, and keep me company for fifteen minutes while meditating on the mysteries of the Rosary, with the intention of making reparation to me."

4. See **Russia Will Be Converted**, 1950, AMI Press, p. 238. (Book currently out-of-print.)

Chapter Four

1) Bishop of Fatima approves Pledge - 2) The "March" begins - 3) Resolved: Take a Pilgrim Virgin statue to Russia - 4) Statue comes to America - 5) Statue enters U.S. on December 8, 1947 - 6) Pledges grow to hundreds of thousands - 7) Lucia pleased with results - 8) Sister Lucia remains as Our Lady's Messenger - 9) Her 1981 message to the Blue Army and to its leaders.

Below: The author with the Most Rev. George W. Ahr, to whom this book is addressed.

THE ARMY
BEGINS ITS MARCH

"And the favors She performs along the way are such that we can hardly believe what we are seeing with our eyes." — *Pope Pius XII*

As mentioned in the first chapter, I had several misgivings as I sat there in the presence of Sr. Lucia with the final draft version of the pledge on the table in front of me.

Firstly, since many must have thought as I did that the Rosary was the central message of Fatima, what would be their reaction when confronted with this particular formula which claimed to embody the essential requests of Our Lady for the conversion of Russia? Was there not a possibility of it becoming a subject for debate?

And secondly, since Our Lady had not mentioned the Scapular but had merely held it out from the sky in the final vision at the climax of the Miracle of the Sun, and since I had previously been identified with the Scapular Apostolate, would not everyone think that I had arbitrarily introduced this into the pledge?

So while I had intended to travel from Porto to Lisbon and thence back to America, I decided it would be wise to see the Bishop of Fatima, to relate the substance of this interview and show him the pledge.

I am sure that Our Lady was responsible for this. But before I narrate what happened, I should mention one other incident from the interview with Lucia which, perhaps, I should have recorded earlier.

The Bishop of Fatima had earlier told me that Lucia had recently received further apparitions from Our Lady, so I began to ask her about these visions and the messages conveyed to her. She said tersely: "I am not permitted to speak of anything which has happened since 1917."

I was completely surprised and told her then what the Bishop had said, which was still very fresh in my mind. It was her turn to be surprised.

There was an awkward silence for a few moments. I could sense her anxiety about speaking of these things, even though the Bishop had already spoken to me about them. So I simply asked: "Sister, could you tell me if I have understood the Bishop correctly?"

She answered that I had, and that gave me the courage to ask: "And Sister, when Our Lady still appears to you, does She always appear the same?"

A most wonderful, yet pitiable look of wistfulness and loneliness seemed to come over her and she almost whispered the answer: "Yes...Yes, always the same."

In that moment I sensed what must be her most acute suffering—her grief of exile. Like Francisco and Jacinta she had seen a reflection of heaven, and now she lived in "darkness." I recalled how the children had literally lived from one apparition to the other, consoling themselves that it would only be so many more days, so many more hours, so many more minutes before they would see the ineffable countenance of Our Lady once more.

And it brought home to me, with keener insight, the essence of the pain of Purgatory, which is the awareness in the soul of the nature of God and His infinite love and goodness, of its own destiny for God, sundered now by a period of separation from Him....

As I approached the Bishop's residence, I wondered what would be his reaction to this "pledge," this formula which was supposed to contain the essential conditions of Our Lady of Fatima for the conversion of Russia and world peace—so different from what I am sure many persons would have deduced from a study of all Our Lady's words to the children.

Almost as soon as I arrived in Leiria, the Bishop took time out of his busy schedule to see me. I explained that while I did not wish to intrude on his valuable time, I was unwilling to return to America with this pledge without having shown it to him and learning whether he, too, would interpret the message of Our Lady in this way.

I had translated the pledge into French on the way and was able to give it to him directly. I shall never forget that moment—and particularly the change of expression on the Bishop's lined face as he read the pledge.

Obviously he sensed the responsibility of a judgment. He was the Bishop of Fatima, and he was asked to pass judgment on what was perhaps the most important of all aspects of the Fatima apparitions—namely, the conditions of Our Lady to be fulfilled throughout the world in order to obtain in return the fulfillment of Her great promise.

There was a slight frown and an intense air of concentration. I expected this to remain and perhaps deepen as he read this pledge: sanctification of duty, aided by the Rosary prayed with attention to the Mysteries, and the wearing of the Scapular as a sign of consecration to Mary's Immaculate Heart.

But instead, with each passing word the frown began to fade. A glow of relief, of eminent satisfaction filled the Bishop's face. And as he finished the last word, he looked up and with a smile which I suppose I would not exaggerate to call radiant, said most solemnly: *"You may promulgate this as coming from me."*

I returned to America satisfied, but in a sober, prayerful frame of mind, conscious now of the full magnitude of the task that lay ahead.

As mentioned in the first chapter, I was engaged at the time in the direction of a Scapular Apostolate under the auspices of the Carmelite Fathers in New York and had a magazine with a circulation of 163,000 copies.

I now filled it with the "March of Pledges."   2

During World War II this apostolate had organized units throughout the nation to make scapulars for servicemen. I now called upon these centers to also promote the pledge. They were urged to get as many persons as possible to sign it, to commit themselves to these basic conditions of Our Lady for the conversion of Russia and world peace.

Within a year more than one million of the signed pledges were returned to our New York office and then the "miracle" of the Pilgrim Virgin statue began.

And we can rightfully call it a miracle since Pope Pius XII himself said of it:

"I crowned Our Lady of Fatima Queen of the World (this was the coronation of May 13, 1946), and the following year She set forth through the Pilgrim Virgin as though to claim Her dominion, *and the favors She performs along the way are such that We can hardly believe what We are seeing. with Our eyes."*

Several books have been written about the wonders and the salutary effects of this Pilgrim Virgin—wonders which continue to the present day.

During all this time I kept the Bishop of Fatima fully informed of the March of Pledges, and apparently he was also receiving very favorable comments from Sr. Lucia—although this is something I can only infer. But because it is important, perhaps I should state my reasons:

The first Bishop of Fatima developed a high esteem for Lucia. Believing she was having authentic revelations, he naturally took advantage of her "direct line" to Our Lord and Our Lady to consult with her whenever the need arose. The Pilgrim Virgin statue was a good case in point.

3   There had been an international Congress of Youth at Fatima in May, 1946. The war had just recently ended, and it was the first *international* event of its kind ever held at Fatima. Indeed, the Bishop remarked on this occasion that Fatima, as a *world* shrine, dated from that occasion.

Perhaps this Congress of Youth would long have been forgotten were it not for the resolution passed there that a statue of Our Lady should be carried processionally from Fatima to Russia.

When the Bishop was asked about this, he questioned Lucia about it. In due course the answer came back:

"Yes, Excellency, and let them take the statue which Thedim has made for you."

In that simple statement lies a significant story.

As you know, Francisco and Jacinta died not long after the apparitions, as Our Lady had foretold. Francisco passed away first, almost two years after the first apparition. At about that time Our Lady gave Jacinta the option of either coming to heaven with Francisco or remaining on earth to suffer more for sinners. And this heroic little girl, who with Francisco is expected to be canonized soon, chose to suffer longer. She was taken to Ourem Hospital (not far from where the three children had been in prison) to endure another kind of imprisonment—suffering alone in a room for two months, away from her family. After that she was taken to Lisbon for a futile operation, and finally, as Our Lady had foretold, died all alone on February 20, 1920, just a few weeks before her tenth birthday.

When Bishop da Silva was appointed the first Bishop of Fatima three months later, one of his first actions was to send for Lucia—who was then 13 years old. The Bishop suggested to Lucia that she should take an assumed name and go to an orphanage in the north of Portugal, where no one would know her, in order to facilitate the work of the Canonical Commission of Investigation and at the same time spare her from the endless interrogations to which she was continually subjected.[1]

Only heaven knew how much suffering this must have cost the little girl. One can only ask: How would *you* have felt at fourteen to have been told that it would be better for you to become a virtual orphan! To leave your home and mother! To change your name and spend the remainder of your childhood among complete strangers.

Lucia was further asked never to mention Fatima, nor indicate that she knew anything about it other than what others might know through normal channels. She accepted these difficult requests graciously and completely.

How she must have missed those places where she had played with Francisco and Jacinta! How she must have yearned and sighed for those prayerful and profound visits to the Cova where they had been so blessed by the appearances of Our Lady! Or to Valinhos, or to the Cabeco where the angel had spoken to them, or to the well behind her mother's house where the angel had also appeared. What a suffering it must have been for her to go to the distant north of her country into voluntary exile, at the request of the Bishop, away from all she knew and loved—and not even to have her own name....

As the years advanced, Lucia aspired to become a Carmelite nun, but was told that her health would not permit it. She then became a member of the community which ran the orphanage: the Dorotheans. It was in one of their convents that I interviewed her in July, 1946.

And shortly before that interview, she had returned to Fatima for the first time in all those years!

Her visit there had not been announced, but the Bishop had decided that she should have permission to visit her home once more. Only a favored few were told of the visit, or happened to recognize her before she was whisked back up north to resume her "exile" in the Dorothean convent.

But during that brief visit she had, of course, visited the Cova, and verified that the Chapel of the Apparitions and the small pillar which it enclosed, were indeed at the exact place where Our Lady had appeared. (She made the identification by the position of the large tree under which the names of Blue Army members are now buried, beneath whose shade the children used to stand to await Our Lady's arrival.)

When she spoke to the Bishop afterwards, she commented on the statue in the Chapel of the Apparitions, remarking that it was indeed beautiful, but that if she were making such a statue, she would have excluded much of the ornamentation on the mantle, that there would only be a single mantle, and that she would change the tassel around her neck for a golden globe.

So the Bishop decided that the sculptor of the original statue of Our Lady of Fatima should personally speak to Lucia and make a new image more in keeping with her exact memory of how Our Lady had appeared.

It was *this* statue which Lucia referred to when she answered the Bishop's inquiry about the Pilgrim Virgin: "Yes, Excellency, and let them take the statue which Thedim made for you."

Your Excellency will remember that recently we drove past Villa Victoria in Trenton which is conducted by the Filippini Sisters and I was telling you that one of my problems is that I cannot *remember* things because I am so taken up with *doing* things. But you said that one even would bring to mind another....

And I remember now that it was at Villa Walsh, the center of the Filippini Sisters where I was giving a lecture in July, 1947, that I thought of asking the Bishop of Fatima for a *second* Pilgrim Virgin statue which might come to America and travel towards Russia from this direction—since there would be little hope that the other Pilgrim Virgin statue, traveling through Europe towards Russia along a path of much-publicized "miracles," might ever come here.

Special tribute is due to Mary Ryan, a wonderful lay woman of New York, who was present at that lecture and who instantly volunteered to pay my expenses to Portugal to enable me to talk to the Bishop and hopefully have the statue made. She has long since passed to her eternal reward. (How many wonderful persons are milestones in this "history!" How many of them will never even be mentioned!)

No one of us can take any credit. The most we can say is that we prayed that Our Lady would use us as instruments, and despite our unworthiness, and despite our many omissions, occasionally She did.

I shall never forget—in the midst of the many things I do forget—the very first words the Bishop said to me on that occasion:

"Oh, we never expected when the statue left Fatima the wonderful things that were going to happen!"

And he gave permission at once and handed me a letter for the sculptor to have a duplicate statue made to travel to the United States. I then suggested to His Excellency that without any publicity, *a third statue could be made which we might try to "smuggle" into Russia* since, with all the publicity of the miracles Our Lady was performing, there was little likelihood of the Russians ever opening their borders to the Queen of the World. **4**

I went back to Portugal again on October 13, 1947, when the Bishop—in the presence of hundreds of thousands of people—blessed those two statues. One of them he crowned, but without explaining. The other he did not crown, but standing before the microphone in the Cova, he told that immense multitude: "You see I do not crown this statue because it will be crowned in America..."

Mrs. Wiley, wife of the U.S. Ambassador to Portugal, was holding the crown, and both statues—the one which was ultimately destined for Russia and the one which was to travel to the Americas—representing the Queen of the World, were taken to the Lisbon Airport in cars of the U.S. Embassy.

Archbishop Vachon of Ottawa had recently held a Marian Congress which was the greatest ever held on the American continent. He still had the structure for the Congress and used it for the reception of the Pilgrim Virgin statue, which was certainly one of the most wonderful receptions of the statue ever to take place on our continent. **5**

One of the Bishops present on this occasion was a Bishop O'Hara, formerly an Auxiliary to Cardinal Spellman in New York, and at that time Bishop of Buffalo. (He later became Cardinal Archbishop of Philadelphia.)

Bishop O'Hara was so impressed by the occasion that he asked to have the statue enter his diocese when it had finished visiting the dioceses of Canada.

One could write several entire chapters on the tumultuous reception of the Pilgrim Virgin statue in the Diocese of
Buffalo. It crossed the border on the Feast of the Immaculate Conception (our patronal feast). Bishop O'Hara was
there to greet it. The statue then went to my former
Carmelite monastery at Niagara Falls as the last stop in
Canada before entering the United States. And the Buffalo
police record that for the visit of the statue to their city,
they witnessed the greatest traffic jams in their history.
One nationally-recognized newspaper reporter, who was
commenting at the end of that year on the greatest news
events of the past twelve months, cited—out of *all the
news* of the world that year—the visit of the Pilgrim Virgin
statue as the most outstanding.

Bishop O'Hara told me at that time that he would
personally be responsible for "booking" the visits of the
Pilgrim Virgin statue to the various dioceses of the United
States and that he would propose it at a meeting of the
Bishops which was to take place a few weeks later.

During the Bishops' meeting, a leading Cardinal said
that it was not fitting, in a country predominantly Protestant, to carry a statue of Our Lady in the streets and that
he thought we should not become involved with the
Pilgrim Virgin. As a result, not a single Bishop answered
the offer of Bishop O'Hara to arrange for the statue to
come to their diocese. As the meeting ended, Bishop
Walters of Raleigh, N.C., approached Bishop O'Hara in
the cloakroom and said: "John, you can send it to me."

So it went to the Diocese of Raleigh, and from there to a
neighboring diocese, then to another, and another
diocese, like a chain reaction, until virtually every bishop
of America had received the statue and almost all of them
had laid their croziers and mitres at Our Lady's feet. In the
end, the Cardinal who had objected, relented, and it was
received into his cathedral in New York (although rather
quietly).

6 All along the path of the Pilgrim Virgin statue, the
pledges multiplied—like myriad tokens of love, a phenomenon which continues to the present day.

Meanwhile, there was another exceptionally important
development, but one which did not become publicly
known until many years later.

Lucia had felt completely helpless, in the restrictive
capacity of a Dorothean nun, to propagate the Message of

Fatima. One by one the prophecies were coming true. The second world war had come, following the extraordinary light in the sky which had caused millions in Europe to think it was the end of the world. Russia had become a "super power" and was disseminating militant atheism "throughout the entire world." The nuclear bomb had been developed and already the atheists were brandishing it in the face of a terrified world, threatening the annihilation of entire nations, which Our Lady had warned of if Her message was not heeded.

So she decided to start an apostolate and drew up the rules—a sort of "handbook" for its operation.

But as the March of Pledges developed, which led to the Blue Army, she abandoned her plans. A Jesuit priest in Portugal, who had reviewed Lucia's "handbook," told us many years later what had happened.

Apparently Lucia came to feel that the "March of Pledges" was our response "to Our Lady's requests at Fatima" (as Cardinal Tisserant put it). She then asked permission to close herself away from the world in a Carmelite cloister.

By this time permission to see her had been greatly restricted. Fr. Lombardi, S.J., founder of the Better World Movement, was one of the last to see her (in 1956) before the Pope himself mandated that only those who had seen her earlier (which fortunately included me!) could see her again, without express permission from the Holy See. This was both to safeguard her from the growing multitude who wanted to interview her (including many notable persons whom it was hard to refuse), and also to prevent her being misquoted (which had happened on several occasions, once involving a seriously inexact reference to the delicate subject of the 1960 Secret).

What a remarkable change I noted in her when I was privileged to see her a second time in 1952! When I had seen her in July, 1946, she had appeared so serious, so full of responsibility, so concerned.

7

But when I saw her again, this time in the Coimbra Carmel, I could not help saying, with an apology: "Sister, I hope you don't mind my saying it, but you seem so much happier and even so much younger than when I saw you last."

She replied with a peal of laughter, such as one expects to hear only in places as close to heaven as a Carmel.

I was with her for about an hour on this occasion. It was an unexpected visit and I had no important questions to ask, so I did what I had failed to do several years before: I rejoiced in looking into the eyes that had gazed into the eyes of Our Lady. I enjoyed listening to the voice that had responded to the voice of the Queen of the World.

Was Lucia so much happier now because something positive was being done to promote Our Lady's message on a world-wide scale? Was she happier because Our Lady Herself, as the Pope had put it, "had gone forth as though to claim Her dominion, and the favors She performs along the way are such that We can hardly believe what We are seeing with Our eyes?" Was she happier because the Blue Army was growing all the time and already there were *millions* who had signed the pledge, and now there were little cells developing in imitation of herself and Francisco and Jacinta, who were living the message in greater depth, so that fewer souls would be lost?

Oh, how we must reproach ourselves *for the little we have done!* How we must reproach ourselves that Our Lady Herself had to take things into Her own hands as She did through the Pilgrim Virgin statue. How we must regret the petty struggles and contests for power that have marred our Apostolate!

God had given me the gift of languages, and although I worked rather earnestly in the early 1950's, traveling to various countries to help establish the Apostolate, I soon grew tired of the interminable travel—and how much time was wasted!

Whether on instructions from Lucia or not, I cannot be sure, but I presume that it was most certainly with her approval and encouragement that the Bishop of Fatima began to look on the Blue Army as the most important of all Fatima activities. He not only encouraged us to build an International Center near the Basilica to foster the Apostolate in the world, but in his last days, *the very first thing he asked his secretary each morning was:* "What news is there today of the Blue Army?"

By then he was immobilized by the affliction he had sustained during his years of imprisonment under the atheists after the revolution in Portugal in 1910, when he had been forced to stand for long hours in icy water. I cannot quite understand the bond of friendship that developed between us because I was more than 3,000 miles away and our communication was mostly by letter, but I could not write this without recording a few personal, intimate and very memorable incidents.

It will be recalled that on October 13, 1947, the Bishop blessed two Pilgrim Virgin statues, one of which would travel openly and publicly in America, and the other which he crowned, without explaining its purpose. This was the one which I brought to America with the idea of "smuggling" it into Russia.

It was in January, 1950, at the very time we launched the first issue of SOUL Magazine, that the statue left that little oratory in Washington, N.J. with Assumptionist Father Braun, on a flight via Helsinki to Moscow!

I felt a great sense of loss when the statue departed. I poured my heart out to the old Bishop in a letter. It was mixed with the sadness of parting and the joy of being able to tell him that the U.S. Government had finally forced Stalin to live up to the Litvinov Agreement and allow a Catholic chaplain in Moscow, and that this chaplain— whom I had previously informed about the statue—had agreed to take it with him.

A few months later I received a notice that there was a large crate at the New York docks addressed to me. When I opened it, I was overjoyed to find one of the loveliest statues of Our Lady of Fatima! And with it was a most beautiful note from the old Bishop which read:

"May Our Blessed Mother, through this image, grant to you, to Ave Maria Institute, to the Blue Army, and to all those associated with the Apostolate, a flood of graces and favors." Through the difficult years which followed, what a consolation the presence of that statue has been!

There is a wonder connected with it, but those who know of it, say that I should not talk about it. So I will simply say that, to me, this statue is "wonderful."

In any case, it brought to us as much a sense of the presence of Our Lady as the original Pilgrim Virgin statue had done for us, for our Apostolate in America, and for the dedicated staff who worked there.

The saintly Bishop's thoughtful generosity and prayer were wonderfully fulfilled!

But there was another dramatic incident that must be recounted:

Shortly before the old Bishop died, his Auxiliary, Bishop John Venancio, was in the room while the old

Bishop had dozed off. Suddenly he awoke with a start. Gazing intently at Bishop Venancio, he said:

"Excellency, let us take Our Lady's statue and carry it into Russia!"

And then the old man dozed off again.

Bishop Venancio (who became the second Bishop of Fatima, and also the International President of the Blue Army) said that he often recalled with a smile the picture that came to his mind on that occasion:

"I could see myself pushing the Bishop's wheelchair across Europe, while he held the statue of Our Lady between his feet and clutched it in his arms."

Remarkably, as we shall see in a later chapter, this picture became a glorious reality.... But it was to be the second Bishop of Fatima who would be holding the statue and carrying it across the Iron Curtain....

8

Before closing this chapter I ought to add that Sister Lucia was not only the source of the Blue Army Pledge, but she has followed the Blue Army constantly with her prayers and sacrifices. Details of this will be revealed later, but I think I should stress here why this involvement of Sister Lucia must be considered of major importance.

When Our Lady told her that she was to remain on earth and to "learn to read and write," we must conclude that she was to continue to be the voice of Our Lady in the world.

Lucia was so afflicted that Our Lady was moved to console her at once with the words:

"Do not be sad. My Immaculate Heart will be your consolation and the way that will lead you to God."

There is no need for us to consider how Lucia must have suffered during the years that followed when it seemed that "nothing was being done" to make known the Message of Fatima. How her heart must have been afflicted when the Infant Jesus appeared to her on February 15, 1926, at Pontevedra, and asked:

"What is being done to establish in the world devotion to the Immaculate Heart of My Mother?"

Lucia answered that she had told the Mother Superior and that the latter said there was nothing she could do.

Jesus Himself had to lament that the superior could do nothing of herself. But if she had the faith, He added, she could accomplish it all because He would assist her.

We never really knew the extent of Lucia's concern for the Blue Army, nor of the joy that she derived from seeing this Apostolate spread throughout the world, until July 5, 1981, when she twice spoke of the Blue Army:

To that lament about evil in the world, the swallowing up of the youth in waves of pornography, drug abuse, and an almost inexorable tide of materialism, Lucia replied:

"Do not be discouraged. The triumph of the Immaculate Heart of Mary is approaching. Look at the United States, a country so often associated with materialism, and yet there is the Blue Army!"

At another moment, the remark was made to her:

"It seems that we do not have great leaders today like Pius X, St. Benedict, and St. Gregory the Great." And Lucia said:

"We do have great leaders but they are not recognized. However, *today there is something more: Today there are legions like the Blue Army in the United States..."*

9

On another occasion, later in the month, Lucia was asked what advice she would give to the Blue Army today. And to our surprise she did not speak of the need for more pledges, greater numbers, television productions on the Message of Fatima, world peace flights, and so many other efforts being made to draw the attention of the world to Fatima, all of which are important.

She mentioned only one thing: She said that the present members of the Blue Army should pray the Rosary with more attention to the mysteries, and should try to be *constantly open to God.* She spoke almost an hour on the importance of a real conversion on the part of Blue Army members—in the sense that the Little Flower used the word "conversion" in her own life. To our surprise she said that there were priests, and even some bishops, who belittle the use of the Rosary and do not sufficiently encourage devotion to Our Lady. She said it was *only our own conversion,* our own greater openness to God in every moment of the day, *which would change the world as is needed in order for the Immaculate Heart of Mary now to triumph.*

We had long since felt the truth of this advice even before Lucia put it into words. In recent years we had been stressing the development of those little "cells" meeting together once a week to pray the Rosary and to consider the Message of Fatima in depth.

In the next chapter I will speak at greater length on the involvement of Lucia in the actual beginnings of the Blue Army, but before doing so I would like to share an experience which Bishop Venancio had when he was a young priest working on the commission investigating the miracle of Fatima under the first Bishop, Dom Jose Correia da Silva.

One Day Bishop Venancio was visiting his sister, whose husband had been suffering for years from a most painful affliction, chronic sciatica. He was speaking about Lucia when the husband, crying out in the desperation of his pain, said something most unexpected and surprising:

"Oh! If she really saw the Blessed Virgin, she could cure me!"

At that moment the pain left him, and never returned.

It was of course years later (after he had become Bishop of Fatima and we were traveling somewhere together) that Bishop Venancio told me this. At once the thought crossed my mind that this wonder had been performed by God because as the Bishop of Fatima he would have so many decisions to make, and God wanted him to know beyond any doubt that Lucia was truly what Our Lady had indicated: Her messenger remaining on earth until the fullness of the Fatima Message should be known.

I thought of it often. Then one day when I was again alone with the Bishop I said to him:

"Your excellency, you recall having told me of your brother-in-law's remarkable cure from sciatica as you were talking about Lucia, and he exclaimed that if she had truly seen the Blessed Virgin she could cure him?"

The Bishop nodded, and I dared to add:

"I have always felt that God permitted this because you were destined to become the second Bishop of Fatima, and He wanted you to have the consolation of knowing beyond any doubt that Lucia is truly Our Lady's messenger."

I was not surprised at the little twinkle that came into the Bishop's eyes and the smile that lit up his face, revealing that he had often thought the same.

But most remarkable of all was the fact that Pope Paul VI, after insisting that Lucia be with him at Fatima on May 13, 1967, literally took her by the shoulders and marched her to the front of that great platform, in front of hundreds of thousands of people, and then opened his arms and stepped back as though presenting her to the world. No words were spoken. But millions, either in person or by television, saw the Vicar of Christ presenting Our Lady's messenger on that 50th anniversary of the apparitions which were destined to change the world.

FOOTNOTES

1. While Lucia was **thirteen** when the first Bishop of Fatima was consecrated and installed, she went to the north of Portugal on the orders of the bishop, in June, 1921, when she was **fourteen.**

Below: Pope Paul VI with Sister Lucia and Bishop Venancio at Fatima on May 13, 1967. The following October Bishop Venancio agreed to succeed Monsignor Colgan as first "elected" International President of the Blue Army.

Chapter Five

1) Important role of first Bishop of Fatima - 2) Important role of Bishop Venancio - 3) Role of Bishop Ahr.

Below, left to right: Cardinal Tisserant (Dean of the College of Cardinals), Cardinal Centro (Apostolic Nuncio to Portugal) and Bishop Venancio (then Auxiliary Bishop of Leiria-Fatima) as Cardinal Tisserant arrived in Lisbon on October 11, 1956, as Legate of Pope Pius XII to bless the new International Center of the Blue Army at Fatima.

WHO WAS THE FOUNDER?

---

*"The Blue Army is the response to the Message
of Fatima."*
— *Eugene Cardinal Tisserant*

So far, in this slightly disjointed "history," we have
made no attempt to distinguish who was the actual
founder of the Blue Army.

Was it Sr. Lucia, who, in the parlor of the Dorothean
Convent on the outskirts of Porto, spelled out precisely
the fundamental requests of Our Lady which must be
fulfilled to bring about the conversion of Russia?

After all, we must remember that *the foundation on
which the Blue Army is built* is that simple pledge. This is
what Catholics all over the world are asked to do. This is
their essential commitment as members of "the Blue
Army." (See declaration of Bishop of Fatima on p. 320.)

The other requests of Our Lady are all tied to that same
foundation, out of which develops, almost of necessity, the
spiritual "cell" of holiness which is the second—or next
higher degree—of Blue Army membership. This spirituality is, as Fr. Joaquin M. Alonso of Madrid[1] has so beautifully expressed it, "the spirituality of Fatima as evidenced in the lives of the children whom Our Lady Herself
instructed."

Should we be more correct however in saying that the
first Bishop of Fatima, the Most Rev. Jose Correia da
Silva, was the founder of the Blue Army?

It was he who had the inspiration, and above all, the
courage to evaluate the pledge at a time when the
essential conditions of Our Lady of Fatima had not yet
been reduced to a simple formula—and to say with all the
authority as Bishop of the place of the apparitions: *"You
may promulgate this as coming from me."*

1

Was there anyone more concerned in the development of the Blue Army than this venerable prelate? How could we forget that during the last months of his life, the very first question he asked his secretary each morning was: "What new development is there today about the Blue Army?"

Indeed his interest in the Apostolate was so great that I remember begging Our Lady that he would live to see the building of the Blue Army International Center in which he seemed even more interested than the completion of the buildings at the Shrine itself (although this could be a subjective exaggeration on my part). Certainly one of the most memorable days in the history of the Blue Army was when the old Bishop in a wheelchair, pushed and guided by Bishop Venancio who was to be his successor, crossed the Cova behind the Basilica to bless the cornerstone of the Blue Army International Center and to preside at the cornerstone ceremony during which Msgr. Colgan and Fr. John Loya (a Byzantine priest) sealed the stone. (I cannot refrain from recalling here with joy that I was privileged to add a bit of the mortar.)

(I want to say a word later about Fr. Loya and an extraordinary experience he had which caused him to become deeply involved in the Blue Army, and which was instrumental in his daughter Martha's[2] decision to dedicate the rest of her life to the Apostolate.)

Before I proceed, there is something else I would like to recall about Bishop da Silva. I believe it occurred during the very last time I saw him before he died.

How many times I had climbed the steps to the second floor of his so-called "palace" in the center of Leiria (opposite the market) which was simply a large apartment over a printing press and some stores.

How many times I had been there since that first visit in July of 1946! How many times I had gone to seek advice and direction from the saintly old Bishop! And how many times I had sought his permission (almost always granted) for matters connected with the International Center being built behind the Basilica of Our Lady, or for the development of the Apostolate, or the propagation of the Pilgrim Virgin statue program!

After the usual brief wait in the parlor, I went into his study—piled on every side with books and papers accumulated through some forty years of his administration of the diocese and one of the most important Marian shrines of the world.

Now, as already mentioned, his legs were quite useless and he was sitting behind his desk. I leaned over as usual to kiss his ring, but he refused and threw his arms wide. To my amazement there were tears in his eyes and he insisted that I bend over the desk so that he could put his arms around me, and touch his cheek to mine.

What is this mystery? I know that I was slightly embarrassed, and yet I know that it was meaningful to him—with the meaning I shall understand one day. I remembered it—and identified it again as a "mystery"—when one day in the Institute, Msgr. Anthony Connell, who became the first National President of the Blue Army in the United States after Msgr. Colgan died, acted in a similar manner three days before he died.

This is a mystery of a love in the Immaculate Heart of Mary, which communicates itself to all those who are united in Her Heart, and can we not expect that those who serve to make known this important devotion in the world, as Our Lord now desires, should participate in this great mystery of Our Lady's Heart?

During the thirty years that you were the Bishop of Trenton and everything we did depended upon your will, how I prayed and "trembled," especially during the early years, when I was summoned to the Chancery Office! And yet there was always, from the very first day I met you, an experience of that same "mystery."

It flourished in a special way between the old Bishop and one of the Canons whom he chose to be his Auxiliary and whom Pope Pius XII finally appointed as his successor.

During all the times that I had been to Bishop da Silva's "palace" in Leiria, I had never even noticed Canon Venancio. By far the most prominent and influential of the Canons was Dr. Jose Galamba de Oliveira. He was the one who acted as liaison between Lucia and the Bishop, as everyone who has read Lucia's Memoirs will know. And I certainly thought that Canon Oliveira would be chosen as the Auxiliary and possibly the successor, and I believe most others did.

Canon Venancio was humble, quiet, prayerful, never in the foreground. I suppose that anyone meeting him would have perceived that he was a holy person, but there was no outward demonstration that he was holier than anyone else. But the old Bishop knew...

To return to the day when I visited Bishop da Silva and he had embraced me, I had some important business to discuss at the time, but did not feel that the old Bishop was quite up to it. By this time Bishop Venancio had been made his Auxiliary, and he was in an outer room. So before leaving, I went to see him, explained the business I had in mind and asked if he would give a decision, or at least his advice.

It would be difficult to describe the attitude of humility with which he explained that since Bishop da Silva was the Bishop, he should be the one to reply. And when I pressed for at least an opinion—a sort of "spiritual direction"— Bishop Venancio softly reaffirmed that he was only the Auxiliary, and that everything depended on "the Bishop."

During some twenty years to follow, I became very, very close to this holy man. The mystery of the love of Our Lady's Immaculate Heart flowing in and through Her children like a golden stream, would develop and flourish here as perhaps in no other relationship in my life.

These are things difficult to talk about, but in revealing them, Your Excellency, I hope I am making it clear that the real founder of the Blue Army was Our Lady Herself, and that the Apostolate flowed from that golden stream of love issuing from Her Immaculate Heart.

Bishop Venancio buried Bishop da Silva in the Basilica, just inside the sanctuary on the left side, not far from the tomb of Jacinta. And on the tomb he placed this simple inscription: *"Here lies the Bishop of Our Lady."*

The great American Jesuit, Fr. Lord, who had distinguished himself in the Sodality work, was writing the story of Fatima and he said something which very few others have observed, but which is very true. He said that most of us think of four personalities involved in Fatima: Our Lady and the three children. But there were really five: Our Lady, the three children, and the Bishop.

Recently I wrote an article in SOUL Magazine titled *Our Lady's Bishops*, and that article really should be a part of this "history." It said that there was not just one Bishop of Our Lady, but, as far as the Blue Army was concerned, there were three: Bishop da Silva, Bishop Venancio, and yourself.

How could the Blue Army have developed without *you*?

In those early days—indeed during all the thirty years that we were blessed to have you as our Bishop—your letters to us were only one or two sentences long, completely businesslike, saying essentially either "yes" or "no."

When Cardinal Tisserant decided to interest himself in the Blue Army, I understand that a letter was sent from the Vatican· to several American Bishops, including, I presume, Cardinal Spellman, requesting any information they had on Msgr. Colgan and myself. After you had answered this letter, you decided to call me to the Chancery Office and share it with me.

I suppose that was during the time of the 1954 Marian Year, or perhaps a little earlier, when we had just undertaken the building of the International Center of the Blue Army at Fatima.

Your letter to the Vatican was two pages long, single spaced, and I literally held my breath as you read it to me word by word.

It was mostly factual, completely objective, and then towards the end came "the hemline." You said that you had always found me obedient.

But you also stated in the letter that we had decided to build an International Center at Fatima and that you were not in favor of this—which of course I had not known until that moment.

So I explained the reasons why we thought that the International Center would be valuable to the Blue Army. But I added that if you were still not in favor of its construction, we would forfeit the money we had already advanced and discontinue it.

Inevitably, I expected you to say "Yes, that will be better," especially since you had already expressed your view on this to the Holy See. But instead, after a moment of quiet reflection on the reasons I had advanced, you said: "I will write to the Holy See and tell them that I have changed my opinion."

The very recollection of these words brings tears to my eyes....

Neither Msgr. Colgan nor myself had thought of consulting you about building the Center at Fatima because it was an undertaking in a different diocese. I know that, for my own part, I was always concerned about the ever-growing volume of work and responsibility we were placing on your desk, that was not, strictly speaking, diocesan, but which came under your authority because the National Center of our Apostolate was situated in your diocese. And the greatest of the burdens was the evaluation of the thousands and thousands of pages of manuscripts that came for your *Imprimatur*, and which were published under your name—bringing down upon you the criticisms of many (not excluding the most influential Cardinal in the country) who were suspicious of Fatima and who objected to the idea of having statues carried in public streets, or did not agree with the emphasis we were giving to this "private revelation."

But for you, beloved Bishop of Our Lady, the Blue Army would never have been born, would never have grown to become the vast international movement of holiness that it is today.

We adopted the motto on your Coat-of-Arms as our own: *"Mary, my hope."*

It was a fitting expression of our united devotion and loyalty to Your Excellency.

FOOTNOTES

1. Fr. Alonso, a Claretian priest and world-renowned Mariologist, was the official documentarian of Fatima. He was chosen by the Bishop of Fatima to gather together and evaluate all the documents of the Apparitions and he worked at Fatima over a period of many years. His total work fills eighteen volumes. Fr. Alonso died suddenly on December 12, 1981, just as this book was going to press. He was writing a book on "the Spirituality of the Blue Army" at the time of his death.

2. For those who may be surprised to learn that Martha's father was a priest, it should be explained that it was permissible for a married man to be ordained in the Byzantine Rite at that particular time.

MARIA SPES MEA

Most Reverend
GEORGE W. AHR, S.T.D.

Below: The 120-room International Center of the Blue Army at
Fatima as seen from the Basilica.

Chapter Six

1) Brother of Saint Maria Goretti joins - 2) Msgr. Colgan's amazing story - 3) Forces joined.

Above: Msgr. Colgan giving Benediction of Blessed Sacrament.

MONSIGNOR
HAROLD V. COLGAN

"We will be the Blue Army of Our Lady against the Red Army of atheism."
— *Msgr. Colgan*

The first person to use the name "Blue Army" was Msgr. Harold V. Colgan. (I constantly refer to him as "Monsignor," although in those early days, of course, he did not have that title.)

He was quite an unusual priest. Very few people ever got really close to him. He had an amazingly childlike simplicity. You know how much he loved baseball. As a young man, he was seriously injured while playing the game. And when we used to go to Fatima to celebrate the 13th of October, it was a great sacrifice for him if we had to miss the end of the World Series. He once quipped that his idea of heaven would be to have a spot just behind the catcher's position for all the World Series games in history.

In the seminary he had made the Act of St. Grignon de Monfort—the Act of Total Consecration to Our Lady—and he really lived it. His greatest interest and greatest concern (as well as joy) was the children. Regularly he went through the school and visited every classroom, and one of my most arresting and vivid memories of him is the following incident:

I had gone down to Plainfield to consult with him about something concerning the Blue Army, and they told me in the rectory that he was in the church speaking to the children.

You will remember that the beautiful St. Mary's Church in Plainfield has a large transept, with entrances on both sides, as well as having the main entrance in the front. I entered through one of the transept doors; Msgr. Colgan was speaking in the nave and so did not see me. I knelt quietly and heard him saying to the children: *"It is better to die than to commit one mortal sin."*

And then he called upon the children to affirm this, and one after the other they made the declaration that they would rather die than commit a mortal sin.

Having chanced upon this scene so abruptly, I could not help but wonder how the children's parents might react if they were kneeling in my place and heard their young ones making this affirmation. Would they not have thought: "But a mortal sin can be forgiven, but if my child died...."

The models whom Msgr. Colgan held up to the children were St. Maria Goretti and St. Dominic Savio—two children who had indeed preferred death to sin and are now canonized.

Could one say anything more to indicate the kind of "pastor" Msgr. Colgan was?

And St. Maria Goretti, through her brother, was to play a major role in the development of the Blue Army for youth.

As Your Excellency knows, the oldest brother of St. Maria Goretti lived in your diocese, only seven miles from the National Blue Army Center in Washington, N.J. He and Msgr. Colgan became good friends and it gave us all great joy when Mr. Goretti not only signed the Blue Army Pledge, but "endorsed" the Blue Army as a movement which his sainted sister would have welcomed. Monsignor would drive up and take Mr. Goretti to St. Mary's so that the children could meet the living brother of the saint.

Although it does not enter essentially into this story, there is an interesting—and perhaps memorable—anecdote connected with the death of Mr. Goretti.

Br. Aloysius, the brother in my book *The Brother and I*, had been visiting me. We drove past Mr. Goretti's house as I was taking Brother to Allentown to visit his Carmelite sister there. We had just passed the Goretti house at about forty miles an hour, when suddenly I realized Br. Aloysius had never met him. I quickly pulled over, backed the car, and drove into Mr. Goretti's driveway.

There was very little likelihood at that time of day (mid-morning) that Mr. Goretti would be home. Surprisingly, we found him sitting on the side porch. It was July 6, a very pleasant day.

As we chatted by the driveway, an elderly woman came walking along the side of the road, turned into the driveway, came up to Mr. Goretti and said: "Sir, I want to congratulate you on your sister's feast day."

There was something strange about her—but I will reserve my personal opinion concerning this because it might seem too extraordinary.

For some reason the liturgy of that day was not of St. Maria Goretti, so neither Brother nor myself had realized that it was the feast day, and Mr. Goretti himself had forgotten! He said to the old lady: "Good heavens! You remind *me*!"

And as the old lady walked away, I turned back to Mr. Goretti and said:

"When have you last been over to see the tomb of your sister, and the great monument that has been made of the house and the very spot where you found her bleeding to death?"

(It was this brother, Angelo, who had been the first to come to the house and find his young sister dying with fourteen stab wounds.)

"Oh, I have not been back since the Canonization," he said. I was amazed and asked why. He explained that he simply had not been able to afford it.

Without any further thought, I put my arm around his shoulders and said:

"Mr. Goretti, as a feast day gift to you from your sainted sister, I am going to give you a free trip to Italy with a Blue Army pilgrimage."

I accompanied that pilgrimage. When we arrived in Naples, I hired a car, and alone drove Mr. Goretti down to a farm outside the city where one of his brothers was living. It was one of those farms with the animals downstairs, and living quarters upstairs. Mr. Goretti's brother had been ill. He came to the upstairs window in a robe— almost unable to believe his eyes when he saw his brother Angelo in the courtyard below.

I had a camera with me, but the emotion of the meeting of the two brothers was so deep that I felt that I could not intrude upon it by taking a photograph.

Subsequently Mr. Goretti visited his sister who was a nun in Taormina, and then went to the old homestead near Nettuno, where he saw the church and the beautiful tomb of his sainted sister, before journeying to Genoa where he visited other relatives. He was returning to the United States on the *Michelangelo* when mechanical trouble developed on the ship, and the vessel had to return to Genoa. While waiting for the ship to sail again, he was dining with relatives in Genoa, when suddenly he collapsed on the dining room table—dead of a coronary.

When I heard the news, I rejoiced that he had been able to visit all the family, and especially the tomb of his dear and sainted sister, thus preparing himself for their final reunion in heaven. His daughter had the body returned to New Jersey, and he is buried only seven miles from the National Center of The Blue Army of Our Lady of Fatima.

But to return to Msgr. Colgan: it was one of his curates who learned of Fatima first—way back in those early days just after the war when all of us were first hearing about Fatima. Shortly after this, Msgr. Colgan developed a heart condition which could have been fatal. He went down to Johns Hopkins Hospital in Baltimore and they said that a long period of absolute rest was essential.

But he was not a man to rest, as Your Excellency knows!

He came back to Plainfield, and another attack sent him back to the hospital where, in the fall of 1947, he realized that he might possibly die. I have never verified the hospital records, but I can tell Your Excellency exactly how Monsignor related this to me on several occasions:

Feeling he might die in the prime of his priestly life, he promised Our Lady that if She would restore him to health he would spend the rest of his life spreading devotion to Her under Her title of Fatima. He also promised to make known, to the best of his ability, Her message of conversion of Russia and world peace.

He suddenly felt convinced that Our Lady had heard his prayer and he wanted to leave the hospital immediately. The hospital, of course, could not yet discharge him, but somehow he managed to get his clothes on and go down to St. Mary's.

His own doctor was present in the Church and stunned to see him come out to say Mass. Knowing that Monsignor could not possibly have been released from the hospital without his authority, and fearing that he might have a coronary even while saying Mass, he went out and called the Archbishop.

Hardly was Mass over when the Archbishop was on the phone insisting that Msgr. Colgan return to the hospital.

But the latter told him of his experience and his feelings and asked permission to go to Johns Hopkins for verification that he was cured.

I suppose all this should be adequately verified, for we are not narrating it as it actually happened, but as Msgr. Colgan believed it to have happened, and as he himself recounted it to us many times later.

Wondering how he might fulfill his promise to the Blessed Virgin, he decided to conduct a Novena in honor of Our Lady of Fatima every Wednesday and he preached on a different aspect of the Message of Fatima each week.

Meanwhile, it must be remembered, he had been very active in the Sodality of Our Lady. As I said in the first chapter, Fr. Daniel Lord had cited him as one of the most outstanding Sodality priests in America. And he received the Scapular Magazine, in which we were promulgating the March of Pledges.

Finally, on the fifth or sixth Wednesday, the thought came to him as he entered the pulpit to ask all present to wear "something blue" if they were going to fulfill the requests of Our Lady so that they could stand up and be counted. Without premeditation he found himself saying: *"We will be the Blue Army of Our Lady against the Red Army of Communism."*

It was not long after this that he had invited me to come and speak about the Message of Fatima in his parish. As I have already mentioned, it was an experience that impressed me deeply and was the reason for my inviting Msgr. Colgan to the farm in Washington, N.J., when I had completed the oratory in which the Pilgrim Virgin statue for Russia was "hidden" until it could go to Moscow.

I lectured a great deal in those days, sometimes averaging 300 or more lectures a year—one for almost every day. This was because it was not unusual for me to give two and three lectures a day when I was on tour.

To me, an "audience" became like an individual person. They differed from place to place. Each seemed to have its own personality, its own identity. Some seemed eager to listen to what was going to be said. Some seemed skeptical and had to be won over. In all there seemed to be a slightly different degree of affinity, either to the speaker, or to the subject.

As I recall elsewhere in this "history," I remember that the audience at St. Mary's in Plainfield, N.J., was one of the warmest and most receptive I had encountered. Msgr. Colgan had certainly prepared them well!

And I noticed there were many in the audience wearing little blue ribbons. When it was explained to me that these were being worn as an outward sign of the commitment to fulfill the requests of Our Lady, I at once thought: "What a wonderful idea!"

As I mentioned earlier, the "right hand" of Msgr. Colgan in this effort was Mrs. Marie Hart, a wonderful person whose husband was in the business of hospital supplies.

It was Marie who prepared most of those little blue bows, and it was she who urged me a year later when I left the Scapular Apostolate in New York, to team up with Msgr. Colgan and spread this idea of the Blue Army on a national scale. Shortly after that I ran into Fr. Lord in a Childs' Restaurant in New York, and after asking his advice, received the answer:

"If you and Fr. Colgan join forces, there will be an explosion for Our Lady."

Neither Msgr. Colgan nor anyone else realized at the time that there was a marvelous biblical foundation for wearing a blue ribbon as a sign of fulfillment of the Blue Army Pledge. It is found in the book of Numbers:

"The Lord said to Moses: 'Speak to the Israelites and tell them that they and their descendants must put tassels on the corners of their garments, fastening each corner tassel with a blue cord. When you use these tassels, let the sight of them remind you to keep all the commandments of the Lord, without going astray after the desires of your hearts and eyes. Thus you will remember to keep all my commandments and be holy to your God.'" (15: 37-41)

Below: Monsignor Colgan with Rev. Andreas Fuhs, President of the European Committee of the Blue Army and later Rector of the Blue Army International Center at Fatima. Father Fuhs died while serving in the latter capacity and is buried in the cemetery of Fatima near the former tomb of the children who saw Our Lady in 1917.

Chapter Seven

1) Father Fox and Msgr. Connell - 2) Msgr. Colgan "remains" with us.

Below: The late Monsignor Anthony Connell with Sister Mary Grace, A.M.I., coordinator of Blue Army national organization, and Sister Mary Joseph, A.M.I., Superioress of the Handmaids of Mary Immaculate who administer the U.S. National Center of the Blue Army in Washington, N.J.

MONSIGNOR COLGAN'S SUCCESSORS

"It is a challenge we must meet." — Most Rev. Jerome J. Hastrich, D.D., Bishop of Gallup

Unfortunately, we have very few personal writings of Msgr. Colgan. He trusted me to write the articles, and even most of the letters. We do have many pictures, however, and the recording of a talk he gave describing his approach to his fellow priests for help with the construction of the Blue Army Center at Fatima. In this he describes his consecration to Our Lady, as explained by St. Grignon de Montfort, and how he readily found cooperation of priests who had made the same consecration.

One of my most vivid memories of him is the last... shortly before his death.

Never in our quarter century of association had he ever refused me anything, and I looked into his clear blue eyes and said: *"Monsignor, please do not leave us! We have no priest to take your place."*

That twinkle of humor one had seen so often in those clear and pure eyes sparkled again. He could not speak. But there was a reassurance, as though saying *that he would still be with us.*

And on the very day of his death we had the most wonderful corroboration of his continued nearness.

We had signed the contract to purchase the convent of the apparitions in Pontevedra, Spain, but could not do anything further because the representative of the Archbishop of Santiago was of the firm opinion that the entire inside of the convent had to be destroyed and that a new structure was needed within just the outer shell of stone.

On the very night of Monsignor's death (April 16, 1972), the wife of a doctor on the outskirts of Chicago had a dream which impressed her so much that she could no longer sleep. She began early in the morning to telephone us to say that she wanted to make a large offering for a convent in Spain which she had seen falling into ruins.

This is so important that I will recall it later in great detail, but as a direct result of this, *the actual convent of the apparitions* of Our Lord and Our Lady (giving the promise of the First Saturdays to the world) *was saved.*

Perhaps even more extraordinary is the story which was sent to us some years later—and which we intended merely to keep in our archives to see whether similar events might develop.

An abandoned mother, with six children, wrote that on April 15, 1981, she was facing a grave problem to which she had not been able to find a solution. It involved a good and dutiful son who had lost all interest in life, and at this time experienced a major setback. She writes:

"As I prayed in desperation I remembered that Fr. Colgan died on April 16, so I prayed so hard that night and the whole next day, April 16, to Fr. Colgan for great help for my son."

The immediate sequence of events (details of which filled a typed page) seemed an extraordinary answer to her prayers. She concludes:

"I was amazed at all this. I am already a full day late in telling of this favor and so decided to bear witness before another day passes. I firmly believe I have had direct help from Fr. Colgan and am going to pray to him often for the much-needed help in my family life and problems."[1]

But what to me is most marvelous and consoling as I recall that last visit with Monsignor before he died is that from the day of his death *we have never lacked a priest to take his place.* And little by little the number of priests who became involved in the Blue Army increased by leaps and bounds.

Fr. Robert J. Fox had begun to mention the Blue Army in his columns in the *National Catholic Register* and in *Our Sunday Visitor*. This was followed by books written on the Message of Fatima, and particularly of that special role of Our Lady as a Catechist...which had always been one of Msgr. Colgan's primary concerns: the presentation of the Message of Fatima to youth.

Not only did Fr. Fox begin to promote this in his newspaper columns and books, but he began to organize pilgrimages to Fatima for young people, and to conduct special catechetical weeks of instruction for them which resulted in the development of the Blue Army Cadets in America and gradually throughout the world, and also resulted in many vocations both to the priesthood and to religious communities of women.

And almost immediately after Msgr. Colgan's death a close friend of his—one of those who had made the de Montfort Act of Consecration in the seminary with him— came to the Ave Maria Institute for materials. I happened to be there alone in my office (on a Saturday) when he arrived.

He was Msgr. Anthony Connell, perhaps one of the most wonderful priests in the entire Archdiocese of Newark. He said that he simply *felt inspired to come and get material on the Blue Army* and to begin to promote it more ardently *since Msgr. Colgan had died*. Shortly afterwards he joined us on the pilgrimage to Paray-le-Monial and Pontevedra for the celebration of the Feasts of the Sacred Heart of Jesus and the Immaculate Heart of Mary in the very year when these feasts were celebrated together for the first time in the Church.

In subsequent stages, *Msgr. Connell came to be the first National President of the Blue Army in the United States, following Msgr. Colgan.*

Msgr. Connell agreed that we should concentrate on organization. He knew that to "switch" the power and the direction of this Apostolate from self-perpetuating trustees to elected officers was going to be far from easy!

Msgr. Connell was suffering this pain with me. Indeed it may be that he was suffering even more than I knew. One Thursday he came to discuss the matter with me and while doing so, suddenly leaned forward and touched his head to my chest and said: "I love you, John."

It seemed that he wanted to console me for calumny and contradictions that were part of this trial.

Two days later, at the eight o'clock parish Mass, after Communion he suddenly collapsed over the altar—and was dead.

I have not the slightest doubt in my own mind and heart that he went straight to heaven—to continue his thanksgiving throughout eternity. Like Msgr. Colgan he had lived the consecration of St. Grignon de Montfort. He was what one could only have described as the "ideal priest."

So we can believe that we have another champion at the throne of heaven who can now see *everything* we need!

Within two years, for the first time after almost thirty years, elections for Blue Army national officers were held, and you, dear Bishop Ahr, became our first *elected* president.

You yourself had just undergone major surgery, and you also were suffering in the throes of this pain of reorganization in addition to all of the many burdens you had to carry in your diocese of some 800,000 souls.

You would not refuse to have your name on the ballot, but now felt that you should not serve. And the Most Rev. Jerome J. Hastrich, Bishop of Gallup (who had been elected vice president) succeeded you and—a year later—became the second elected national president.

In his first published statement to the national membership of the Blue Army, which was published in SOUL Magazine, Bishop Hastrich said: "I see the Blue Army as a tremendous force for good in the world today."

As I think of you, of Bishop Hastrich, and of the Most Rev. Nicholas T. Elko—an outstanding member of the American hierarchy who succeeded Bishop Hastrich as vice president for a one-year term, I seem to see the smiling, reassuring blue eyes of Msgr. Colgan as I remembered them shining up at me from his death bed when I said: "Do not leave us!"

We continue to know that he is with the Apostolate today in a different, but perhaps far more important way. He is buried in the crypt at the Holy House at our National Center in Washington, N.J.

As I will tell elsewhere, one sometimes hears "angelic voices" above this crypt in the Holy House and one might wonder whether this is because of the stones of the original Holy House of Nazareth imbedded in the walls or because of this wonderful priest, so dedicated to Our Lady, who in his early years in the seminary made a total act of consecration to Our Lady in the spirit of St. Grignon de Montfort and lived that consecration in its totality every moment of his life.

FOOTNOTES

1. A photostatic copy of the original letter may be had on request from the Blue Army, Washington, N.J. 07882.

Below: Bishop Ahr blessing the replica of the Holy House at the Blue Army's U.S. National Center in Washington, N.J. Preceding Bishop Ahr are Bishop Venancio (the Bishop of Fatima and International President of the Blue Army) and Father Modestus Papi, O.F.M. Cap., Director of the Universal Congregation of the Holy House (Loreto, Italy). Behind Bishop Ahr is the Rt. Rev. Anthony J. Connell who succeeded Monsignor Colgan as U.S. President of the Blue Army. Monignor Colgan is buried in the crypt of this "Holy House" chapel.

Chapter Eight

---

1) First International Secretary - 2) Center needed at Fatima - 3) First great leader in Europe: Abbe Richard - 4) "First" Cardinal of the Church gives support - 5) Fatima Center redesigned by Russian priest - 6) Role of Saint Joseph - 7) Auditorium for special meetings.

Below: The Blue Army International Center at Fatima, showing top of major dome of Byzantine chapel, with "onion" dome and Russian-style cross atop it.

INTERNATIONAL CENTER AT FATIMA

"The Blue Army should make (it) known to the whole world." — *Eugene Cardinal Tisserant, Dean of the Sacred College of Cardinals*

Your Excellency will recall that dramatic, and to me very moving, moment when you decided, after hearing the reasons for building an International Center of the Blue Army at Fatima, to write to the Holy See to say that you had changed your opinion about the advisability of this.

The history of the Blue Army as *an international movement* is tied directly, almost essentially, to the building of that International Center.

Bishop da Silva had a multi-lingual secretary named Dona Maria de Freitas, a tiny woman who had moved to Fatima with an invalid sister.

Her name should be written in great capital, golden   1
letters in the history of this Apostolate.

She knew about the Blue Army from the very beginning, because although I knew French and Spanish well enough, it was so much easier for me to correspond with the Bishop in English and Maria de Freitas translated all the correspondence. Since she was also translating most of the other international correspondence, she realized that the only true effective Apostolate of Fatima that was developing in the world was the Blue Army. So when I asked her if she would become our first International Secretary, although burdened with a very substantial volume of work, she readily accepted, without even a moment of hesitation.

She was so humble, so unassuming...and yet she was an absolute master of English, French, Spanish, Italian, and even German! And what is equally impressive, to those who do not know the intricacies of the Portuguese language, she was also a master of her own language. Many articles flowed from her pen, and appeared in prominent Portuguese periodicals, always signed with a pseudonym.

Most of us acquainted with Fatima know of Fr. John DeMarchi's masterful book *The Immaculate Heart of Mary*, but few know that the real author of that book was Maria de Freitas! And most of the work on my own book *Meet the Witnesses* was done by the indefatigable Maria.

Never in my life have I met so capable and industrious a person who was also, at the same time, so completely self-effacing. She always remained behind the scene, giving the impression of being worthless, while her saintly heart, as well as her mind, were contributing more to the Apostolate than anyone could have dreamed.

One would have wondered at such virtue — but she had a special secret: an invalid sister confined to bed, who constantly offered her helplessness and suffering for the triumph of Our Lady's Immaculate Heart. The two lived in a small house on the south end of the only road that went from the parish church of Fatima to the Cova. Maria supported them by teaching languages to the children of the area, and by renting rooms to pilgrims.

As I explained to Your Excellency that day you read to me your letter to the Vatican: I had believed in Fatima before I went there, but it was only when I was actually there that I *realized* the importance and urgency of the Fatima Message. It was only when I stood there where Our Lady had opened the ground and shown the children a vision of hell, and touched the spot of the little tree upon which She had stood and foretold the rise of atheistic Communism in the world, and said if Her requests were heard, the tide of evil would be turned back, Russia would be converted and there would be peace.

And I suddenly asked myself: "What are we doing?"

A tremendous sense of responsibility came over me on that July day in 1946 — only a short time after the end of the great war which Our Lady had prophesied at that very spot, if Her requests were not heard.

As we began to develop the Blue Army, I felt that if we were going to have leaders of the Apostolate, we would have to have persons *who realized the importance of the message* and if we could get them to Fatima, they might also become suddenly and totally convinced and committed.

But there were no facilities at Fatima at that time. There
was not even an English-speaking office of any kind.
There were only primitive houses for pilgrims.

Clearly an English-speaking center was a priority. My
initial thoughts envisaged something very modest: a
simple building with two small chapels at either end, one
Latin and the other Byzantine, thus symbolizing in one
building the union of East and West which Our Lady had
promised if Her requests were heard.

The fact that the Blue Army was gradually becoming a
vast international movement made the establishment of
this Center at Fatima increasingly urgent.

With the endorsement of Bishop da Silva, I went with
Msgr. Colgan on a trip to several countries of Europe in
1951 with the purpose of seeking out Marian leaders who
might start centers of our Apostolate.

At a meeting in London we talked with Douglas Hyde
and the Honorable Henrietta Bower, who subsequently
founded the All-Night Vigil movement and who raised
funds for a room at our International Center in the name of
Great Britain.

But our greatest "find" on this trip was in Paris where,
at that time, there was an Auxiliary Bishop exclusively
concerned with Catholic Action.

This prelate gave me the names of four or five Marian-
minded priests, and I invited each of them in turn to a
lunch or a dinner and finally decided that the most desir-
able "candidate" to head our Apostolate in France was
Abbe Andre Richard, who was, and still is, editor of a
prestigious newspaper in Paris called *l'Homme Nouveau*
and a co-founder of an ecumenical movement called *Pour
l'Unite*. The sign of membership in this unity movement
was a small blue cross. Abbe Richard already knew about
the Message of Fatima and felt that it could become part of
their movement for unity because of the promise of Our
Lady to convert Russia.

Almost at once, however, Abbe Richard found a great
deal of opposition within the Movement for Unity to the
introduction of the Message of Fatima. Much of this was
undoubtedly chauvinistic. To this day the Message of
Fatima is considered of very secondary importance in
France, where Our Lady had appeared at Lourdes.

As this opposition mounted, and as Abbe Richard's own conviction of the importance of Fatima deepened, he decided to go to Rome and seek advice.

4 By the providence of God, the Cardinal to whom he addressed himself was none other than His Eminence, Eugene Cardinal Tisserant, Dean of the Sacred College of Cardinals.

His Eminence had already been reading *l'Homme Nouveau,* and at the very beginning of the interview, he praised Abbe Richard for having introduced the Message of Fatima into the movement and heartily supported this action. The Abbe then asked if the Cardinal would give them some kind of written endorsement.

The result was a magnificent article from Cardinal Tisserant describing the Blue Army as *"the response to the message of Our Lady of Fatima,"* and quoting the Scripture attributed to Our Lady, namely that She is "like an army in battle array," and that the Queen needs this spiritual army for Her victory.

Later Cardinal Tisserant was to give the Blue Army its greatest mandate when he said: *"The Blue Army should make known to the whole world, and not just to Catholics, what is necessary in order that peace may reign at last in the whole world."*

In other words, His Eminence not only saw that it was fitting for Our Lady to have an army, but since this army was formed, His Eminence pointed out that its members had the *obligation* to make known the Message of Fatima *to the entire world*.

In addition to being Dean of the College of Cardinals—and therefore the most important Cardinal in the Church, Cardinal Tisserant was also an intimate of Pope Pius XII and perhaps had more influence with the Pope than any other member of the Curia.

Your Excellency will recall that shortly after this—or perhaps before the Cardinal wrote the letter to *l'Homme Nouveau*—a questionnaire had come from the Vatican to several American bishops concerning Msgr. Colgan and myself. And it was undoubtedly due to the answer given by Your Excellency that the full endorsement of the Pope and of Cardinal Tisserant followed.

In any event, when we decided with the permission of the Bishop of Fatima to build the International Center behind the Basilica, Cardinal Tisserant took a special interest in the fact that we had planned to put a Byzantine Chapel in the building and he even suggested a priest who could be chaplain.

He was Fr. Pavel Bliznetsov, a former captain in the Soviet Air Force who had flown his plane to Germany after the war and then walked to Rome to become a Byzantine priest. Cardinal Tisserant took him under his wing and sponsored him through the Russicum (Russian College) in Rome. He then offered to send him to Fatima as the first chaplain of our "Byzantine Center of the Blue Army's International Secretariat."

Fr. Pavel was a true Russian not only in nationality, but in character. When he saw the unpretentious plans that I had drawn up—providing for only a few rooms with two very small chapels at either end of the building, he exclaimed: "These plans are unworthy of such an important project!"

So he went down to Lisbon, found an architect, and ordered a new set of plans. This was done without our knowledge, and the bill from the architect was a large fraction of the total I had expected to pay for the entire building!

Fr. Pavel wanted to go ahead at once with the construction and expected to have a free hand in the project. He asked that the necessary funds be sent to him to begin work immediately.

Of course we had no funds. We had nothing at all! And after waiting impatiently at Fatima for the deadlock to be resolved, Fr. Pavel asked the Cardinal to send him to work among Russian immigrants in Germany until such time as we might be ready to begin the construction of the Center.

I keep interrupting this "history" with little anecdotes which would otherwise be lost, but which are really not essential to this particular account. I feel compelled, however, to add a touching anecdote here concerning Fr. Pavel which was published in SOUL Magazine under the title of *"The Russian Who Wouldn't Take 'No' for An Answer."*[1]

Before he left Fatima, Fr. Pavel made a determined effort to see Sr. Lucia in the Carmelite Convent at Coimbra. Despite being told by the Bishop of Fatima's secretary that it was impossible to see the famous visionary and that even the many bishops who had requested to see her while they were en-route to the Second Vatican Council had all failed, Fr. Pavel persisted with characteristic Russian obstinacy.

He resolved, on the eve of his departure for Germany, to visit the Coimbra Carmel and speak to the Mother Prioress.

Waiting by the grille in the convent, he saw the Prioress enter, accompanied, as was the custom, by one of the other Sisters of the community. Fr. Pavel told her the moving story of his flight from Russia, of how he had been an engineer, aviator and officer in the Soviet Air Force. He spoke of his imprisonment, his flight, of how he had no faith...and then he had found it, and decided to belong to God even more than he had once belonged to the Soviets. In Rome, he had become a priest, a Catholic priest of the Byzantine Rite.

The interview came to a close. "Reverend Mother," Fr. Pavel pleaded, "please pray much for my poor country, for my countrymen, and tell Sr. Lucia to pray much for Russia."

The Mother Prioress straightened, pointed to the silent Sister at her side and said simply: *"This is Sister Lucia!"*

The astonished Russian gave his blessing to them both and then departed, full of joy and satisfaction for his holy obstinacy.

As Your Excellency knows, there was a wonderful relationship between Msgr. Colgan and myself which lasted almost a quarter century—until his death. There was never a disagreement between us. The only time I did not agree with him in principle, and when he was quite definite about it I agreed with him in obedience, was on the difficult question of beginning the building of the International Center at Fatima before we had raised a substantial amount of the necessary money. He simply decided that this was something that had to be done, that Our Lady would provide the means, and therefore we should make the commitment and commence the building in good faith.

6

I thought this implied that I was to be the one to raise the money, but really it was Our Lady and St. Joseph—upon whose shoulders we immediately placed the burden—and upon the active workers of the Blue Army who were being reached through SOUL Magazine.

Before the building began, despite the appeals in the magazine, no great amount was forthcoming. So someone suggested that we invite a few prominent persons to a dinner at a New York hotel, present them with the need and ask for substantial support.

One of the persons we invited to that meeting was Rose Saul Zalles, whose family owned a great deal of real estate in Washington, D.C., and whose father had founded one of the prominent Washington banks.

She was the only person at the meeting who offered even one dollar, but her offering was quite a lot more! She said quietly that she wanted to pay for the Byzantine Chapel, and a week later we received a check for $25,000! (The Chapel ultimately cost about $200,000, but that $25,000 was all we needed to begin the work.)

We finally agreed that the "grand plan" of Fr. Pavel Bliznetzov was what Our Lady really wanted, and that we should build that great building of 125 rooms, with a Byzantine Chapel whose dome would become a Fatima landmark.

Today the building is one of the most impressive structures at Fatima and is the closest building to the Basilica for receiving pilgrims.

Always preoccupied with the need for having people come to Fatima and experiencing its reality for themselves, in order that they may take upon themselves its responsibility, I wanted an auditorium with multi-lingual facilities in which seminars could be held.

The Vatican Pavilion of the World's Fair at Brussels had such simultaneous translation equipment, and I arranged for its purchase two years before our auditorium at Fatima was completed.

It is truly a beautiful auditorium, with seats for 500 people. Important meetings on the Message of Fatima have been held there through the years. Perhaps one of the most significant was the 1969 international seminar over which Cardinal Ursi of Naples presided and in which we were discussing the advisability of petitioning the Holy See to declare the Rosary a "liturgical prayer." The Cardinal spoke with the authority of the Holy Father in saying that we should not pursue this debate and that we should realize that the importance of the Rosary does not depend on its being a liturgical prayer.

But probably the 1971 international seminary on the Immaculate Heart of Mary was of the greatest historical importance to date. We chartered a plane to bring the top Mariologists of the world from the recent Marian

Congress in Zagreb, Yugoslavia. The Bishop of Fatima had sent invitations to all the bishops of the world to attend, either in person or through a legate. During this important seminar, the way was prepared for the Collegial Consecration of Russia to the Immaculate Heart of Mary. One of the principal speakers was Father Luigi Ciappi, O.P. (later Cardinal), theologian of the Papal Household. He spoke on the doctrine of devotion to the Immaculate Heart of Mary and the meaning of the consecration.

At the instruction of the Bishop, the discourses of the six major speakers were published in a book[2], which was translated into several languages, and sent to all the bishops of the world.

While I was a prime organizer of this seminar, as the International Lay Delegate of the Blue Army, I had not the remotest intention of participating as a speaker. But the Bishop of Fatima insisted that I speak on the "practical application of the Message of Fatima," which, of course, is the Blue Army.

Something happened at this seminar which is important to recall:

Up to this time, there were many who felt that the Scapular had been "dragged into" the Blue Army Pledge by myself because of my previous close connection with this devotion and the books I had written about it.

This feeling not only persisted, but some violated the statutes of the Blue Army and did not include the mention of the Scapular in their use of the pledge. And in the international meetings, in which the statutes were repeatedly reexamined, the Scapular was mentioned, not as a necessary, but as a *fitting* sign of our consecration to the Immaculate Heart of Mary. This was dramatically changed during that historic seminar on the meaning of devotion to the Immaculate Heart of Mary.

FOOTNOTES

1. SOUL Magazine, May-June 1963, p. 12.
2. A Heart for All, AMI Press, Washington, N.J.

Above: Barn on the farm bought by John Haffert which, with the growth of and need for promotion of the Blue Army, was converted into the Ave Maria Institute ca. 1949. Below: The barn is beginning to assume the now-familiar lines of the business office of the U.S. Blue Army. (Picture below does not show later addition now housing data processing, bookkeeping/accounting, and administrative offices.)

Chapter Nine

1) "The Rosary and the Scapular will save the world"
2) Study of these devotions is needed - 3) How to know the Rosary - 4) The Voice of the Church: Importance of Papal pronouncements to the Blue Army - 5) Some of the most outstanding leaders within the ranks of the Blue Army

On May 13, 1967, Pope Paul VI issued the encyclical SIGNUM MAGNUM and paid a personal visit to Fatima. His Holiness said that the two principal Marian devotions for our time, in keeping with Paragraph 67 of LUMEN GENTIUM, are the Scapular of Mt. Carmel and the Rosary (the two principal devotions promoted by the Blue Army).

VATICAN II AND THE PLEDGE

"The Scapular and the Rosary are inseparable."
— *Sr. Lucia, August 15, 1950*

One of the speakers at the aforementioned seminar on the Immaculate Heart of Mary in August 1971 was the Archbishop of Coimbra, a city some 60 miles to the north of Fatima.

Coimbra is an old and important diocese. Lucia, sole survivor of the three children who saw Our Lady at Fatima, is a Carmelite nun in the Carmel in that city.

(Many of us who are particularly interested in the Holy House of Nazareth, now in Loreto, Italy, will remember that in past history it was the Archbishop of Coimbra who obtained from the Pope a stone from the Holy House, and then fell into an illness which seemed mortal until the stone was returned—and that there is a document in the archives of the Holy House to this day with the seal of the Bishop, testifying that Our Lady had appeared to a nun in his diocese and told him that he would only recover when he had returned the stone to Our Lady's house.)

The present Archbishop who spoke at the Seminar was a Dominican and had been an active member of the committee of Vatican Council II which had prepared Paragraph 67 of *Lumen Gentium* (Constitution on the Church in the Modern World).

During his talk, the Archbishop said that he had argued with other members of the committee that the Rosary should be explicitly mentioned in that paragraph of the Constitution of the Church as one of the traditional devotions which is to be most encouraged at the present time.

"It was the judgment of the committee," the Archbishop said, "that they should not mention *any devotion* in the Vatican Document but that *it should be left to the Holy Father at any given moment in history to indicate which devotions were of greatest importance.* ''

This very important ''note'' to the action of the Second Vatican Council might have been lost in history. And in view of the action taken by the Pope (Paul VI) just a few months after the promulgation of *Lumen Gentium*, it is of crucial significance.

Three months after he had promulgated *Lumen Gentium*, Pope Paul VI sent this instruction to the Marian Congress held that year in the Dominican Republic:

"You will make known our will and our exhortations which we base upon the dogmatic constitution of the Ecumenical Council, Vatican II, which is in complete conformity with our thought and indeed upon which our thought is based:

" 'That one ever hold in great esteem the practices and exercises of the devotion to the most blessed Virgin which have been recommended for centuries by the Magisterium of the Church.' (67) And among them we judge well to recall especially the Marian Rosary and the religious use of the Scapular of Mount Carmel...a form of piety which is adapted by its simplicity to the spirit indeed of everyone, and is most largely widespread among the faithful for an increase of spiritual fruit.

"In these times when we instruct the Christian people, it is necessary constantly and clearly to inculcate the realization that insofar as the Mother is honored, so the Son...for Whom all exists [cf. Col. 1:15-16]...will be known, loved, glorified as He should be, and that His commandments will be observed [#66, Constitution de Ecclesia, cited above]; it is also necessary to advise the faithful that piety toward the Mother of God is not to be found in a sterile and passive sentimentalism nor in a certain vain credulity, but on the contrary that it proceeds by that true faith through which we are carried towards a recognition of the eminence of the Mother of God, driven to a filial love toward our Mother and to the imitation of her virtues... Mother of the church, Mother of Grace and of Mercy, Mother of Hope and of Holy Joy, she by whom we have access to Jesus and to the sources of salvation which are in Him, by a royal, direct way."

This papal statement is the most important endorsement of the pledge, as well as of the Blue Army itself.

As Your Excellency knows, many years ago when I was doing research for *Sign of Her Heart* (which was first published under the title of *Mary in Her Scapular Promise*), I came across a very old Latin text of Ventimiglia, in which he told of a meeting of St. Francis, St. Dominic, and St. Angelus at a street corner in Rome during which St. Dominic prophesied that "one day, through the Rosary and Scapular, Our Lady will save the world."

When I wrote the book, I never included this extraordinary prophecy! I felt that while the Rosary and Scapular were important devotions, they were not *so important* that they would one day be instruments to *"save the world."*

Then when I first went to Rome in 1946 and visited the Generalate of the Dominicans, known as Santa Sabina, I was shown the room in which St. Dominic died, and over the door a painting of St. Angelus, St. Francis and St. Dominic, commemorating the historic meeting of the three saints recorded by Ventimiglia.

But I was still reluctant to use the prophecy for fear that it might not be authentic—that it might have become distorted and exaggerated with the passage of time.

When I learned that Our Lady had appeared at Fatima holding out the Scapular and the Rosary and promised to save the world, I realized that, independently of the prophecy attributed to St. Dominic, these devotions were of paramount importance, being the ties of Our Lady's children to Her Immaculate Heart—the Heart to which, as Jacinta said, "God has entrusted the peace of the world."

Still there persisted some opposition within the Blue Army regarding the Scapular as "the sign of consecration to Her Immaculate Heart." On August 15, 1950, Lucia was asked by the Very Rev. Howard Rafferty, O. Carm., who visited her on behalf of the General of the Carmelites, whether we were right in insisting that the Scapular was an important part of the Fatima Message.

She stated positively that those who denied this were wrong, and stressed: *"The Scapular and the Rosary are inseparable."*

Pressed further, and asked why Our Lady held the Scapular out of the sky in that final vision during the Miracle of the Sun, Lucia replied:

"Because She wants everyone to wear it. It is, as Pope Pius XII has said, the sign of consecration to Her Immaculate Heart."

One day I received a letter from the Mother Provincial of the Carmelite Sisters in Coimbra—Lucia's Carmel. She asked permission for their community to translate my book *Sign of Her Heart* into Portuguese.

It was the Archbishop of Coimbra previously mentioned who wrote the preface to the book. And in it were repeated all of the quotations of Lucia mentioned in her interview with Fr. Howard, alongside the prophecy of St. Dominic:

Perhaps it is a good idea for us to look at them together:

"The Rosary and the Scapular are inseparable." (Lucia)

"One day, through the Rosary and the Scapular, Our Lady will save the world." (St. Dominic)

But it is one thing *to say* that the Rosary and Scapular are inseparable, and that these two devotions have great power to change us.

It is another thing *to understand*.

It is probably wrong of me to say that *everyone* should read *Sign of Her Heart*. But oh, how I wish everyone in the world could read it!

I have never mentioned this before, and hope I may be forgiven my lack of humility for recording it here:

Sometime after this book was first published, I happened to go into P.J. Kennedy and Sons Bookstore on Barclay Street in New York. An elderly man—whose name I do not recall—served me, and when he saw my name, he said: "You are the author of *Mary in Her Scapular Promise*!" (Now known by the title of *Sign of Her Heart*.) I said, "Yes."

He replied that he had been a "reader" for P.J. Kennedy for many years, and had evaluated manuscripts by the dozens, and he said that all Marian books up to this time had been more or less "derived" from the books of St. Grignon de Montfort and St. Alphonsus Liguori. But then he said:

"Your book on the Scapular is the most important I have read since *True Devotion* and *The Glories of Mary*."

I think Your Excellency once told me I was not much of a writer, and I wholeheartedly agree. I have always been one to put down on paper anything that seemed to be important to say. The writing of *Sign of Her Heart* was not *my work*. I can read it today as though someone else had written it entirely.

By contrast I do not feel the same about some of my other books, notably *The Brother and I*. How I disliked ever having to look up anything in that book! It went out of print and despite requests for it, years went by before I could bring myself to have it reprinted. I wrote it in two weeks—and only did it because I thought it would help build up the Scapular Apostolate.

It did, because the apostolate was based on that extraordinary mystical experience between Bro. Aloysius and me—something that was very private, and that I would have preferred to remain private. Certainly there is no need to recount such things here because that book has already been written.

Concerning the Blue Army pledge, there are really two books which should be read by anyone who wants to understand the pledge: *Sign of Her Heart* and *Sex and the Mysteries*. The latter is a book *using the Rosary,* which is the best kind of book *about the Rosary.*

Pope John XXIII said the fifteen decades of the Rosary each day, and he was able to write in his 80th year, as he was examining his conscience for his whole life, that he had never sinned against purity and he attributed this to his constant devotion to the daily Rosary. And he added that he had found in the Rosary *all the strength and light that he needed, not only for his personal life, but for the governing of the Universal Church!* 3

He wrote very few encyclicals, and the encyclical he wrote on the Rosary was simply *his own example of meditations.*

Sex tests everyone. And while the title of that book on the Rosary may seem a little daring, and even shocking to some, is it not one of the most needed books of our time?

Paul Hallett, brilliant analyst and a book reviewer for the *National Catholic Register,* did a rather pleasant and favorable review when the book first appeared. And then a couple of months later he wrote a stronger and lengthier review in which he said that this was the best book on the subject of sex in a "sea" of such books.

I surmised that Paul Hallett had looked over the book for the first review, but had *used the book before he wrote the second.*

We can understand the power of the Rosary and the Scapular only by *using them,* and we cannot use them well without help.

We may have no difficulty in understanding persons who say about the Scapular that they could not believe in such a superstition, nor wear such a "talisman," and so on. And we can understand people who find the Rosary monotonous or who do not, as a Vatican official said to me, "find it relevant in their lives today." But for those who know—for those who understand these devotions—nothing could be more keenly relevant!

I think my greatest regret after so many years of promoting the Blue Army Pledge, which more than 25,000,000 around the world have already signed, is that so few understand it. We must rely on the Blue Army cells for this. We must depend on them to take the books and read a chapter or so at each meeting until, over a period of time, they will have absorbed the sublime meaning of these great devotions, and the manner in which they unite our hearts to the Immaculate Heart of Mary—Heart full of grace and reservoir of the Holy Spirit for the world!

As we said earlier, the essential request of Our Lady of Fatima is the sanctification of our daily duty. She stressed with the most compelling earnestness that men must "stop offending God."

This, of course, is what the prophets have said from the beginning. But at Fatima, God did not send us a prophet, but *the Queen of Prophets,* His own Mother!

And She came—not merely to tell us that we must stop offending God, that we must accept whatever He chooses to send us in our daily lives and offer up the sacrifices required in order to keep His laws, but She held out Her Rosary and Scapular to save us!

This is what makes Fatima so different. This is what makes Fatima so full of hope. This is why Our Lady can say, while declaring that "sin is the cause of war," that She can bring about the conversion of Russia and world peace if Her requests are heard. She knows if we use Her devotions of Rosary and Scapular, *She will share the light of Her Immaculate Heart with our hearts* and not only make it possible for us to comply with the laws of God, but to *sanctify our daily duty* in the manner *which will repair for the sins of many* "who do not believe, do not adore, do not trust, and do not love." When enough people are doing this, Her Immaculate Heart will triumph.

No wonder Padre Pio could confidently say that the Blue Army is an ideal apostolate, and that Russia will be converted "when there is a Blue Army member for every Communist."

I am a little concerned that some readers may not realize *the tremendous importance* of the explanation of paragraph 67 of *Lumen Gentium* by Pope Paul VI, and that it is a confirmation of the Blue Army Pledge.

In summary, we must recall that the commission which drew up paragraph 67 of *Lumen Gentium* (perhaps the most important of all the Vatican II documents) wanted to include the Rosary as one of those devotions traditional in the Church which must be fostered at the present time.

4

After long debate, the commission decided that it would be up to the Pope *at any given moment in history* to indicate the devotions which were most important. Within four months the Pope said *that the two devotions to be stressed particularly in our day,* in conformity with that paragraph, *were the Scapular and the Rosary.*

These two devotions were never before linked in a single apostolate until after the meeting with Lucia in 1946 when the Blue Army Pledge was drafted, seventeen years before the promulgation of *Lumen Gentium.*

There are also many other Church documents which are most important to the Blue Army and to the fulfillment of its mission in the Church and in the world.

Indeed, it would be difficult to say which papal pronouncements of the past century are not of direct and vital meaning to this Apostolate which bears the burden of bringing about the triumph of the Immaculate Heart of Mary through the conversion of individuals to become wholly alive and vital members of the Mystical Body.

The Immaculate Heart of Mary was a source through which the Mystical Body came into the world, and as She gave it its first life, so the principal and ultimate fruit of devotion to that same Immaculate Heart is a vital Christian life.

Just consider the apostolic exhortation of Pius XII on evangelization: *almost every paragraph of that important document finds its fulfillment in our Apostolate.* It specifies how we are to carry through the principles of catechism given by Our Lady to the children, making them alive within us through the cells, as the children at Fatima did in their daily meetings and prayers and mutual spiritual support.

And then there are the social encyclicals. Hamish Fraser, a convert from Communism's militant atheism, wrote what I have always considered one of the most important books of our century, describing his own conversion and foretelling what the conversion of Russia would be and how it would come about.

Fraser had become disillusioned with Communism when it turned into the totalitarian dictatorship experienced in Russia and China and the satellites. Then, almost by accident, he learned of the social doctrine of the Catholic Church. He saw that the dream he had beheld in Communism was possible of realization only in the Church. He wrote:

"Had Marx not lived, Marxism would nonetheless have been invented: for, given a Christless society, Communism *is* inevitable, and the expropriating socialist-communist state is no more than an instrument of that collective hatred which with Marx becomes a religion, and with Lenin a Church."

Long before we were amazed at the number of affluent Italians and Frenchmen who espoused Communism, and of the numbers of middle class and wealthy persons who also became Marxists in America and other parts of the world, Fraser said:

"For me, the path to Moscow is paved with a desire for self-justification, emotional and intellectual revulsion from Protestantism, *abysmal ignorance of Catholic teachings,* and an insatiable craving for a faith capable of ordering my own existence as well as providing a solution to the problems of the crisis-stricken world."

Before he was able to believe in the Eucharist, Fraser believed in *Quadragesimo Anno,* and *Rerum Novarum.*

"The simple truth," Fraser said, "is that man cannot live without a faith." In that celebrated book mentioned above, Fraser said that it was the task of an apostolate *like the Blue Army* to awaken in the Christian world an awareness of its obligation as defined in the social encyclicals of the Church.

5   Our Lady asked for the sacrifice required by our daily duty, and *our duty in the workshop, the factory, in all our social obligations, has been clearly defined for us by the Vicars of Christ.* And Our Lady expects us to hear their voice and to obey.

I personally never spoke much about Fraser's marvelous book, and his great apostolate to awaken the Western world to the social encyclicals of the Church, because the Blue Army was constantly being accused by the Communists of political motivation. And it seemed to me that to acquit ourselves of our social obligations we must be involved to some extent in political action.

But the Message of Fatima is obviously connected with this. Ultimately the Blue Army members—whether they are explicitly directed to this or not—will be inspired by Our Lady *to obey the teachings of the Popes* and to become vibrant, vital, truly "converted" members of the Mystical Body.

Indeed, as was said above, is it not the central mission of Our Lady to fulfill this role for each of Her children, even as She gave birth to Christ Himself and to His Mystical Body?

It is touching to read Hamish Fraser's testament to Mary—the testament of a man of great intellect and fiery disposition, who had served as a Communist Commissar in the Spanish Civil War and was an organizer of Communists in one of the most politically sensitive areas of Great Britain. His book, *Fatal Star* (published by Burns, Glasgow, 1954), unmasks the heresies of Communism and materialism within the Church itself. "Heresy is never more dangerous," he wrote, "than when its ideas win admittance to the minds of the faithful." And he says it happens first by the permeation of the Marxist ideas which have infiltrated everywhere, and secondly as a result of Catholic apathy and the fact that the faith of many is not grounded "in the recognition of the necessity of strict orthodoxy." In a word, it is our failure to listen to the voice of Jesus speaking through His vicars in Rome.

In 1952, Hamish Fraser spoke to the Blue Army Rally in Paris at the *Parc des Expositions,* filled to the doors with more than 13,000, and with more waiting outside for lack of room. During the rally someone let some doves fly. One came down and rested for a few minutes on the head of Hamish Fraser just after he had said:

"I know that prayer can convert Communists, because I was a Communist and someone's prayer converted me."

I often felt that I was negligent in not stressing the social encyclicals, and the significance of the obligations of our daily duty with regard to political and social life as well as personal life. But as the years have passed I have felt confirmed in the conviction that *it was proper for the Blue Army to stress only the spiritual,* and that when we are truly spiritually converted we will not only listen to the

voice of the Church, but we will study and cling to every
word as we begin to live the words of Jesus:

"Who is mother, who are brethren to me?...anyone
who does the will of my Father...." (Matt. 12:48-50)

Below: Msgr. Colgan is shown blessing the first Blue Army banner in 1951. The three white stripes and four of blue represent
the three conditions and recommendations of the Blue Army
pledge.

In 1954, when the Blue Army became international, the dove
and hearts were changed to the now-famous Blue Army symbol
of peace through prayer: two doves forming the praying hands
and the motto "Orbis Unus Orans" (One World Praying).

Below: A most beautiful view of the Blue Army's Shrine of the Immaculate Heart of Mary, whose construction was urged by the late Msgr. Anthony J. Connell in answer to Our Lord's plea of "What is being done to establish in the world devotion to the Immaculate Heart of My Mother?" Construction of the Shrine was approved by Bishop Ahr, and His Excellency dedicated the Shrine on October 13, 1978.

Chapter Ten

1) Another daring Russian - 2) Padre Pio accepts
3) Spiritual sharing with millions - 4) Our greatest
privilege - 5) Sabbatine privilege conditions realized in
fulfillment of Blue Army Pledge.

**Below: Padre Pio is shown venerating Pilgrim Virgin statue. He
accepted all who honor their Blue Army pledge as his own "spiritual children."**

REWARDS

"What better thing could you do?" — *Padre Pio*

Padre Pio's words just quoted were given in reply to a
question by one of his celebrated spiritual children,
the Marquesa Boschi. She had asked him whether it was a
good thing to join the Blue Army. The famous stigmatist
replied:

"This (the Blue Army) is not only an act of prayer—it is
also an apostleship. *What better thing could you do?"*

One would be quite justified in interpreting these words
to mean that the Blue Army is an "ideal" apostolate.

It would take an entire volume to recount the roles of
such holy and eminent persons as Padre Pio in this Apostolate, but we have only space here to say a few words
concerning the identity of Padre Pio as "spiritual father"
of the Blue Army.

This wonderful development was largely due to an extraordinary man, Alex Pernitzky, a Ukrainian whose
father was killed for his faith, in the Ukraine. Distressed
and bewildered, he succeeded in making his way to Rome.
There he became a student at the Russicum, a college
founded in Rome by Pius XI to train priests for work in
Russia, and to be ready to go into Russia to help after the
conversion promised by Our Lady of Fatima, when there
would be a great need for priests.

Alex completed courses of study for a doctorate in
theology, a doctorate in philosophy with very high marks
and mastered several languages with absolute fluency—
but in each instance he refused to take the actual
doctorate. Eventually he became a devoted follower of
Padre Pio in the following manner:

Under the strain of separation from his homeland, accused on one side of being a Communist spy, and on the other of being a spy of the Vatican, he had a nervous breakdown. He had heard of Padre Pio's mystical powers and decided to seek his blessing at San Giovanni Rotondo.

As he knelt in Padre Pio's confessional for the first time, Alex suddenly felt as though there was an explosion within him and something terrible went up and out of him. He went back to Rome for a while, but felt attracted to return to Padre Pio again and again. Finally he took up residence in San Giovanni Rotondo where he acted as an interpreter for pilgrims, and not only attended Padre Pio's daily Mass, but prayed close to Padre Pio as often as he could, frequently going to confession for Padre Pio's advice, even on the smallest matters.

Alex already knew about the Blue Army because I had met him in Rome in 1946 when I visited the Russicum, and I had begun to give him a little personal help at that time. Like all Russians in exile, and particularly those who have suffered the persecution which Our Lady of Fatima had foretold, he was anxious to see the requests of Our Lady of Fatima fulfilled.

When Alex realized that Padre Pio saw the Blue Army as a providential apostolate, his concern and interest in the Blue Army knew no bounds. He founded a cell in San Giovanni Rotondo, and soon Blue Army posters were appearing on the front of the Church of Our Lady of Graces where hundreds of thousands were coming to see their "spiritual father."

It was after looking at one of these posters that the Marquesa Boschi asked Padre Pio if indeed it was a good thing to join the Blue Army and received the memorable reply: *"Could you do anything better?"*

Nothing gave Alex greater joy than seeing Blue Army pilgrimages coming to San Giovanni Rotondo. He not only arranged for me to serve Padre Pio's Mass, but each time Msgr. Colgan arrived, he arranged for him to meet the saintly stigmatist. In the back of Alex's thoughts was the remote, but glorious, possibility that Padre Pio might accept *all who had signed the Blue Army Pledge as his spiritual children.* Only a true spiritual child of Padre Pio could understand how important this was.

Padre Pio had a special mission to make persons holier than they were, in addition to his mission of bringing back persons who had lapsed from the faith. But Padre Pio would not always accept everyone who asked to be his "spiritual child" because in doing so, he was accepting a heavy responsibility according to his own words: *"I shall stand at the gates of Paradise and shall not enter until all my spiritual children have entered."*

But since the Blue Army was an apostolate of holiness—an apostolate using the instruments of the Immaculate Heart of Mary to become united to that same Immaculate Heart full of grace—Alex dared to hope that anyone who would join this Apostolate might be accepted by Padre Pio as his own spiritual child. One day he told Msgr. Colgan to ask the saintly stigmatist for this singular favor.

To the great joy of Alex (and to the perpetual wonder of all of us who follow), Padre Pio agreed and said that he would accept them all as his spiritual children provided only "that they behave well," which was understood to mean as long as they would sincerely strive to live up to their commitment.

2

Only in the future, when the Church may well have glorified Padre Pio, may we expect all who sign the Blue Army Pledge to realize their great good fortune.

And there is an interesting corollary:

After Padre Pio died, there was no longer any way to become one of his spiritual children. He was no longer there to be asked: "Father, will you accept me as your spiritual child?"

Then the Capuchins at San Giovanni Rotondo remembered that Padre Pio had agreed to accept anyone who had joined the Blue Army as his spiritual children! And they printed a little card as a reply to those who were now writing in after Padre Pio's death and asking to be inscribed as his "spiritual children." The card stated that if they belonged to the Blue Army, they were already his spiritual children, or they could become one by joining.

After Padre Pio's death, Alex devoted himself full time to traveling throughout the world showing slides of Padre Pio and slides of Fatima, and persuading as many as he could (and they were in the thousands in many nations) to join the Blue Army.

Like Fr. Pavel Bliznetsov, Alex was a true "Russian," and often his character rubbed other persons the wrong way. But this humble man persevered through all obstacles. Often he was assisted by a very learned Roman prelate, Msgr. Carlo Carbone, once head of the Catholic Action of Italy, an editor of several books, and a Canon of the Basilica of St. Peter's. On many occasions Msgr. Carbone traveled with Alex and humbly introduced him to audiences.

Something which has impressed me very deeply about these outstanding contributors to the growth of the Blue Army, such as Maria de Freitas and Alex Pernitzky, has been their refusal of all honors. A most unusual and dedicated man (Bill Ponce), who often worked 80 hours a week in our publishing department, never even permitted his name to be used. He was a person of *inestimable* value. It was almost as though Our Lady had sent an angel in the form of a humble man to undertake Her work in total self-abnegation. Several times he printed *The City of God* in his free time because he wanted the work to be a gift to Our Lady. Similarly he produced the book *"There is Nothing More,"* a synthesis of important writings on the Blue Army as a fulfillment of the Message of Fatima and on the elements of the Blue Army pledge.

But when one stops to think of it — is it not a true mark of a devotee of the Immaculate Heart of Mary that She seems to convey to Her special children the readiness and ability to say in all truth: "He has regarded the lowliness of His handmaid."

Nevertheless, in this world where honor is so avidly sought after, such self-abnegation must remain a wonder...and it must cause us to ponder on the sacrifice of all those who have contributed to the growth of the Blue Army throughout the world and whose names are written only in heaven — as they themselves would wish.

3   While speaking of this great benefit to Blue Army members of being the spiritual children of Padre Pio, is it not fitting and proper to recall that *by the act of signing the pledge,* and then having one's name buried in the same ground at Fatima, all these members of Our Lady's spiritual army *share in their mutual good works and prayer?* Is not the ultimate strength of this army the union of so many hearts with the Immaculate Heart of Mary? And does this not connotate the power which flows through and by and with them all?

One of the things that has concerned all of us in recent years — and I am sure was a concern to Your Excellency when you asked me to write this "history" — has been the continuity of the Apostolate. We know that after Russia is converted, the triumph of Our Lady's Immaculate Heart is to develop necessarily over a considerable period of time. The "era of peace for mankind" will not come like a flash, but through a whole series of individual conversions and a whole series of forward steps in the life of Grace until the reign of the Eucharistic King will be with us.

I long to speak of this now, but first — because I think this is the appropriate place — it would be fitting to mention a reward even greater than that of the communion of merits among the members of the Blue Army — namely the Sabbatine Privilege.

The Privilege was granted as a sort of "super indulgence" by Pope John XXII in the year 1322 and I think it is to be presumed that a comparative few — perhaps very few — profited by this great privilege before the founding of the Blue Army.

Indeed *Our Lady told Pere Lamy*, a 20th century French mystic who died in 1931 and who was regarded by his bishop as a "second Cure d'Ars,' *that very few obtained the Privilege*. And yet Pope Pius XI, whom Cardinal Tisserant considered the greatest Pope of our century (and certainly the most scholarly) said: *"This is the greatest of all of our privileges from the Mother of God."*

For some who read this and may not know about the Privilege, a brief explanation is necessary here.

Our Lady had appeared in the 14th century to Pope John XXII while he was yet a Cardinal. As evidence that he was truly seeing Her, She prophesied that he would be the next Pope, and then asked that he promulgate this Privilege: *That those who observe chastity according to their state in life and practice two other devotions to Her would be free from Purgatory by the first Saturday after death.*

It is called the "Sabbatine" privilege because the Bull issued by John XXII was known as the *Bulla Sabatina.*

In modern times, especially at the turn of the century, there have been arguments about the authenticity of the present copy of the Bull, but the Church has again and again reaffirmed the Privilege itself. Even when St. Pius X granted permission for the use of a medal to replace the Scapular (with a good and sufficient reason), he said that he conveyed to the medal all of the indulgences that could be gained through the Scapular "not excluding the Sabbatine Privilege." And there is, of course, the famous letter of Pope Paul V authorizing the teaching of the Privilege to the Church.[1]

When this Privilege was first promulgated, the Rosary devotion had not yet become widespread in the Church, but it was common practice for those who could read—if they were not bound to say the Divine Office—to say the Little Office of the Blessed Virgin.

So the original conditions to obtain the Sabbatine Privilege were the wearing of the Scapular and the daily recitation of the Little Office (or fasting on Wednesdays and Saturdays for those who could not read). Priests with the faculty to do so could commute either of these last two conditions (the Little Office or the fasting) to some other prayer or pious work. As the years passed, it became common practice to substitute the Rosary, or seven Paters, Aves and Glorias.

About a year after the Blue Army Pledge was promulgated by the first Bishop of Fatima, the General of the Carmelite Order granted to those who signed the pledge the permission to have the Rosary substituted for the Little Office or the fasting.

Perhaps it would not be too presumptuous if we speculate that it was always in the mind of Our Lady that this great privilege should exist in the Church and be prepared and ready for the day that She could use it to reward those who join the Army of Her Immaculate Heart.

It is indeed, as the learned Pius XI said, "the greatest of all our privileges from the Mother of God"—because it extends even after death!

Essentially, it is a promise that we shall be holy by the time we die!

The recently-published book, *Revelations of Martha Simma,* points up the greatness of this privilege which caused the celebrated mystic St. John of the Cross to exclaim as he died (on a Saturday):

"The Mother of God and of Carmel descends to Purgatory with grace on Saturday and delivers those souls who have worn Her Scapular. Blessed be such a Lady who wills that on this day of Saturday I shall depart from this life!"

All of this is contained in my book *Sign of Her Heart.*

And please God some day someone will write an entire book on the meaning of this great privilege in relation to our personal sanctification and with regard to the importance of avoiding or shortening one's stay in Purgatory.

St. Teresa of Avila, who saw the transition of thousands of souls, saw only three who went straight to heaven. Two did not astonish her in the least. They were St. Peter of Alcantara and St. John of the Cross. But the third amazed her because, as she remarked in her autobiography, *she knew who that person was!* Then she added that she was given to understand that this soul had obtained the Sabbatine Privilege.

In other words, the soul of this person, who was so ordinary and who seemed to have lacked the exceptional graces and total purity of St. Peter of Alcantara and St. John of the Cross, had died in the same radiant whiteness of soul!

I love to recall—and can never tire of doing so—the wonderful example of St. Alphonsus de Liguori who, after describing the Sabbatine Privilege in *The Glories of Mary*, added: *"If we do a little more than Our Lady asked, can we not hope that we will not go to Purgatory at all?"*

Imagine! If we do a little more than just wear the Scapular and say the Rosary, and thus united to Mary's Immaculate Heart observe chastity according to our state in life, we shall—like the greatest of saints—fly straight to heaven at the moment of death!

If any ordinary person had said this, we would certainly consider it not only unbelievable, but an exaggeration of the worst kind.

But St. Alphonsus de Liguori is a Doctor of the Church, and we have been given to know that it was his book on Mary and Her glories, far more than his moral theology, upon which the Church based its decision.

Of course we know that St. Alphonsus did more than a "little more," so it is not surprising that when the great saint died, it seemed that Our Lady came for him at the last moment. He had been in a coma for some time, and then suddenly he sat up fully alert, staring in front of him. Reaching out his arms and pronouncing the name of Mary, he then slowly sank back in death.

Then, extraordinary to relate, when his tomb was opened forty years later, everything corruptible within the tomb had turned to dust with one solitary exception: lying there in the midst of the corruption of the grave, in the midst of the buckles and bones, was the saint's brown scapular perfectly preserved!

I have seen that original scapular 200 years after it was taken from the tomb—and it was almost like new, with the stitching around the edges, the picture and the woolen material which should have disintegrated long ago!

This sign, which Our Lady held out in Her final appearance at the climax of the Miracle of the Sun at Fatima—the sign of consecration to Her Immaculate Heart—shone from the corruption of the tomb of St. Alphonsus de Liguori as though emphasizing those daring words of the saint concerning the Sabbatine Privilege: "If we do a little more than Our Lady asks, can we not hope that we will not go to Purgatory at all?"

Oh, how fortunate we are to live in this time of the revelation of Our Lady's Immaculate Heart! How fortunate we are to live in this time when Her simple devotions of consecration to Her Heart and of entering into the mysteries of the life of Christ through Her Heart (through the Scapular and the Rosary) have become a reality to so many millions through the Blue Army!

In a time of unusual evil, Our Lady has given us an ideal apostolate of holiness simple enough for the smallest child and yet of such rich theological content that it commands the admiration and awe of savants.

FOOTNOTES

1.   Cf. **Analecta O. Carm.**, vol. 4, p. 250.

This is a photograph of the marvelously incorrupt scapular of St. Alphonsus after forty years in his tomb where everything else corruptible had turned to dust. The saint, and Doctor of the Church, suggested that those who "do a little more" than Our Lady asked (for the Sabbatine Privilege) may not go to Purgatory. The Blue Army fulfills the conditions of the Sabbatine Privilege, and these words of St. Alphonsus are a great encouragement to those who "do a little more."

Chapter Eleven

1) Statutes submitted to Rome in 1956 - 2) Forces of division - 3) Constitution mandates elections - 4) First U.S. elections contested - 5) New elections and new Constitution for U.S. Blue Army

By 1960 our Blue Army television program was being aired on over 100 stations. Below, Monsignor Colgan with famous newspaperman James Kilgallen.

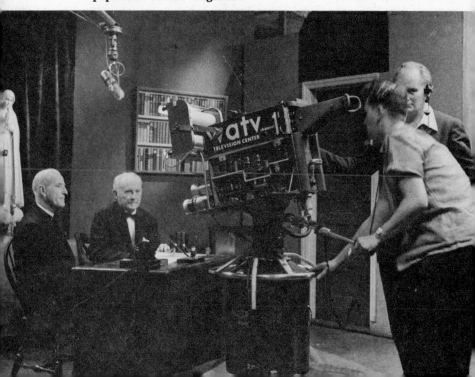

ORGANIZATION

"Concentrate on Organization." — *Deathbed*
advice of William A. Haffert, Sr.

I presuppose everyone thinks that his mother was the most wonderful woman who ever lived, and his father was one of the greatest men who ever lived. So I shall be excused for saying that I think my father was an exceptional, and perhaps great, man.

He is very important in this story.

Largely self-taught, at the age of 17 he was Advertising Manager of the *Atlantic City Press*. He fell in love with the daughter of a prominent lawyer and judge in the neighboring mainland town of Somers Point, not knowing that the owner of the *Atlantic City Press* and the judge were on opposite political sides. In order to get on the good side of the judge, he edited a political paper for him. When the owner of the *Atlantic City Press* discovered who was writing the political articles, my father was soon out of a job.

He was still in his twenties when he owned his own newspaper, which in time became the second largest weekly in America. As the years passed, he came to own several newspapers and three printing plants.

After the depression, he analyzed the publication field and on finding that agricultural publications were the most reliable, he began to build a "stable" of agricultural publications which later included *Poultry Digest* and *Business Farming*.

When I came out of school, my father had great hopes that I would enter into his small publishing empire. He could not understand when I told him that I felt called to a Marian apostolate. He could see no "future" in it. (And, of course, there was none to see!)

But then—as I relate in my book *The Brother and I*—he had a mystical experience which convinced him that he should permit my sister (his only daughter) to enter Carmel, and that he should help to launch my work. He then founded the Scapular Press, published my first book, and put me on my way.

He died in 1976 and I spent as much time with him as I possibly could during the last weeks of his life. He confided to me that the greatest satisfaction he had, in looking back over the years, was to think of the Blue Army's International Center standing behind the Basilica of Fatima, and of the spreading of the Blue Army.

I reckoned that I myself had not many more years to live—already in my sixties—and I was anxious to know how my father felt I might best use my remaining time.

"Concentrate on organization," he said.

I argued that there were pledges to be obtained, there was a world to be awakened without further loss of time to the importance of the Message of Fatima, upon which would depend the conversion of Russia and world peace.

"*Concentrate on organization,*" he repeated.

"But, Dad," I said, "would it not be best to produce one major documentary series on Fatima for television, and to use that medium at this late hour to convince millions of the importance of this heavenly intervention as we are poised so close to the edge of atomic war?"

"Any television program will be ephemeral," he said. "But the task of the Blue Army is perhaps more in the future than in the past, and it will not survive without organization."

And this is certainly one thing that I had grossly neglected, although as I mentioned in a previous chapter, I had always been concerned about the continuity of the Apostolate because I knew that it will, perhaps, be even more important in the forthcoming era of the triumph of Mary's Immaculate Heart.

I had felt confident that the international statutes, which had been drawn up at the order of the first Bishop of Fatima, provided all the organization we really needed. And I also felt that the very existence of our international building at Fatima, administered by an International Council based on the statutes, was a guarantee of continuity. And I resented the loss of time and emotional energy in meetings called to develop "organization."

Our own National Center of the United States was governed by a Board of Trustees, and the president of the Board at that time was Mr. Joseph Plevyak, a businessman who kept stressing in every meeting that we had to have organization, we had to have rules and forms and methods of reporting. It was always a penance for me to sit through this because there were projects for action which I wanted to introduce for approval.

Bishop da Silva had appointed Dr. Lourenco, a Canon of his diocese, to draw up the statutes for the Blue Army, and the then leaders of the movement—like Fr. Andre Richard from Paris, Fr. Andreas Fuhs from Germany, Msgr. Strazzacappa of Italy, and other great men, participated.

It seemed to me that the discussions went on endlessly over individual words—but finally, in a solemn meeting, which was attended by Cardinal Tisserant, the statutes were adopted, and then presented to the Holy See for approval. The Congregation in charge of such matters (before the Council) gave them approval *"ad experimentum"* (which was the normal procedure).

I suppose everything came just a little too easily in those days when the Bishop of Fatima was taking the initiative, and we had Cardinal Tisserant—the right hand of the Pope—assisting in Rome!

We were forgetting that any apostolate of Our Lady, and particularly this one which bears the promise of the triumph of Her Heart, has potent enemies—enemies who know how to intrude on the slightest pride and fault of character in order to sow dissension and bring even the mightiest apostolate to a grinding halt.

What a terrible, almost violent example we had in the case of the Sodality and the Queen's work! Who would have dreamed that this, perhaps the greatest Marian apostolate in the world, could actually cease to exist just a few years after the death of Fr. Lord? There had been 81 employees in a "skyscraper" in St. Louis handling the work of this vast apostolate, and yet within two years of Fr. Lord's death, only one employee remained in that great building, and soon the entire Sodality of Our Lady—after existing for *hundreds of years*—came to an end!

And I had the example in my own life of the Scapular Apostolate, which had also become a major apostolate in America, and had begun to spread to other parts of the world. We had acquired our own 4-story building in New York, next to a church which had been redecorated as a "national shrine," and some half a million persons were reading our magazine, and there were centers of the apostolate in cities from coast to coast.

Yet within five years after I left that apostolate *it ceased to exist.*

2

Was it possible that the Apostolate of Fatima, of which the Bishops of Fatima became the principal sponsors, would also cease to exist one day because it depended on one or two persons—and with their passing, there would be no adequate organization to carry on?

A few years before my father died, Msgr. Colgan died, and his successor (already mentioned) was Msgr. Anthony Connell, another totally Marian priest.

When I told him of my father's dying wish, Msgr. Connell not only agreed, but also began urging me to do all that was possible to stabilize the organization by implementing the international statutes with an amendment of the national constitution for the United States which had been drawn up on a preliminary basis in 1973.

Since that was an important milestone in the history of the Apostolate, perhaps it would be fitting to recall it briefly here.

Fr. Richard Ciurej, a fine priest from the Archdiocese of Omaha, obtained a leave of absence for one year and came to Washington to work on a National Constitution of the Blue Army upon which his friend, Joseph Plevyak, had been insisting for so long.

Many hours were spent, week after week, drafting the Constitution and after one year the leaders of the Blue Army throughout the United States were invited to come to a meeting at the Blue Army Center in Detroit to discuss it. The Bishop of Fatima, who by then had become International President of the Blue Army, flew from Portugal to preside.

The Constitution was adopted unanimously. It placed temporary power over the Blue Army in the hands of the Trustees of the Ave Maria Institute—which was the corporation I had founded with the permission of Your Excellency back in 1952 for the publication of SOUL Magazine. (*Ave Maria Institute* was the name I had given to the enterprise for which I had obtained permission from Bishop Griffin in 1949.)

The Constitution provided that when *half* of the dioceses of the United States had Blue Army diocesan organizations, elections would be held, and the power of the administration of the Blue Army would then pass to a National Council, and a National Executive Committee. **3**

Msgr. Connell had an unexpected and sudden death on October 16, 1976. He was succeeded by his personal friend, Msgr. Charles B. Murphy.

Two of the Trustees who feared, perhaps, the loss of their positions with national elections, urged that a new Constitution be passed by the Trustees, without ratification at a national meeting, which would perpetuate the power of the Trustees over the Blue Army. Msgr. Murphy had called a meeting of the national members of the Blue Army in May, 1978, to consider this new Constitution. In that meeting the members voted that the 1973 Constitution should be amended, and that while it was in force, elections should be held the following year, whether or not the Blue Army had been organized in half the dioceses of the country.

As it turned out, by the time of the next national meeting, the Blue Army was indeed organized in 90 different dioceses. (It had centers in many more, but in only 90 dioceses did it have centers which were operating in proper cooperation with the National Center and with the approval of the bishop of the diocese.)

So in the convention of October 13, 1979, national elections were held in which Your Excellency was the *first elected* National President of the Blue Army. And the Most Rev. Jerome J. Hastrich, a wonderful Marian bishop (from Gallup, N.M.) accepted the nomination of Vice President.

I had asked if you would accept the presidency and you had not replied. I presumed that you were considering it — and many prayers were said that you would be able to accept. But at this time—even as we were meeting—you were unfortunately undergoing major surgery.

Some of the previous trustees of the Institute, who would now no longer have jurisdiction over the Blue Army, contested the validity of the elections on the grounds that the Trustees themselves had not authorized them. Indeed, under threat of some scandal, they had insisted that I send a letter out to all those who were coming to the meeting to say that, according to their **4** orders, elections were not to be held. (When the members came, they decided of their own will that, after so many years, it was the Blue Army leaders of the country who should be running the Apostolate, and they insisted on the elections.)

In January, 1980, during a meeting in Rome which lasted for five days, the officers of the International Council for the Blue Army heard the objections of the previous trustees and finally voted—after long and difficult decisions—that the elections of the Blue Army of the United States had indeed been valid and that they recognized the newly-elected officers.

The elections had been for only one year, and so, in October, 1980, the leaders of the Blue Army were back again in another convention.

This meeting was larger and much better organized than the previous one. Bishop Hastrich presided. Officers were now elected for another term, and a revised National Constitution was adopted. This was based on all the work that had been done prior to 1973 and in the years following, under the leadership of Msgr. Connell and Msgr. Murphy. It incorporated the best efforts of all the wonderful men who had spent hundreds of hours in this task.

Bishop Hastrich became the second elected National President, and Archbishop Nicholas T. Elko—who had helped the Blue Army many times over the past quarter century—was unanimously elected Vice President.

I confess to Your Excellency that these elections were a surprise to me. I had thought, as some of the previous trustees wished, that elections would not be held, that we would simply recognize the officers elected in the previous year for one more year, and that another election would be postponed until 1982. So I was unprepared when Archbishop Elko was nominated, and you can imagine the Archbishop's surprise when he received a telephone call from us at the very moment of his nomination asking if he would accept!

He asked quite simply, "Do you think I could be of service?"

I answered: "I think, Your Excellency, that if you accepted this, it would be another rose that you would be placing in Our Lady's crown."

"Then I accept," he said quietly.

Shortly afterwards a beautiful letter came from him,

which was published in our national Blue Army leadership magazine:

Dear Mr. Haffert:

This is to acknowledge my acceptance as vice president of the National Blue Army.

I always deem it a privilege to do as you do in tendering any contributive effort to the promotional advancement of Our Lady of Fatima. Your organization, the National Executive Committee and other officers are vital to the orderly and effective management of the ever expanding membership of the Blue Army.

In my prayers for you and your associates, I will pray that God bless your administrative labors with an ever increasing respect among the episcopacy, priests, Religious, and laity.

With every best wish and remembrance in my daily Masses, I remain

Yours in Christ,

Nicholas T. Elko, Archbishop
October 28, 1980

And now, who was our first nationally elected President to serve in that capacity? Who was Bishop Jerome J. Hastrich?

He was the bilingual Bishop of the Diocese of Gallup, New Mexico, which is a diocese containing the largest number of American Indians in the United States.

In his desire to bring the Indian tribes to God, Bishop Hastrich (devoted from childhood to Our Lady) began to turn more and more to Our Lady of Guadalupe. Annually he conducted pilgrimages to the site of the apparitions in Mexico City, taking as many of the Indians with him as possible to see the miraculous portrait of Our Lady.

He was appalled by the lack of devotion to Our Lady of the Americas in the United States, and by the fact that there was no place in Mexico City where English-speaking pilgrims could be received and instructed in this sublime and meaningful apparition. After striving for several years to do something about it, he learned of my own interest in Our Lady of the Americas and wrote to me. I responded at once by helping him to the best of my ability. Soon, the Queen of the Americas Guild was founded and eighty American bishops (Your Excellency was among them) sent letters of support to Bishop Hastrich in this worthy cause.

It was in this manner, through the miraculous image of Our Lady of the Americas, that Bishop Hastrich and I came to know each other. As we were nearing an organizational crisis within the Blue Army in our own country, I dared to ask him if he would volunteer to serve as a national officer.

When he generously accepted, he did not know the full extent of the organizational problems involved and when he faced them at our meeting on October 13, 1980, I would not have been surprised if he had said when nominated at that meeting for the position of president:

"I have my own diocese to administer, and many other projects, and I am glad to have served for one year, but I would not be able to continue."

To the contrary, he not only accepted, but a few days later, the following beautiful message (slightly condensed) came from him to be published in SOUL Magazine:

Having been previously elected as the President of the Queen of the Americas Guild, how do I see my position as President of the Blue Army? With Bishop Venancio of Fatima, I see in the Blue Army a great rallying force for all people of good will who are desirous of following the teachings of Christ as He continues to exist in His Church. I see it, too, as a means of coordinating various devotions to Our Lord in the Blessed Sacrament and His Blessed Mother.

After all, there is no other organization quite as large and strong, promoting devotion to the Blessed Mother or to our Eucharistic Savior. Should not the Blue Army be listening to what Our Lord is telling us in well-authenticated private revelations of His Blessed Mother? The revelations at Fatima are the most recent acceptable revelations of our Blessed Mother for the world. Do they not, as it were, sum up and give us final directions for personal conversion and sanctification and the conversion of the world? The Blue Army emphasizes this through the intercession of the Blessed Mother and the Adoration of Our Lord in the Blessed Sacrament.

I see the Blue Army, too, as a conservator of the true teachings of the Church today.

Hopefully, my position will help me to clarify to the Bishops what the Blue Army really is, and what it is not.

I see the Blue Army as a tremendous force for good in the world of today.''

Our organizational problems have not been entirely resolved. Indeed, I am sure they will be with us for years to come, but giant steps have been taken to resolve them.

When I was tempted to ignore the problems, trusting that they would solve themselves, I remembered the advice of my dying father:

"Concentrate on organization."

In a personal letter to me shortly after he was elected president, Bishop Hastrich confided that he had realized instinctively that this was what was needed, and that this was why he had accepted the office.

On May 21, 1981, His Excellency wrote: "We have to try to picture the Blue Army existing without our aid, and when we are no longer around. It is a real challenge to be able to create an organization that will last beyond a person's life, but it is a challenge we must meet."

Below: A rare picture of the author with his uncle, the Rev. John J. Haffert, O. Carm., and his father (center) who gave his son much practical advice and support. Father John, for 27 years a Novice Master of the Carmelites, was the author's spiritual advisor.

Chapter Twelve

1) Could Madison Avenue help? - 2) Almost unbelievable setbacks - 3) The Pope finally speaks - 4) Pope refers to Fatima in the Council - 5) Collegial Consecration still to come - 6) Explanation of the 1960 Secret 7) Pope personally goes to Fatima - 8) Bishop of Fatima becomes Blue Army International President.

Below: Msgr. Colgan leaves for Europe carrying the Blue Army Award for Outstanding Achievement to German Chancellor Conrad Adenauer.

AFTER 1960:
SUFFERING AND TRIUMPH

"What is important is the public Message of Fatima." — *Cardinal Ottaviani explaining silence of Pope on 1960 Secret*

To this day I am amazed that all of our efforts to make the Message of Fatima known to the world seem to have had little effect on the vast majority, even of Catholics.

First, we "played up" the 1960 Secret. We had a television program in New York every Saturday night at 9:00 p.m. in which we discussed the Message of Fatima. We called the program "Zero, 1960" and later, "Crisis."

We were not implying that there would be some kind of catastrophe at that time. We implied, rather, that the Message of Fatima was not something that happened in 1917 and was finished, but which *began* in 1917 and would not be consummated until Russia was converted. Even after that, it would continue to be fulfilled in the "triumph of the Immaculate Heart of Mary" and "an era of peace for mankind."

We had some of the most celebrated figures of our time on the program, including President Kennedy, Senator Humphrey, and many others! The program was picked up by over 100 stations throughout the country and for over a year had a "star" rating in *The New York Times*.

And the Pilgrim Virgin statue was traveling from diocese to diocese, with the message delivered to tens of thousands in every diocese on a "person to person" basis. I began to think we just did not have the right techniques and that we should go to Madison Avenue and find the best professional help we could buy. I made inquiries and found one agency whose accounts included the nation of Portugal, the Philippines, and the *Catholic Digest*.

Armed with a half million dollars I had raised in a rather desperate effort, I chose this agency and told them of the urgency of our message and that they should find a way for us to "break through" to the consciousness of the general public.

They prepared a concentrated test program using newspapers, radio and television. St. Louis was the city chosen for the test.

Harris did a poll after the test to see how many people were aware of the Message of Fatima, how many people understood it, and how many people felt they should respond to it.

The result was unbelievably poor. We had used the word "atheist" in the presentation, referring to the prophecy of Our Lady that "error will spread from an atheist Russia." And many people did not even know what that word meant!

But the test also revealed something else that probably contributed to the poor result:

Many television stations refused the spots because of their religious nature. They had a policy of not accepting any religious message on a commercial basis.

A new test was prepared, this time with Cleveland as the test city, and the results were hardly better.

We had spent the largest single sum on propaganda in our history, and when it was all over the Madison Avenue experts gave us this advice:

"The best way to spread this message, based on all of our studies and tests, is *by developing your own organization* in individual parishes and having it spread by one person to another."

Meanwhile Russia was continuing to spread her errors throughout the world, and we were catapulting towards another war in which the prophecy of Our Lady might be fulfilled: "Several entire nations will be annihilated!"

On top of all this, my wife (the former Anne Kraushaar whom I had married in 1942 and who died in 1975) developed an atrophied thyroid (not discovered until years later). When I tried to persuade her to move from an apartment in New York in an area which had become dangerous because of street crime, she threatened to separate from me rather than move. I had to insist because we had a twelve-year-old daughter who was walking that street—which had the highest crime rate in the entire city—to and from school each day. Your Excellency knows the painful time which followed, and which should have done more damage to our Apostolate even than the attempt by the United Steelworkers' Union to organize the employees of the Institute.

I am sure she suffered even more than I because of the allegations which were printed in the newspapers. And at that time you did not even ask me if they were true. You simply presumed that they were false.

Of course, because of the damage to my name, I offered to resign, but neither yourself nor Msgr. Colgan would hear of it. On top of that, 1960 came and went and the Pope—to whom the Secret had been confided—did not make it public. He did not even make known the fact that he had opened it.

The silence from Rome lay heavily on all of us. People began to murmur that Fatima must have been a fake, that there was no Secret, that the 1960 Secret was "a hoax." During all this trying time Your Excellency never once said how you felt. I often wondered. Clearly your faith and your confidence in the words of Our Lady, and in the Blue Army as the instrument of Our Lady in the fulfillment of Her message, never wavered.

Meanwhile we were taken up with Vatican Council II— and with the work of the Council and the responsibility of your diocese—eighth largest in the nation with 800,000 souls—certainly you had little time to think about anything else.

As Your Excellency knows, it was a time of terrible trial for my wife. I decided to use the advantages of my traveling privileges through the Fatima Travel agency and to take her to Rome. Because of the Council it was an exciting time: I would be able to see Bishop Venancio constantly and also work on the book which I had dreamed of writing for several years on the subject of the Holy Eucharist.

We all had so much to suffer at that time! *It seemed as though*, about 1960 or shortly before, *Satan and his demons had been given special power in the world.* Indeed, had not Venerable Anna Katerina Emmerich prophesied 200 years ago that it would be about 1950 or 1960 that this would happen?

Poor Bishop Venancio! How he suffered! He was bedridden during much of the Council.

Our concern was greatly increased by the tensions which seemed to build up in the Council itself. Many had hoped that the doctrine of mediation would be advanced at this time. But instead all work in that direction was halted. And many of the Council Fathers were shocked on hearing one of their members parody the words of a saint and earlier Doctor of the Church by saying:

"De Maria iam satis."

3   But then came that dramatic moment on November 21, 1964, when Pope Paul VI decided to renew the consecration of the world to the Immaculate Heart of Mary in the presence of all the bishops of the world.

Some of us had been circulating petitions among the bishops for the Collegial Consecration. One single petition had been signed by 500 bishops.

And then just two weeks before the close of that session, during which the Pope was going to promulgate the most important document of the Council (Constitution on the Church, also known as *Lumen Gentium*), the Pope sent word to all the bishops that immediately after the closing of the Council they were to meet with him at the Basilica of St. Mary Major later that same day, November 21, Feast of the Presentation.

I remember two bishops (one of whom is now a Cardinal) visited me in my apartment. They both thought that this had something to do with the petitions for the Collegial Consecration and wondered whether I might have any "inside" information. Both said that problems were involved because many prelates, knowing the time the Council was going to end, had made their travel reservations and had not intended to remain in Rome.

Through the "grapevine," I felt certain that the Pope had decided to implement the Collegial Consecration that day, and of course we knew that when this took place Russia would be converted—and all our efforts and prayers over the past years would finally see their reward.

I forget whether it was to Bishop Venancio or to Abbe Richard that one of the French bishops said on learning of this:

"You will get something," and the bishop waved his finger almost as though in anger, "but it will not be that Collegial Consecration!"

To me the antipathy of some bishops towards the idea of the Collegial Consecration seemed beyond all understanding and while I did not ask the question then, I could not help but wonder afterwards how the *Collegial* Consecration could possibly have taken place with so many bishops not really willing it.

Your Excellency can hardly imagine the sense of anticipation and concern as the day was nearing, and yet I had to leave Rome! I was traveling with the Pilgrim Virgin statue on a pilgrimage, and on November 21 we would be in the Holy Land.

I found out that the Bishop of Nazareth would be there two days later, on which day I would be in Haifa. So I called the Bishop and asked: "Excellency, what happened at St. Mary Major's on the 21st?"

"Nothing," the Bishop answered.

There was a moment of incredulous silence on my part and then I said: "But did not the Holy Father invite all the Bishops to join with him at St. Mary Major's after the closing of the Council for some special event?"

"Yes," the Bishop said, "and many of us were there, but nothing special happened."

As I hung up the phone I could hardly believe my ears. My disappointment was profound.

Since I was traveling, my correspondence did not catch up with me. It was only weeks later that I learned what had really happened:

When Pope Paul VI realized that many Bishops could not go to St. Mary Major because of their travel plans, His Holiness decided *to do in the Council* what he had planned to do in St. Mary Major, namely, to proclaim Mary, Mother of the Church, to renew the consecration of the world to the Immaculate Heart of Mary, and to announce that he was sending a "mission to Fatima."

Bishop Venancio was just one of 3,000 bishops in mitre and cope (together with Your Excellency) in the nave of the great Basilica of St. Peter's as the Pope promulgated the Constitution of the Church, and then proclaimed Our Lady Mother of the Church *and mentioned Fatima*.

And Bishop Venancio said, when he heard the word "Fatima" mentioned in the Council, together with the renewal of the consecration which had been previously made by Pius XII, that "it was as though my entire being leaped up within my cope and mitre, although I suppose my body did not actually move."

The Pope had mentioned Fatima in the Council—perhaps the first time that a Pope had ever referred to a

4

private revelation in an Ecumenical Council, and *in the presence of all the bishops of the world*, he had renewed the solemn consecration of the world to the Immaculate Heart of Mary made by his predecessor Pius XII in 1942 (which had also referred to Russia, though not by name).

Were we now to see the great miracle Our Lady promised?

As Your Excellency knows, the Pope also disclosed in almost the same sentence that he was sending a "mission to Fatima" with the Golden Rose, and His Holiness had these words inscribed on the Rose: "To you, O Mary, I confide the Church."

What an affirmation of Fatima!

While I could not be in Rome on the previous November 21, I was in Fatima the following May 13 when the Pope's Cardinal Legate arrived with the Golden Rose. I asked Bishop Venancio: "Excellency, do you think that the consecration required by Our Lord and Our Lady has now been made and we will see the conversion of Russia?"

He was not sure, but he hoped that since this was the Pope's intention that God might accept it and that Russia might now be converted.

However, as time passed it became absolutely clear, as Lucia was able to confirm after a colloquy with Our Lord, that this had not been a truly "collegial act." It had been an act by the Pope himself, only in the *presence* of the Bishops and not with their consent. Indeed, most bishops had not even known in advance that the consecration was to be made.

Once again, in retrospect, can we not ask how it would have been possible for the Pope to have made a Collegial Consecration when a number of bishops did not will it? Was there still not more preparation needed?

This is what the Blue Army had in mind when, under the direction of Bishop Venancio, theologians from all over the world were invited to a Seminar at the Blue Army's International Center to discuss all aspects of devotion to the Immaculate Heart of Mary, including the question of the Collegial Consecration of Russia. As I mentioned to Your Excellency before, Bishop Venancio sent letters of invitation to every bishop in the world, and hundreds responded.

Prior to this we had begun in many other ways to help prepare for the Collegial Consecration, which Lucia said

Our Lord had "insisted" should be done in exactly the way requested, because He wanted *"My entire Church to know that it is through the Immaculate Heart of My Mother that this favor* (the favor of the conversion of Russia) *is obtained."*

We began to place great emphasis on the Queenship of Mary and I suppose one of the most brilliant pages in the history of our Apostolate was written from 1967 until 1971, when pilgrim statues of Our Lady of Fatima were crowned simultaneously by 50 bishops, for more than 70 countries around the world.

But even after the Pope had mentioned Fatima in proclaiming Our Lady "Mother of the Church" at the close of the third session of the Vatican Council on November 21, 1964, the effect of the long silence concerning the 1960 Secret still seemed to hang over us like a pall.

Three and a half years later the Pope finally took direct action concerning this.

Early in 1967 the Vatican announced a press conference would be given concerning the 1960 Secret of Fatima by Cardinal Ottaviani, Prefect of the Holy Office.

The conference was given in one of the largest halls of Rome. It was overflowing to the doors and windows on February 11, 1967, when Cardinal Ottaviani explained that Pope John XXIII had opened the Secret, read it, and then decided that it should not be made public.

"What is important," said the Cardinal, *"is the public Message of Fatima."* And His Eminence stressed that all that the world needed to know was contained in the parts of the Message of Fatima already revealed, and what was now required was the response of the faithful to that message.

6

I later learned (from the former Secretary of Pope John XXIII, who became the Archbishop of Loreto, and of whom Your Excellency knows because of the correspondence establishing our Holy House, U.S.A.) that Pope John XXIII shared the secret with several others including his confessor, his secretary and Cardinal Ottaviani, so that he could have their opinion as to whether it should be made public. All agreed with him that it was a message intended *for the Pope alone,* and that it should not be made public.

(I have often wished that the Vatican had possessed a good public relations office, and had simply made this clarifying statement seven years earlier!)

Your Excellency has never said anything about it, but I have wondered (and hoped) that when the Pope *mentioned Fatima* in the Council just after promulgating the Constitution of the Church that you, too, must have felt a great joy, *a confirmation of the courageous decisions you had taken for more than 15 years,* not only in permitting, but having encouraged, the Blue Army—and on one occasion of having absolutely saved its life.

7

But the greatest triumph of all came three years later when the Pope suddenly announced *that he himself,* despite opposition from some members of the Curia, from political opponents of Portugal, and from many other sources, *was actually going to Fatima!*

To make it clear that this was not a trip to "Portugal," the Pope flew to a private airport near Leiria, and went straight to Fatima "as a humble pilgrim, to pray for peace in the Church and in the world," and returned to Rome the same day.

His Holiness brought Cardinal Tisserant with him, and the Shrine was filled to overflowing with hundreds upon hundreds of thousands, perhaps millions, of pilgrims, with the banners of the Blue Army everywhere waving in that vast sea of prayerful, jubilant humanity. It never occurred to me to try to reach the Cardinal. I thought he would be constantly with the Holy Father and the Papal entourage. Later His Eminence wrote to me from Rome and said that he sat waiting for someone from the Blue Army to come and take him to the Blue Army International Center. (How sadly we remember our omissions!)

This visit of the Pope to Fatima was carried by television to the four corners of the world. Unfortunately it was seen only very early in the morning in the United States, but it made a tremendous impression all over Europe.

Perhaps the most significant aspect of that memorable occasion, from the Blue Army's point of view, was the fact that the Pope had asked that Lucia be permitted to leave her cloister on this particular day and *to be at his side* as he prayed to Our Lady for peace in the Church and in the world.

It is difficult to realize the immense significance of this act. The Pope wanted the living visionary of Fatima at his side, not because he wanted to see her, or touch her, or look into her eyes, but because he apparently *wanted to affirm his belief* that she actually saw the Blessed Virgin, and that she has been left on earth *as Our Lady Herself foretold, as Her continuing messenger.*

The Pope made this most evident in a gesture which certainly surprised me — and I suppose surprised many others even more. In the midst of the ceremonies, His Holiness took Lucia by the arm and marched her to the front of the platform before that immense crowd and the clusters of television cameras which were carrying this incredible sight to hundreds of millions around the world. Leaving Lucia standing there in the foreground, the Pope stepped back and spread out his arms in a gesture of presenting her to the world.

And it was she who prepared the Blue Army pledge, containing the essential conditions to be fulfilled in the world for the conversion of Russia, the triumph of Mary's Immaculate Heart, and "an era of peace to mankind."

I mentioned to Your Excellency earlier the lengthy illness of Bishop Venancio during the long months of the Council.

After the visit of the Pope to Fatima, what new energy filled him! He seemed ready to "tackle the world," and six months later, in October, even though Msgr. Colgan was still living, he accepted the position to which all the national officers of the world wished to elect him as the first *elected* International President of the Blue Army. 8

He had confided to me before that he did not want to be the International President because, as Bishop of the diocese, he had jurisdiction in any event over any actions that were taken at the International Center and if he actually presided over the meetings of national leaders, he would become a part of the decisions that were made and therefore would not, as the Bishop, have the reserved right of vetoing those decisions later.

But now *he felt that the Blue Army needed the prestige of his leadership, and also his active participation.*

How true!

There was one little sentence buried somewhere in the pages already past that Satan and all his hordes are constantly working upon our apostles, breaking in wherever there was the slightest crack in the door of a person's pride or through other moral defects, to create dissension, doubts, even downright scandals where none really exist.

But with His Excellency presiding at the meetings of the Blue Army leaders, what a difference we experienced!

Those who were trying to assert petty authority, or striving to be sure that their opinions were heard, spoke with respect. We began to "concentrate on the issues."

I cannot tell Your Excellency how much I suffered at some of these international meetings! Many European members seemed to resent the fact that the Apostolate originated in the United States—and how outnumbered I was at those meetings! It was once in sheer emotional exhaustion that I took the house car (which I rarely did) and drove over to Ourem to visit the Castle of Blessed Nuno. It led to a development which proves again that out of each cross and each suffering a "victory" is won.

I had been coming to Fatima for some twenty years and as related earlier, had "rewritten" a biography of the third Count of Ourem, Blessed Nuno; yet I had never traveled those six miles to visit that historic site where the children of Fatima had several times gone to pray to Blessed Nuno.

When I arrived at the beautiful old castle town I was amazed to see that one of the principal buildings, just next to the great Castle church, was for sale. The thought occurred to me, "What a wonderful thing it would be to own something that had been a part of the Castle of Blessed Nuno." And when I found out that the building was only $3,000, I decided at once to buy it!

The next day, in a more somber moment, I had the carpenter from our International Center go over to look at the Castle building. He said that it was in such a bad state of ruin that it would have to be totally demolished and rebuilt. I was disappointed because I had thought of this "identity" of Fatima with Blessed Nuno as being particularly significant. I inquired whether there might be something else for sale. It turned out that there was a very beautiful house with a private chapel, which had recently been remodeled by the Swedish millionaire who owned Sveda. I got him on the telephone at 2 o'clock the following morning and bought the house—and this led to a whole new apostolate, and one which played a major role in saving Portugal from Communism in the coup which followed a few years after the death of Salazar.

But that is another story and can be left for another time...or another writer.

In a word, a program was developed at the Castle (for which I used personal resources) presenting the Miracle of Fatima in the light of Portugal's history. Thousands of

Portuguese from all parts of the nation have seen it, and at the present time the Portuguese government is making major improvements there.

It is as though Blessed Nuno had returned to his Castle...to continue his work for Our Lady and for Portugal.

Below: Bishop Venancio watches as Portuguese Minister cuts ribbon opening the Medieval Banquet Hall of the Castle of Ourem.

Chapter Thirteen

1) No better name found - 2) Soviets recognize the Blue Army's importance - 3) Our Lady's color - 4) Pontmain Chapel in Moscow

Below: The author and the Bishop of Fatima conversing in the Blue Army's International Center at Fatima. Large map in background depicts the BLUE and the RED WORLD, with red lines from Moscow to Soviet capitals and political centers of the world, and blue lines from Fatima to the more than 100 nations where the Blue Army strives to bring about fulfillment of the requests of Our Lady of Fatima.

THE BLUE ARMY'S
NAME AND PONTMAIN

"It is good that they did not change the name..."
— *Most Rev. John P. Venancio, D.D.,*
Bishop of Fatima

As I mentioned earlier, at first Bishop Venancio had not wanted to accept the presidency of the Blue Army because he wished to have a chance to review any decisions taken by the International Council at leisure, so that, as Bishop of the diocese, he could approve or disapprove them insofar as they came within diocesan jurisdiction.

Strangely the name "Blue Army" gave us more trouble than any other particular aspect of the Apostolate. Every time a new nation joined the International Council, we could expect a long statement from the representatives of that country to the effect that the title "Blue Army" was not acceptable in their part of the world.

Usually Msgr. Colgan was present at these meetings. I would sit at his side as an interpreter. The common language of the meetings was normally French (but as Your Excellency knows I was also able to communicate in other languages, which was a tremendous asset in these international exchanges).

In one particular meeting we were truly "worn down" by the constant opposition. To my surprise Msgr. Colgan suddenly lifted up his hands in a gesture of resignation and said to me: "John, tell them that if they want to change the name, it is all right with me. Let them vote for another name."

There were perhaps representatives of some 25 countries. Ballots were passed, suggestions were made, and finally there was a vote.

Even before the vote was taken, it was evident that *there*

1

was no other name which seemed to fit the Apostolate quite as well. They thought of "Crusade," but the representative from Italy made it known that Pope John XXIII specifically said that he did not like the word "crusade" to be used because of its recollection of the actions of some of the "Crusaders" who had stormed Constantinople. *In the end, an overwhelming majority confirmed the name "Blue Army."*

I was telling the Bishop about this later, and to my surprise he remarked with great firmness:

"It is good they did not change the name, because I would have vetoed that decision."

The average person might think there was nothing unusual about this, but to anyone who knew Bishop Venancio, this was indeed unusual because he was a man who invariably recognized the will of the majority of any authorized committee. And at the moment, and ever since, I have felt that he could only have been so positive about the name of the Apostolate because Lucia herself must have spoken to him concerning the Blue Army and its name.

But as time passed, the Communists were indeed able to "smear" the name of the Blue Army—which, as it turned out, they considered the number one deterrent to the success of their world revolution.

In this, of course, they were identifying the Blue Army with Fatima *itself*. And certainly Fatima, and the message of Our Lady concerning Russia, has been a tremendous force in deterring that spread of "error from an atheist Russia throughout the entire world."

(Forewarned is forearmed, and it was at the very moment of Lenin's triumph that Our Lady foretold that "error will spread from an atheist Russia throughout the entire world, fomenting further wars... the good will be martyred, the Holy Father will suffer much, several entire nations will be annihilated... but if my requests are heard, Russia will be converted and an era of peace will be granted to mankind.")

In October, 1967, the very year that the Bishop of Fatima agreed to be the first elected International President of the Blue Army, the official Soviet magazine dedicated to the atheistic revolution published an analytical article on the progress of the revolution over the previous fifty years. The title of the magazine is *Science and Reli-*

gion, and almost a half million copies were printed of this issue of the jubilee year of the Communist revolution.

The article, titled "Tragicomedy in Four Acts," cited three factors which, in Soviet eyes, had prevented the atheistic revolution from having taken over the entire world in the fifty years since the success of Lenin's storming of the Winter Palace in Leningrad. The first was Hitler, the second was the Cold War, *and the third was The Blue Army of Our Lady of Fatima.*

It was a somewhat lengthy article, and perhaps it should be recorded when the real history of the Blue Army is written, so we will add it as an appendix to this book. Anyone who wishes can turn to it now.

I suppose it was flattering in a way to Msgr. Colgan and myself that we were immortalized in that Soviet article—as the founders of this greatest deterrent to the success of world communism!

But, of course, both the Blue Army, and our small role in it, were greatly exaggerated by the Soviets. They were merely identifying the apparitions of Fatima—which are the real force—with the Blue Army.

But what a wonderful compliment!

It is said that the Devil recognizes his due, and certainly the Message of Fatima will have no power against him unless it is *applied,* and the Blue Army is—as Cardinal Tisserant said so well—"The response to the Message of Fatima... It is the application of that message in our personal lives."

But the Soviets have spent many millions of dollars in propaganda and we can be sure that vast sums are concentrated on fighting this deterrent and striving to destroy it. Their incessant and violent attacks have certainly damaged us on more than one occasion.

We know, for example, that the name of the Blue Army fell into such disrepute in some parts of the world that it became necessary to use another name, one which the Blue Army adopted long ago as an equally "official" name: *"The World Apostolate of Our Lady of Fatima."*

I suppose it is a more pretentious and meaningful name than "Blue Army," but the latter is simple and as Cardinal Tisserant said, it connotes that the Queen needs an army, *a spiritual force* against the black legions of the Prince of Darkness.

And there is no doubt as to why we call it the *Blue* Army.

3   We associated blue with Our Lady. It seems that in every major apparition *She always wore something blue* — which is exactly what the members of the Blue Army do!

Of particular importance was Her appearance in 1871 in the small French village of Pontmain, which I, personally, have regarded as foreshadowing the Blue Army, its message, and its ultimate triumph.

When Our Lady appeared at Pontmain at the height of the Franco-Prussian War, She disclosed that "My Son has heard your prayers" (for peace). At Fatima, She promised not only peace, but also the conversion of Russia. She appeared in blue, crowned as a Queen, with two crosses next to Her head — one East and one West. Four candles were burning in an oval which surrounded Her. And as the Rosary was prayed, the entire apparition increased in size in the night sky.

There were many other meaningful details, but of special significance is the last part of the apparition of Pontmain: Our Lady's crown, with Her blue aura and four burning candles (like the four elements of the Blue Army pledge), remained. Your Excellency will remember that one of our greatest efforts during the past decades was the simultaneous coronation of Our Lady's statues by bishops all over the world on May 13, 1971 — the 25th anniversary of the coronation of Our Lady of Fatima by Pius XII as "Queen of the World."

It was also *the centenary of Pontmain*.

We had worked for several years to prepare for this worldwide coronation. The Bishop of Fatima had made two world flights with us, and one special flight all around Africa, delivering Pilgrim Virgin statues to the individual bishops and then crowns, which had been blessed by Pope Paul VI.

As we neared the deadline of the jubilee, there were only a few countries in which the coronation had not yet been successfully arranged. One of them, to our surprise, was France, a country which had been repeatedly favored with Marian apparitions over the past 150 years.

Earlier, I had learned that the original history of the apparitions of Pontmain, which had been written within a few days of the event, had never been translated into English and that the Rector of the Sanctuary of Pontmain wanted the translation for the centenary. So I offered to undertake the task and publish it. I then took advantage of the impending worldwide Coronation of Our Lady and told the Rector how fitting it would be to have the Coronation for France take place in the beautiful Basilica of Pontmain on the occasion of the centenary of the apparitions of Our Lady of Pontmain.

He agreed, and the Bishop of Laval consented to perform the act of Coronation. And I must confess, Your Excellency, that I little dreamed or suspected at that time how significant this would be—not even after I had translated the entire authentic and beautiful story of those apparitions.

I was in Moscow for the coronation of Our Lady's statue there (the same statue which had left Washington, N.J. in 1950). And I discovered that the chapel in Moscow was named the "Chapel of Our Lady of Hope"...Our Lady of Pontmain. But to return to my account: **4**

In order to obtain the final consent of the Bishop of Laval, I needed a letter from Bishop Venancio very urgently.

The Director of Fatima Travel, Mr. Camille Berg, was going to Luxembourg to visit his mother for Christmas, and I persuaded him to go via Portugal so that he could deliver my message to Bishop Venancio and obtain the Bishop's signature to a letter to the Bishop of Laval.

Your Excellency remembers Camille Berg well. What a glorious and providential man in our history!

After we had built the International Center of the Blue Army in Fatima, I asked the Portuguese government to recommend suitable and capable applicants who might manage the House. One of the persons recommended was Mr. Berg, who was at that time managing a small hotel at Fatima, where I could easily evaluate him.

I stayed in the hotel a couple of days. After seeing how efficient he was, I offered to double his salary if he would come to the Blue Army House.

He looked sad, and then said how glad he would be to accept, but that two elderly people owned this small hotel, and that they could not replace him on short notice, not even within six months. But if I would wait until after October 13 (which was the day when I would most need him because Cardinal Tisserant was coming then to dedicate the House!), he would be glad to accept.

I made up my mind at once that this was the man for us. He was not only capable, but also placed the interest of his employer above his own.

He turned out to be one of the most valuable persons ever associated with us in any capacity. From the very beginning he managed the Blue Army House without debt, until one day I received a fateful letter stating that he had been offered a better position by a restaurant chain in America. He had decided that he would like to live in America.

He was not really "Blue Army" as he was essentially a professional hotel manager. But how, I wondered, would we run the House at Fatima without him? He had not only managed the Center, but with his knowledge of languages he had been invaluable in our international correspondence. And he was a man whom we could trust—and trust was so important in a project as complex as our Fatima House, which included some twenty employees.

That was when I conceived the idea of developing a travel agency and of making him the manager. Fortunately, he accepted. Within two years, he had developed it into what is known as a "million dollar agency." It became a most important factor in the development of the Blue Army in the world—organizing pilgrimages not only to Fatima, but around the world and around Africa with the Pilgrim Virgin statue, besides making my many journeys cost-free to the Blue Army.

Camille willingly accepted my commission concerning Pontmain to the Bishop of Fatima, and who would have dreamed of the result? As he was driving up to Fatima with his son, Nuno, he began to feel weak. His son saw the blood draining from his face.

The Bishop had been ill and had risen from his sick bed because of the urgency of the visit. As Camille entered the Bishop's parlor, he suddenly collapsed in the prelate's presence, but managed to murmur repeatedly: "But John said this letter is so important."

The Bishop assured Camille that he would take care of the letter, and then, unable to get help at the moment, he aided Nuno in getting Camille down to his car and to a hospital.

Camille never returned to America. He died in Lisbon, his last service having been to honor the Queen of the World as a "working member" of the Blue Army.

Below: Bishop Venancio and author look on as Pope Paul VI venerates statue blessed by His Holiness for Blue Army for tour of Africa on October 15, 1969.

Chapter Fourteen

1) Camille Berg: Providential man - 2) Agency expanded
to keep him at our side - 3) Personal resources used -
4) The Columbus fleet - 5) Difficult choice!

Below: On May 13, 1967, Pope Paul VI prays before the statue of
Our Lady of Fatima while Bishop Venancio speaks to the crowd
(more than one million). Between 1960 and 1967, the Apostolate
of Fatima had suffered unexpected reverses in many parts of the
world. The visit of the Pope to Fatima opened a new period of development. Bishop Venancio, according to the wishes of Monsignor Colgan and of the Blue Army International Council, became the first "elected" International President of the Blue
Army shortly after the Pope's visit to Fatima.

IN THE DEVIL'S TRIANGLE

"Lesson from a Storm at Sea"

So far in writing this "letter of memories" I have rejoiced to have been able to cover some major events in a few paragraphs. I am sometimes tempted to indulge in so many details that volumes rather than mere chapters would be needed.

But I think it would be a mistake to pass over the wonderful role of Camille Berg and of Fatima Travel in mere paragraphs. Some of the greatest advancements of our Apostolate throughout the world were due to the fact that we had the *Fatima Travel* agency, and therefore had expertise in planning trips (*even operating our own airline around the world!*). People were willing to pay their way to go on these trips, and at the same time made them "cost-free" to the Apostolate.

Our flight around the world in 1978 with our plane "Queen of the World" cost almost half a million dollars, so it is evident that this contribution was indeed very important. And even though the visible effects of that world flight were little short of the spectacular, I think that only in heaven will we know the truly enormous contribution it made to the final triumph of Our Lady's Immaculate Heart and the recognition of Her Queenship.

Camille Berg, whose first name was really "Camillus," was from Luxembourg. He was handsome, ambitious, and brilliant. He was still in his early twenties when he had become assistant manager of the biggest hotel in Berlin, considered at that time one of the finest in all Europe. When war came, Luxembourgers—who because of their Catholic faith and independence were not trusted by the

1

Nazis—were sent to the Russian front after minimal training. Of his entire regiment, he was the only survivor.
Those who had not died on the battlefront, died during
their two years of imprisonment in Siberia.

Gifted in languages and charm, Camille made friends
with the doctors in the Siberian camp, and traded food for
cigarettes—which were "currency"—and little by little,
accumulated enough "wealth" to bribe guards and to
obtain enough medicines to enable him to survive.

He married into a well-known Portuguese family with
some deliberation—because after the white horror of
Siberia he had always dreamt of living in a warm climate
(and Portugal is semi-tropical).

The degree that he had from his Swiss School of Hotel
Management which advanced him at a young age to the
position of assistant manager of the big Berlin hotel now
stood him in good stead in Portugal, where he took a
position in Fatima as manager of a small hotel. He did so
well that he attracted the favorable attention of the Portuguese Tourist Department. And there, as Your Excellency
already knows, is where I met him.

I have been told often in my life that "no man is irre-
placeable," and I suppose, in an absolute sense, this is
true. But where, except by God's providence, could we
ever have found a man with the qualifications, the disposition, the honesty of Camille Berg? Everyone I knew liked
him and many loved him, including, eminently, Msgr.
Colgan. He and Camille became the closest of friends.

2 Ever since we completed the Blue Army Center at
Fatima, I had been promoting trips there at cost, in order
to help the Center financially and to fulfill our even
greater and more important purpose of getting people to
Fatima *to experience its reality*.

At first we did this as a Blue Army venture, but shortly
thereafter we were informed by the steamship companies
that only a duly-established travel agency was entitled
to commissions, so I formed a small agency, separate
from the Blue Army, but with no intention of making
a profit.

When I received that fateful letter from Camille saying
that he was accepting a job with a restaurant chain in
California, I knew this meant that I would have to go back
to Portugal (since I was the only one of the organization
who spoke languages) and perhaps have to spend a great

deal of time there setting up a new management. And I was quite sure that I could never hope to be so fortunate as to find another man with Camille's rare qualities.

I thought that we would need something to do in winter as well as summer (not foreseeing how rapidly the agency would develop) and hit upon the idea of the "Columbus Fleet"—three schooners of approximately the same size as the three in which Columbus had discovered America. We would operate these in the Bahamas where Columbus actually landed.

In the back of my mind I was thinking primarily of youth. Most of those going to Fatima were older persons, often retired. No young people seemed to be attracted to Fatima. I felt that a sail in the West Indies, with daily Mass and a bringing home to young people of the almost miraculous nature of Columbus' original voyage and the subsequent apparition of Our Lady of Guadalupe, would open the door to their minds and hearts.

I knew boats well because I had been born on the Atlantic Coast and before the Blue Army began I had owned a Stadel schooner. (I later sold it in order to help finance the beginning of the Blue Army.)

Perhaps it might be of interest to explain how the Blue Army was at first financed.

Fortunately, I was always very sensitive about accepting payment for doing Our Lady's work and therefore had sought other financing. Shortly after the Carmelites had sponsored the Scapular Apostolate for me in New York, I considered that the income from any lectures or writings should go to the apostolate. In return I took a salary, first of only $25.00 a week, and ultimately, for almost all the rest of my life, of only $100.00 a week. And Divine Providence rewarded me in a most extraordinary way, especially through my father.

With the earnings from the press my father had established for me before the Scapular Apostolate, I bought the Stadel schooner. It was a remarkable little ship, considered by *Yachting Magazine* to be "the most seaworthy of her size ever designed." Of the six built at that time, one had been commissioned by the British government as a pilot boat in the Straits of Madagascar. I would not have hesitated to sail around the world, but, I had little spare time and it was really a weekend escape. As I became increasingly involved in the apostolate, those escapes became progressively rarer. One of them, however, led to the purchase of a house on Long Island.

When I decided in 1950 to launch SOUL Magazine and promote the Blue Army as an extension of the "March of Pledges," the schooner and house were sold. The latter brought *six times what I had paid for it only five years before*, and the schooner realized four times what I had originally paid!

Thus I had a very substantial "nest egg," and I am pleased to recall this here because it gives me the opportunity (as I said before) to acknowledge the great debt all of us owe to my first wife, Anne, who readily agreed to this sacrifice.

4 But as the years passed, and the Apostolate mushroomed like the proverbial mustard seed, the Blue Army was able to reimburse me to a large extent for property and equipment. It was with these funds that I now decided to expand the travel agency to keep Camille Berg at my side, to multiply the trips to Fatima, and also to launch the "Columbus Fleet."

I found the "flagship" in Miami. It was a wonderful old schooner which had been built in Greenwich, N.J. in 1901 and was well preserved because Atwater Kent, one of the early inventors and producers of radios, had turned it into a private yacht. When he died, it was stored out of water and there it was discovered by two men who had decided after the war that they were going to escape the coming atomic destruction by sailing with their families to Bora Bora. One of them was a ship's carpenter, and they spent two years completely rebuilding it.

Although they were good carpenters, they knew nothing about sailing and they had not gone far from New Jersey when they were caught in an ocean gale and swept 300 miles off course. When they got back to port, one of the two left and turned the ship over to the other, who, fearing the ocean, sailed it all the way down to Florida on the Inland Waterway. There it remained tied up for seven years in the Miami River.

The Nina and the Pinta were each forty feet long, and were reconstructed from ocean-going fishing boats. These boats had gone to sea almost every day with a crew of nine and when the fish left our Jersey shores after the war, they were virtually abandoned.

There is no need to go into the details of all this because they relate little to the Blue Army. But regretably, as it turned out, the youth were not interested in the West Indies with the religious twist, anymore than they were interested in going to Fatima. And we soon learned that running a travel agency—certainly the way in which Camille developed ours—was more than just a summertime business!

(Incidentally, the Nina and the Pinta were sold to the Cubans during the time when many of them were escaping from Castro. The Flag Ship, the Santa Maria, had a longer and even more interesting history, but it need not be recorded here, except for the following anecdote, which explains the reason I have spent so much time telling Your Excellency about our maritime venture.)

On the first test-sailing of the *Santa Maria* to the Bahamas, I had three men with me. Only one had ever had any sailing experience, and that was in small boats.

Our only charts for the Devil's Triangle at that time were the old British Admiralty charts of 1836 and 1890, marked in fathoms!

Because of this, it was customary to sail in those islands only in daylight when one could see the coral heads through the clear water. There were very few navigational aids. The only ones I can recall were the Isaacs Light on Bimini, the harbor lights of New Providence, and two or three on the outermost islands.

So we set sail at sunset, expecting to make a landfall in Bimini next morning. The weather report called for northerlies of 20 to 25 knots, but I felt confident that the big (110 ton) schooner would welcome any winds of less than hurricane force.

I did not count on the human factor—or the marvelous design of our American sailing ships which had been refined to a peak of efficiency by the turn of the century when these commercial sailing vessels depended on speed for business advantage.

As we crossed the Gulf Stream, the waves were so large that looking back over the gallows (a giant rack upon which the boom of the mainsail rests when not in use), we could see the waves were towering above it. And soon my three man crew became so violently ill—even though none of them had ever been subject to seasickness, that I was sailing alone. They were in such a distressed state that I am sure they did not care whether the ship sank right there, or plowed up on the coral reefs of Bimini.

I would leave the wheel and dash down into the aft cabin to check the chart, and then back up to the wheel, trying to plot my course, allowing for the flow of the Gulf Stream and leeway from the force of the wind.

Because of the schooner's speed, I was off the rocky coast of Bimini *four hours earlier than expected.....*and in pitch blackness!

5   I had to choose between coming about (which would have been virtually impossible without a crew), or of heading northward, close to the wind, in the hope of clearing the Bimini reef altogether.

Of the two points of reference needed to get one's position, I had the Isaacs Light alone to guide me and I could only calculate my position by estimating where I was when I made my northward turn (which was little more than a guess!) and heading towards the light, which I expected to be on the extremity of the reef.

As I came closer and closer to the light, seeing its flashings weirdly reflected on the sails, it suddenly occurred to me that maybe the light was *not* on the extremity of the reef. When this thought hit, with beating heart I plunged back down into the cabin to check the chart.

There were three miles of breaking reefs to the north of the light! I would have to round them in the dark without any further point of reference!

I held the ship as close to the wind as I could, the spray-lashed darkness, the roar of the waves and howl of the wind adding to the tension of that fateful decision of estimating just when I would have passed three miles north of the light.

Nor could I tell, of course, exactly how fast the ship was going, otherwise I would have known when I had traveled the three miles. Your Excellency can imagine how I held my breath when I finally decided to make the fateful turn to the east. For minutes which seemed like hours, the ship plunged forward into the unknown darkness. I saw the light come abeam to the south and sailed on with a rising sense of relief into the famous "tongue of the ocean," now with 2,000 fathoms of water under the keel!

This episode reminds me so much of the crisis we had in 1979, but which need not be included in these reminiscences. I feared at that moment that the entire Blue Army

Apostolate in the United States was in danger of foundering, but you were constantly guiding me. Then at the last moment, when the most important direction was needed, I telephoned only to find that you had been taken to the hospital for an emergency major operation and could not be reached! I had to take that dangerous turn alone, not knowing whether I was leading the Blue Army onto the rocks, or into the safety of open waters which would lead to the calm harbor.

The experience of that stormy night off the Reef of Bimini was mild by comparison!

Below: Photo of author's yacht, the SANTA MARIA, referred to in this chapter. This yacht, shown here anchored off Conception Island in the Bahamas, played an important role in the decision to write THE WORLD'S GREATEST SECRET.

Chapter Fifteen

1) The mystery of Conception Island - 2) An aside: God's goodness shown in a marvelous way - 3) Each nation's special devotion to Mary

Below: The Most Rev. Jerome J. Hastrich presents a picture of the Mother and Queen of the Americas to Cardinal Corripio of Mexico City. It can be called "a picture of devotion to the Immaculate Heart" which Father Alonso describes as a devotion to Our Lady's INTERIOR life. Bishop Hastrich became U.S. National President of the Blue Army in 1980. In every nation Blue Army members are urged to honor Our Lady in a special way according to their own national traditions.

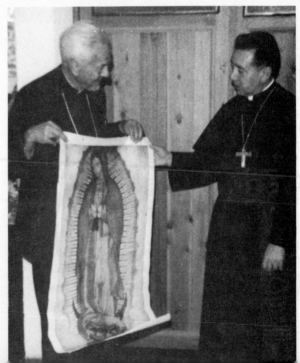

OUR LADY OF THE AMERICAS

―――――――――――――――――――――

"Special Mother to Each One...to Each Nation"

We made our landfall at two o'clock the following afternoon at the top of the Berry Islands. We had averaged an incredible twelve knots an hour!

I could not stay away from the office very long, so I left the ship in New Providence, but decided to continue exploring the islands and particularly to continue to my planned destination: San Salvador, where Columbus had made his first landfall.

There are actually three islands which comprise the first landfall of Columbus. The first was San Salvador itself (now called Watling Island). The second was Conception Island (which he named after the Immaculate Conception of Our Lady). The third was Holy Mary of the Conception (now called Rum Cay).

None of these islands has a harbor and thus they are very rarely visited by other than supply ships.

The two islands which have been renamed are inhabited. The first (San Salvador) has a radar tracking station operated by the United States government and has completely shed its primitive nature. But the second (Santa Maria de la Conception) would seem almost like the dream island in a South Pacific movie. (Since only one or two yachts dare to sail those waters in the course of a year, we received a warm welcome from the friendly people who lived there, many of whom probably had never traveled away from it.)

There remained Conception Island, still uninhabited, and one of the few small navigational aids (although not always reliable) was mounted on that prominence.

Many years ago there was a small harbor there but the entrance had filled with coral. Just outside, the water plunges straight down to a depth of almost 200 feet.

1 Why had Columbus named this island "Conception" in 1492, long before the proclamation of the Dogma, and the apparition of Our Lady at Lourdes? It was 39 years before Our Lady was to appear at the geographical center of the Americas and say in the Nahuatl or Aztec language what to the Spaniards sounded like "Guadalupe," but which, to the Indian who heard Her, seemed as incomprehensible as the words "Immaculate Conception" to Bernadette at Lourdes.

Had Our Lady saved this virgin island, with its exceptional little hill, as a lasting memorial of the "miraculous" voyage of Columbus?

I don't think any of us realized how truly "miraculous" that voyage was until a few years ago when, under the sponsorship of the *Saturday Evening Post,* a group of hardy men decided to re-enact it. It took them almost double the time to cross the Atlantic, and they realized that Columbus must have had *continually following winds* to have arrived at San Salvador when he did. And to think that he arrived just as it was being decided that they would turn back if land was not discovered that very day!

When they sighted that first island, they gathered at the rails of the ships and sang the "Hail, Holy Queen," and after naming the first landfall in honor of the Holy Savior, they named the next two after the Immaculate Conception and Our Lady of the Conception of Jesus!

As I was anchored off that same island, in a schooner almost identical in size to that of the flagship of Columbus, I couldn't help wondering whether Our Lady had brought me here for some purpose.

When I arrived back in New Providence, I went to see the Bishop of Nassau and told him of my thoughts. To my surprise the Bishop said that this very island *was responsible for the Catholic faith throughout that area of the West Indies.* A Benedictine monk had been shipwrecked just off Conception Island. Stranded there, he felt that God had done this to indicate that He wanted these islands evangelized. The holy priest then made a vow that if he were rescued from that desolate spot, far out in the vast ocean, he would remain in these islands and bring other Benedictines to teach the faith to the natives.

I therefore wrote to influential men proposing that Conception Island be set aside as a national monument and that a statue of the Immaculate Conception be placed on that little hill as a lasting memorial of the dedication of the Americas to the Immaculate Conception.

Subsequently the Bahamas became an independent nation, and the area around Conception Island has now been declared a national park. Bishop Haggerty, the Benedictine Bishop of Nassau, has endorsed a project to have a statue of Our Lady erected on Conception Island. May we hope that this can be done by 1992, the 500th anniversary of the miraculous voyage of Columbus under the protection of Our Lady, the Immaculate?

My hopes in this were increased when Bishop Hastrich, so devoted to Our Lady of the Americas, became the first active nationally-elected president of the Blue Army—and he was the founder of the Queen of the Americas Guild.

The sea is my great escape. I cannot help feeling that, by God's providence, my love of boats and the occasions that I have had to "escape to the sea" were of great importance to my work. My lifelong spiritual director, Fr. John, was so concerned with the intensity and unrelenting work schedule which I maintained that he once wrote to my father (I did not see the letter until after my father's death) that he was praying that I would get another boat!

How often I have exclaimed: "Oh, how the good Lord spoils those who serve Him!" I remember the time that I had gone to Coimbra to see Sr. Lucia, accompanied by Msgr. Colgan and an American millionaire, hoping to get them in at least to greet her. But it was impossible, even on contacting the Archbishop of Coimbra, to obtain permission for them.

As we were returning by train to Lisbon, I was sitting in the compartment with the millionaire, who had fallen asleep, and I could not help reflecting that I was more fortunate than the richest man in the world. And yet—and I say this most sincerely and for the benefit of others—I have never hesitated to place the needs of the Apostolate above all others.

I had sailed in and through, up and down the Devil's Triangle in the *Santa Maria*, but Our Lady was always there!

The one thing I regretted about these trips was my inability to get to daily Mass and Communion. I suppose that back in my subconscious mind the main reason that I had originated the idea of the Columbus Fleet, with a chaplain aboard and Daily Mass, was so that I could indulge in my favorite hobby and still remain close to Our Eucharistic Lord.

3   Perhaps by 1992, when we celebrate the 500th anniversary of the discovery of America, our continent will appreciate far more deeply the special love of Our Lady "for all in these lands" (Her words to Juan Diego, December 12, 1531).

It is fitting for members of the Blue Army to acknowledge their special national devotion to Our Lady in whatever country they live. Our Lady of Fatima is Queen of the World, and what nation does not have some special and "personal" manifestation of Her love? What nation does not have its own special Marian shrine(s)?

France has so many that one wonders what degree of responsibility this places upon France for her own people and for the world.

Recently Belgium has been greatly honored by "Our Lady of the Golden Heart" and the revelations of Berthe Petit. England has Walsingham and Aylesford. Ireland has the extraordinarily meaningful yet "silent" vision of Knock. And so on, and on.

Should not all Marian movements of a nation or a continent recognize *the personal intimacy of Our Lady* expressed in their own shrines? Certainly it seems commendable that Our Lady's Blue Army tends to do so. She is Queen of all. She is the Mother of each one of us, and of each individual nation.

Below: Following the 1976 Eucharistic Congress in Philadelphia, ground is broken for the Blue Army's U.S. National Shrine in Washington, N.J.

Bishop Venancio (who had come from Portugal for the occasion) was asked to break ground as International President of the Blue Army. His Excellency quietly insisted that the Blue Army is not the work only of the Bishops but of all together. He therefore asked that John Haffert join him. This happy occasion reflects the spirit of cooperation between clergy and laity (and especially of reverence for the authority of the Bishops) which has been a major foundation stone of the Blue Army.

---

Chapter Sixteen

1) Our Lord's sweet legacy - 2) The Voice of God for us -
3) Fatima emphasizes Bishop's authority - 4) Blue Army
is diocesan-based apostolate - 5) Bishop Luna succeeds
to international leadership.

**Below: Bishop Ahr speaks in the pulpit of St. Mary's in Plain-
field, N.J. during the Blue Army's first national congress in
1953. His Excellency developed the theme of his own motto,
"Mary, My Hope." No one present could have realized the
major efforts this Bishop would undertake in the years which
followed, not only to prevent the Blue Army from destruction,
but to lead it to success.**

16

ROLE OF THE BISHOPS

"So that My entire Church will know..."
— Words of Our Lord to Lucia concerning the
Collegial Consecration

W hen Bishop Venancio retired as the second Bishop of Fatima, his successor (the Most Rev. Albert Cosme do Amaral) had only one major piece of advice for us: *"Always be obedient to the Bishop."*

As the years have passed, the Bishop of Fatima has repeated this exhortation under every circumstance as *the first and last commandment* for all Blue Army apostles.

For those who will read this "history," I would like to add that we should look upon our bishops not only as symbols of authority but as spiritual fathers. How can we separate the Voice of God from the Love of God?

Your Excellency knows that I originally thought that the path for the realization of my vocation was in the Carmelites, and when I made vows of poverty, chastity, and obedience for three years, I had not the slightest doubt that I would soon be renewing them forever. What was most difficult for me when I was faced with the open world in which I was to find the path of my vocation, was my lack of a religious superior who would be the Voice of God to tell me which way to go. Then I remembered the Bishop!

Since I was now back in my father's house in the Diocese of Camden, New Jersey, I went to the Bishop of Camden, the Most Rev. Bartholomew Eustace, and poured out my heart to him.

Most of us are "afraid" of bishops, and certainly I was conscious of this awe on that occasion. I just hoped that a bishop, who must necessarily be one of the busiest persons in the world, could find time to listen to the needs of one of his thousands of children.

But Bishop Eustace immediately understood my problem, and (I am sure, by the Light of God) also understood that I had some kind of special vocation. He said that he would pray to Our Lady during the entire month of May, and that on the 31st of May (which at that time was the feast of Our Lady's Mediation) he would hope to have a definite decision.

I was there on that day, and the Bishop told me, in effect, that he would have liked to have invited me to become a priest in his diocese, but he recognized that if I were to become a priest I would undoubtedly be attached to pastoral work. I would not be able to fulfill the special vocation that I felt to spread devotion to the Blessed Virgin and that he was therefore *convinced* that I should remain in the lay state, even though he did not know how that apostolate would ever be fulfilled.

I came out with all the paths still stretching to the horizon and not knowing which one I might take, but convinced that the path would be there.

Recently, in preparation for writing this history, I had occasion to go through some old correspondence and I found the letters from Bishop Eustace which I don't think I had read for almost thirty years.

In order to give me a source of income and to "start me on my way," he had written to every parish in his diocese suggesting that they invite me to give a lecture on Our Lady! And what an experience that was! I lectured in parishes which had not had any such outside lecturer in the memory of the parishioners!

Apparently the reports the Bishop received concerning these lectures from the various pastors were favorable, and little by little I was invited to just about every parish in southern New Jersey. This work had hardly finished when the General of the Carmelite Order arrived in New York, driven from Italy because of the war, and his Assistant General, the Very Rev. Gabriel Pausback, came down to see me and proposed that I come to New York, where the Carmelites had a church dedicated to Our Lady of Mount Carmel, to start a national apostolate of devotion to Our Lady of the Scapular (Mt. Carmel).

When I wrote and told Bishop Eustace, I can imagine the joy of that saintly man who had for 31 days prayed to Our Lady for the light to guide me! He wrote:

Dear Mr. Haffert:

I am delighted that at last such a wide scope, with such a splendid backing, has been given you for the fulfillment of your holy ambitions. It looks as though your prayer had received an almost miraculous answer.

I think by all means you should accept the offer given you. Work at the thing that God has put into your hands and about further ambitions we can later see. But throw your whole heart into this project which God, through the instumentality of His Carmelite Sons, has given you.

I trust you will keep in touch with me both by letter and by personal visit and I close by saying I am proud of my noble son.

With every best wish and blessing, I am
Sincerely yours,

+Bartholomew Eustace
Bishop of Camden

Now, of course, the Carmelite Provincial in New York became my superior, and I was again able to tread the solid path of obedience even up to that sudden bitter moment when a letter from Cardinal Spellman recommended that the Carmelites should not continue to have a layman at the head of their apostolate. And shortly afterwards I moved to the Diocese of Trenton, when first Bishop Griffin, and then Your Excellency became for me the Voice of God.

As Bishop Venancio has so often told our Blue Army leaders at meetings at Fatima, and in his visits around the world: "Always obey the Bishop, and if he says no, do what is permitted, and quietly persist, quietly continue to knock as Our Lord commanded."

Sometimes the Voice of God says "no" because there has been insufficient preparation, insufficient unselfishness and humility, perhaps insufficient prayer and sacrifice—without which no seeds of the Apostolate would take root. But what bishop in the world would say "no" to an apostolate of holiness in his diocese if he were convinced that those promoting it were sincere and that the Apostolate was a sound one?

I feel that this is a very important statement to make in any "history" of the Blue Army—because our entire Apostolate has been built upon this awareness of the authority of the bishop and his role as the Voice of God, as well as of the expression of God's fatherliness.

It was therefore somewhat of a shock for us to hear at the meeting of the International Executive Council of the Blue Army, which was held in Rome in January, 1980, that the Cardinal Prefect of one of the congregations expressed the opinion that since the Blue Army was a lay apostolate it should not have a bishop at its head.

Canon Jose Galamba de Oliveira (mentioned earlier as the most influential Canon during the time of the first Bishop of Fatima) presided at this meeting. A vote was being held to approve or disapprove the recent election of national officers of the Blue Army in the United States in which Your Excellency and Bishop Hastrich were elected President and Vice President respectively. And Canon Oliveira urged all the members of the committee to abstain from voting because of the Cardinal's opinion.

There followed an important (and I would presume historic) discussion as to whether or not the Blue Army is a *lay* apostolate, such as the Legion of Mary might be considered.

While Bishop of Fatima, Bishop Venancio had written a very important and detailed definition of the Blue Army and its role, and of the persons who should be involved in the Apostolate. Indeed this is so crucial that it is an appendix to this book. (The reader might find it advantageous to read that appendix now.)

The Bishop emphasized that perhaps one of the unique aspects of the Blue Army is that its membership is open *to every person, in every walk of life,* and it eminently includes bishops, priests and religious, as well as laity. It is an Apostolate of holiness, in response to the message of Our Lady of Fatima (to use the phrase of Cardinal Tisserant once more).

Your Excellency will recall that the first Bishop of Fatima had appointed Rev. Dr. Lourenco, a Canon of the Diocese of Leiria, to draw up statutes for the Blue Army, which were later studied by the international leaders and finally approved at a meeting under the presidency of Cardinal Tisserant and presented to the Holy See.

In that first international constitution, it was specified that the president of the Blue Army would necessarily always be a priest.

I remember that we were all unanimous in this. This is a spiritual Apostolate, and it is fitting that it should always have at its head an ordained minister of God.

Later Msgr. Dalos, of the Vatican's Council of the Laity, told me, when we had reported after five years concerning the progress of the application of the statutes, that the Holy See had found no objection to the statutes except for the clause that a priest would necessarily be president. He said that since Vatican Council II, when this Council was established and the apostolate of the Blue Army was placed under the jurisdiction of this Council, they felt that while a priest could be president, a lay person should also be eligible for this office.

So when the constitution was revised in an international meeting a few years ago, the leaders of the Apostolate from all over the world reluctantly changed this, but then introduced a new statute to the effect that if a lay person were elected President, there would be an International Spiritual Director (either a bishop or a priest) who would be on a level with the President.

How often has Our Lady Herself emphasized the importance of the role of bishops in the Church!

3

In that very intimate and wonderful apparition which took place at the dawn of our own history on Tepeyac Hill, Our Lady's first instruction to that model of lay apostles, Juan Diego, was "Go to the Bishop."

And what greater lesson could we have concerning the role of bishops than that God has chosen in our own day to require, as a decisive condition for the conversion of Russia and world peace, a *Collegial Consecration of Russia* to the Immaculate Heart of Mary—an act made by the Holy Father "together with all the bishops of the world!"

We had not heard much about collegiality before Vatican II, but in 1929 Our Lady revealed that Russia would be converted only after the Holy Father, together with all the bishops of the world, consecrated Russia to Her Immaculate Heart. And subsequently, on several occasions, Our Lord Himself spoke of the absolute need of this consecration in order that Russia be converted. Even after the Popes had repeatedly made the consecration themselves, and even after Pope Paul VI had done so in the presence of all of the bishops in Vatican Council II, Our Lord's words, spoken in 1936 to Sr. Lucia, were still not fulfilled to the letter.

Our Lord had explained: "I desire that it be done in this way so that *My entire Church will know* that it is through the Immaculate Heart of My Mother that this favor (the conversion of Russia) is obtained."

As we have somewhat breathlessly been working towards, and waiting for, this Collegial Consecration, it has become absolutely clear that it has to be truly *collegial*. It has to be truly the bishops with the Pope, and not the Pope simply commanding it, and then acting without the bishops having been fully informed, and without the *willing* participation of at least the vast majority.

Oh! Is there not a great mystery in this! Is not God, through the Immaculate Heart of Mary, asserting the importance of the role of the bishops in the world today as Our Lord asserted it when he chose "the Twelve" 2000 years ago? Also strongly emphasized in the Message of Fatima, and therefore through the Blue Army, is the need of respect and prayer for His Holiness, and of a kind of "devotion" to him as the Vicar of Christ.

How can anyone fail to be deeply moved at recalling that remark of Jacinta to Lucia after two priests had spoken to them about the need of praying for the Pope—of whom these children had heard very little, if anything—before the apparitions of Our Lady?

Jacinta thought that these priests must have known something of the Secret, and from the moment those two good priests spoke to the children of the need of praying for the Pope, their hearts responded generously and not long after, Jacinta had that profound vision of the Holy Father "in a great house, his head buried in his hands," with people storming outside. Often after that Jacinta would say, as she remembered the vision: "O, the poor Holy Father! O, we must pray for the poor Holy Father!"

And she persuaded her brother and Lucia to add three Hail Marys "for the poor Holy Father" to every one of their Rosaries.

Therefore, the Blue Army is a "diocesan-based" Apostolate. Any Catholic, anywhere, can sign the Blue Army pledge and thus become a member of the Blue Army. And any two or three can gather together in their homes to pray the Rosary together and thus form a Blue Army "cell." But when they want to promote the devotion in any public way within a parish, *they must obtain the permission of the pastor.* And when they want to form a center extending beyond the boundaries of the parish, *they must have the permission of the bishop.*

4

It cannot be expected that every bishop will occupy himself, in even a small degree, with this Apostolate, but certainly he will appoint someone whom he feels qualified to represent him—and to that representative the Blue Army apostles owe the same unswerving obedience as to the bishop himself.

Perhaps the growth of the Apostolate in this manner has been a slow one, but it is built on the solid rock of the Church itself.

In the historic Rome meeting of January, 1980 already described, despite the exhortation of the acting President, after a long discussion the members of the International Executive Committee voted unanimously (with four abstentions) to ratify a bishop as President of the Blue Army of the United States, and to emphasize hereafter that this Apostolate is *not exclusively a lay apostolate*, and that in their opinion it is only fitting (and often perhaps advisable) that bishops and priests should be principal officers, while at the same time they do not exclude the possibility that lay persons could be elected to principal offices. (Incidentally, I think we strike an excellent balance in the Blue Army, as evidenced in our present national officers in the United States, and our international officers—two of whom are lay persons: the International Lay Delegate, which is the highest office next to the President, and the International Secretary.

As I look back over forty years of active apostleship, I think there could be no more effective combination than a sincere priest and a sincere layman working in harmony together, and this becomes all the more important and effective when, on the national or international level, it is the close cooperation of a lay apostle and a bishop (with the lay apostle able to give his full time, and the bishop able to give his enlightened and authoritative direction).

The Blue Army has been singularly blessed in having the direct and personal attention of the Bishops of Fatima, and of Your Excellency as Bishop of the Diocese in which the National Center of the Blue Army of the United States was formed and from which it has spread throughout the world.

We were subsequently blessed in having Bishop Jerome Hastrich become the first elected National President of the Blue Army to serve in that capacity, and then to have the Most Reverend Constantino Luna, 5 former Bishop of Zacapa, to succeed the second Bishop of Fatima.

Bishop Luna had been associated with the Blue Army almost from the time of his consecration as a Bishop in 1956. He had been designated by the Bishop of Fatima to dedicate the Latin Chapel of our International Center at Fatima in 1965.

Bishop Luna had gone to the international meeting at Fatima in 1981 (following the Centennial Eucharistic Congress in Lourdes) with no thought whatever of being elected to any office. But to the delegates from all six continents of the world came a growing realization that he was the ideal person to succeed Bishop Venancio. When the latter was asked, he at once responded: "He would be ideal to lead the Blue Army now!"

The vote was unanimous. Bishop Luna, who in that same year was celebrating his 25th anniversary as a Bishop, assumed an active leadership by drawing together some of the factions that necessarily show themselves in electoral meetings. He told the Blue Army leaders of the world an extraordinary personal story:

He had an audience with Pope John XXIII in which he confided to the Pontiff his desire to be totally consecrated to Mary. When he knelt for the Pope's blessing, the Holy Father placed his hands on Bishop Luna's head and told him that he belonged entirely to Mary!

A short time later Bishop Luna assisted at a Mass for invalids in Rome. As he left the altar, a woman came up and spat in his face! He was told the woman was possessed by the devil. That same evening, at the request of the local ecclesiastical authority, he performed an exorcism for her. When he called upon Our Lady to drive Satan out, she was delivered.

"We have Satan with us," the Bishop said, "but Our Lady is the Queen and we need merely to live our consecration to Her. She will overcome Satan, who fears and hates us because he fears and hates Her who brings about the reign of Christ."

I had the privilege of a long personal visit with Bishop Luna while we were waiting for a delayed flight back to America after the meeting at Fatima. As we were walking in a park in Lisbon, His Excellency suddenly stopped, looked up at me and said:

"You know, it is marvelous to have been a Bishop during the time of the Second Vatican Council. It seems as though all of those days, months and years of the Council are all here," and he made a circling gesture over his head.

Bishop Luna never tires of saying: "The Church is our Mother. We cannot fail in following Her in every slight detail!"

Bishop Luna's own story is truly extraordinary. He was born in the Province of Venice, Italy, received his doctorate from Toulouse University in France and a master's degree in Chinese literature in Peking. He speaks ten languages, including Chinese (because he began his religious service as a missionary in China). When he was expelled from China, after several times expecting to die there, he was made a Bishop and sent to Guatemala to found a diocese, which he consecrated to the Immaculate Heart of Mary. He was perhaps the first Bishop to establish the Blue Army throughout his diocese. Twenty-five years later, when he left the diocese to a native Bishop, the Rosary was being prayed in every parish daily, and he had personally distributed 50,000 rosaries blessed by the Pope as farewell gifts to his people.

"We cannot separate Jesus and Mary" is one of Bishop Luna's most frequent sayings. And another:

"The only true path for a member of Our Lady's Blue Army is the path of obedience to pastor, to Bishop, to Pope.

Bishop Luna blessing the Latin Chapel of the Blue Army International Center at Fatima in 1965.

Chapter Seventeen

1) Vatican approval muted - 2) Vatican rejects Blue
Army link with *Pro Fratribus* - 3) Vatican behind scenes
when Pilgrim Virgin comes to Rome - 4) Nothing done
without Vatican approval - 5) Bishop of Fatima gives
direction - 6) World flights prepare for Collegial Consecration - 7) Some Vatican officials oppose participation
by Holy Father - 8) Bishops around the world intervene -
9) Holy Father responds directly

Below: Most Rev. Thomas A. Boland, Archbishop of Newark,
crowns Pilgrim Virgin statue at Blue Army Rally in New York's
Carnegie Hall as Msgr. Colgan looks on. Archbishop Boland
said: "The very next person to sign the Blue Army pledge may
be the last one needed by Our Lady to bring about the triumph of
Her Immaculate Heart."

The Coronation of statues of Our Lady of Fatima are "acts of
consecration" because recognition of Her royalty is also
recognition of Her rights over us as the Mother of God and
Queen of the World.

17

SPECIAL ROLE
OF BISHOP OF FATIMA

"Here lies the Bishop of Our Lady." — *Inscription on tomb of first Bishop of Fatima*

I have already related how the March of Pledges, which developed into the Blue Army, really began with Sr. Lucia, and then officially with Bishop da Silva, first Bishop of Fatima, who said: "You may promulgate this as coming from me," and how he subsequently encouraged us to build the International Center at Fatima. He appointed a Canon to draw up statutes which he then presented to the Holy See for formal approval, thus establishing an official International Apostolate of Our Lady of Fatima (known as the Blue Army) with the approval of Rome.

The latter was never very vocal! Indeed it was so muted because of the Vatican's *Ostpolitik* and Soviet pressure that one sometimes wondered whether Rome was really in favor of the Blue Army. The Soviets claimed that the whole Message of Fatima was a trick of the Church against Communism, and that the Blue Army was a worldwide political maneuver backed by the CIA, to throw a "monkey wrench" into what the Soviets considered their legitimate goal: a world atheist revolution by "free choice" of the oppressed workers of all nations.

Bishop da Silva did not live long enough to sense this reluctance on the part of Rome. I think Bishop Venancio not only sensed it but suffered because of it. There are two incidents in this "history" which I think important to recall—not simply because they are events in the history of the Blue Army, but because they may have an important bearing on the future.

When Bishop Venancio was about to retire as the

second Bishop of Fatima, his health was of major concern to all of us in the international leadership. We were concerned and anxious about who should be his successor.

At that time, we became aware of an apostolate that was emanating from Rome called "Pro Fratribus." It had been founded in Rome by Bishop Hnilica, a fairly young bishop who had been consecrated in secret behind the Iron Curtain. He had exercised his episcopacy in the underground Church until he was finally discovered, and escaped under circumstances so extraordinary that the bishop does not hesitate to regard them as miraculous.

Now exposed and unable to return to his work behind the Iron Curtain, the bishop took up residence in Rome where he completed studies that he had been unable to pursue before he had become bishop. Then he began a very active and vocal campaign of prayers for those languishing in prisons behind the Iron Curtain for the faith (and often dying for it), without even the moral support of their brothers in the free world.

Everything the bishop wrote and said was almost parallel to the message of the Blue Army, except that it gave a new, greater and very vocal emphasis to the importance of remembering "our brothers" in the Church of Silence.

When the Pope came to Fatima in 1967, Bishop Hnilica was there beside the Pope and was seen in news photographs of the Pope and Lucia.

In Italy, Bishop Hnilica had become a sort of "spiritual director" to the leadership of the Blue Army, albeit not in an official capacity. In Italy there is a national association of all Marian movements, with a bishop at its head. The Blue Army in Italy is a member of that association.

Therefore Bishop Venancio began to consider the possibility of inviting Bishop Hnilica to come to our International Center at Fatima and make it a center for "Pro Fratribus" (which would have helped his cause greatly), and at the same time to succeed him as the International President of the Fatima Apostolate. But as was always his wont, the Bishop went first to the Vatican to ask the opinion of the Holy Father.

On this particular occasion the Bishop invited me to go with him, and I shall never forget that experience in the

Vatican Secretariat of State.

The Bishop had never told me—but one of the highest officials in that important section of the Vatican was a priest of his own diocese. The Holy See had asked him for a priest who was intelligent, capable, and able to keep secrets, and this priest is now very frequently to be seen close to the Pope.

We knew that the Vatican was necessarily having very delicate dealings with the Soviets for the freedom of the Church behind the Iron Curtain. For this reason they could not endorse open protests of the persecutions, nor could they show as much open approval to the Apostolate of Fatima as we would have liked.

We experienced this ourselves on the Queen of the World flight, when we brought the Pilgrim Virgin statue to Rome on May Day, 1978. The Pope had appointed Cardinal Poletti to supervise personally all the arrangements and ceremonies, and it was perhaps *the greatest religious demonstration in Rome in this entire century.* And yet, our group which had brought the Pilgrim Virgin statue in a special plane was not given even a special place at the public audience. But I was asked to go to the Vatican Radio, where I was interviewed in three of the languages in which I was sufficiently fluent, concerning the purpose of the World Peace Flight, and to explain the Blue Army. This was then broadcast by Vatican Radio to all the countries of Europe, with translations into several other languages I did not know.

The next publicized stop of the World Peace Flight was Poland, and the effect of the tumultuous reception in Rome, together with the Vatican broadcast, was that the Russians met the plane at the airport and refused to let the International Pilgrim Virgin statue enter Poland. This unleashed something of a silent revolution in Poland, even among the armed forces, which resulted in the first great capitulation of communism in that nation, from which only months later, the successor to both Paul VI and John Paul I was elected to the Papacy!

But the Blue Army had to act almost without Vatican approval!

While we have been obedient to the Bishop of Fatima, he in turn has always been utterly and completely obedient to the Holy See, even in matters which he might have decided on his own authority. That has also been true concerning Fatima from the very beginning.

Of course at the time that Our Lady appeared, there was an atheistic government in Portugal. All religious communities had been suppressed and there was such a violent persecution of religion that the atheists were openly boasting that they would wipe out the Faith in Portugal within two generations.

4 So when these three children claimed that they were seeing a vision "from heaven," and above all, when they predicted that a miracle would take place "so that all would believe," the reports were immediately sent to Rome by the Patriarchate in Lisbon. Everything concerning the investigation of the apparitions, the final approval of the miracle, and the development of the Fatima Message was continually filtered through Rome. Therefore, it is certainly not surprising that permission to see Lucia after 1956 could only be obtained *directly from the Holy See, and in some instances from the Holy Father himself.*

Bishop Venancio, of course, was following in the steps of his predecessor in referring everything to Rome, and I would like to recall one illuminating example:

I once suggested to the Bishop that it might be useful to invite scientists from all over the world to come to Fatima while there were still so many living witnesses to the miracle, so that they could verify the fact of the great solar prodigy and thus help to publicize it through the world, since it had been reported in only a limited number of newspapers in 1917.

It certainly was within the province of the Bishop to take this step, and he said that he would consult Rome. When no answer came to his letter, that was the end of it—even though it is most probable that the letter just got lost in the Vatican bureaucracy.

To Bishop Venancio, no answer was "no." For him the "Voice of God" had spoken in silence.

5 He is the beautiful example of every virtue and truly one of the holiest men I have ever been privileged to know. But sometimes the laity do not realize—when they hesitate to give obedience—that those to whom they owe obedience are also practicing this same virtue! And when we get down to it, obedience is an essential part of the theological virtue of Faith.

Over the years Bishop Venancio came to know me well, and he often trusted me to translate for him when he spoke to audiences at Fatima. (However, I am sure that he did not develop this trust without asking others whether I had translated faithfully and without interpolation!)

We traveled more than once around the entire world, around the continent of Africa, and throughout the United States promoting the Blue Army and the message of Our Lady, and in particular preparing for the worldwide affirmation of Our Lady's Queenship on May 13, 1971.

(I hope someone will someday write a book on the Queenship of Mary, perhaps based on the 1954 encyclical of Pius XII in which His Holiness said that *in this doctrine of Mary's Queenship lies the world's greatest hope for peace.* It is a doctrine and devotion most intimately linked with the apparitions of Our Lady of Fatima, and above all with Her message and the promise of Her triumph.)

We felt that to prepare for the Collegial Consecration of Russia throughout the world there was needed the consecration of individual nations to Our Lady. Pope Paul VI had said as much in *Signum Magnum*, issued on the occasion of his visit to Fatima on May 13, 1967.

The perfect way to make this consecration, as previously described by Pius XII in *Ad Coeli Reginam*, was to recognize Mary's Queenship. For if we recognize Mary as a Queen, we acknowledge that we "belong to Her"—that She has "rights over us."

Therefore, on May 13, 1971, on the 25th anniversary of the proclamation of Pius XII of Our Lady of Fatima as "Queen of the World," we planned to have bishops on all the continents, and preferably *the presidents of the Bishops Conferences in each country,* crown a duplicate of the Pilgrim Virgin statue which would remain in that country as a "National Pilgrim Virgin."

Naturally it was impossible to have statues delivered to *every* country, but at least every major country was covered, and Czechoslovakia, Poland, and Hungary were the chosen countries in the Soviet bloc. The original Pilgrim Virgin statue in Moscow was to be crowned by a legate of the Bishop of Fatima.

In South America, only one statue was to be crowned for the entire continent, and this was a statue which had been delivered by the Bishop of Fatima at the Eucharistic

Congress in Bogota, and then "presided" at the conference of all the South American bishops which followed that Congress.

Here in the United States, the Cardinal Archbishop of Washington was to crown the statue in our National Shrine of the Immaculate Conception. (Incidentally, Blue Army members *filled* the great shrine on that occasion.)

The simultaneous crownings took some three years of preparation. As I have mentioned before, Bishop Venancio himself had participated in world flights in which statues blessed by Pope Paul VI at Fatima in 1967 were delivered one by one to the capitals of the various nations, and subsequently crowns blessed by the Pope were delivered, for the Act of Coronation.

But something important was missing.

There had been no indication whatever of Rome's favor towards this worldwide affirmation of Mary's Queenship!

We understood, of course, the problem of the *Ospolitik*. But since *principal bishops of the world* had by now agreed to the coronation, could it be considered complete if the Pope did not participate? The problem was almost like having the Collegial Consecration in reverse — with the bishops ready to perform an Act of Consecration for their own nations, but without participation on the part of the Vicar of Christ.

So Bishop Venancio told me that he would like me to go to Rome to speak personally with the Holy Father and ask whether he would consider participating in the simultaneous coronations, because it might be easier for a layman to "discourse."

It was one of the few mandates — certainly of such importance — that the Bishop had ever given me. Naturally I took it very seriously. The moment I arrived at Rome Airport, I took a taxi and drove straight to St. Peter's, where I prayed before the tomb of Pius XII, who 25 years before had crowned Our Lady of Fatima "Queen of the World," and who in 1954 had issued the encyclical stressing that in affirmation of Mary's Queenship lies "the world's greatest hope for peace."

I then went to my hotel and made my application for the audience with Pope Paul VI.

It was not difficult to see the Holy Father on this occasion, and when I explained the Bishop's message, the Holy Father said simply: "I will consider it."

I had no further opportunity for "discourse."

After I had left Rome, I realized I had not completed what the Bishop had intended me to do. So I decided to let a reasonable interval pass and if there was no indication from Rome that the Holy Father had considered the Bishop's message I would return to see His Holiness again. As it transpired, I heard nothing, but when I returned to Rome, I found every door closed. Fr. Balic, president of the Pontifical Marian Academy, told me that everyone "on the inside" knew of my request to the Pope and that this time I would not get an audience. "Even if you should," Fr. Balic added, "it is almost certain that the Holy Father will not agree. There has been a storm of protest about this crowning of statues."

Writing now, some years later, I think I can perceive the probable reason, which I will explain in a moment.

However, I could not bring myself to believe that the Pope would really refuse the request if he fully understood it, and so I was determined to "find a way." I said to Fr. Balic that I would see Cardinal Wright. He agreed to come with me. He knew the Cardinal well because the latter had once been the Pope's delegate for the Pontifical Marian Academy (which could be regarded as the official arm of the Pope for things Marian).

Cardinal Wright agreed to see me even though, as I learned only later, he gave up his lunch that day to do so. Apparently, he was already informed, and as I pleaded my case, he said that he himself had difficulty in seeing the Pope at this particular time and that he thought the arranging of an audience for me would be most difficult. And then he said something rather extraordinary:

As Your Excellency knows, his office of the Congregation of the Clergy was at the end of the Via della Conciliazione, and the windows faced directly on the entrance to St. Peter's. Nodding in the direction of the great Basilica he said:

"John, you have always worked close to the people. Why worry about what happens across the street" (with an inclination of his head towards the door of St. Peter's)?

"But, Your Eminence," I exclaimed, "how can we have a total recognition of Our Lady's Queenship by bishops all over the world without the participation of the Holy Father?"

And then he suggested that the Bishop of Fatima write

again to all the bishops who had agreed to the coronation and invite them to write to the Holy Father, asking for his participation.

Why had we not thought of this eminently practical idea earlier?

I at once phoned Fatima to ask permission of Bishop Venancio to do this—as there was now only about six weeks left before the date of the coronation.

To my dismay, the Bishop was not in Portugal. He was traveling somewhere in Europe, and no one knew his exact whereabouts.

After moments of agonizing doubt, I dared to presume permission to send a letter to each of the bishops asking them to petition the Holy Father's participation.

8   Despite the opposition of many around the Pope (and I emphasize *around the Pope*), most of the replies came directly to the Bishop of Fatima and were extremely favorable. The Cardinal Archbishop of Manila, for example, wrote that he had asked the opinion of the Priests' Conference of his nation and they had overwhelmingly agreed that he should make this petition to the Holy Father.

But one letter, a solitary *terrible* letter, came from Poland to the Holy See asking with great indignation how an individual Bishop could be making a petition concerning something for the whole Church! (Cardinal Wyszynski later indicated that he had not written this, as I shall tell later.)

The Holy See forwarded that "terrible letter" to Bishop Venancio! But if His Excellency thought I had acted unwisely, he did not indicate it. He knew that I had at least acted in good faith.

Time was now getting very short. Two weeks before the great day of the coronation, when there were still a few crowns which had not yet been delivered, I was organizing a special "tourist group" to take the crown to Moscow. Bishop Venancio had designated a wonderful American priest, Msgr. Frederick J. Schwertz, Chancellor of the Diocese of Wheeling, W.Va., as his delegate to crown the Pilgrim Virgin statue in Moscow. There was so much to do and now so little time!

9   Meanwhile, the Bishop of Fatima had given me all the letters he had received from the bishops of the world and I went back to Rome. This time I did not go through any

special channels, but simply went to the office in the American College on the Via d'Umilita where anyone can get a ticket for a papal audience. I explained to the priest who was in charge that week that I had these letters from the various Bishops and asked if he could help me prepare a dossier. He kindly put a secretary at my disposal and we made photostats of all the letters which then went up to the Vatican through the ordinary channels—and reached the Pope!

Fortunately, I was able to see the Holy Father. I had with me the last six crowns to be blessed, and I asked him quite simply:

"Your Holiness, do you understand that there are bishops around the world who are going to renew the coronation of Our Lady as Queen of the World which was made by the legate of your predecessor at Fatima in 1946?"

"Not only do I know it," His Holiness said, "*but I have read every word of the documents you have sent to me.*"

I felt a deep sense of relief and gratitude. Inwardly I was now certain that if the Holy Father *knew*, those around him who had been trying to prevent his participation could not prevail.

His Holiness solemnly blessed the crowns and then prepared to depart. Suddenly he stopped. Then slowly turning, he looked me in the eyes and with an expression I shall never, never forget, he said quietly:

"*Pray for me.*"

His words went through me like a spear and in that instant, I had a sudden recollection of Jacinta's vision in 1917 of a "suffering" Pope. Was this the Pontiff she had seen, kneeling before a statue of the Immaculate Heart of Mary with tears in his eyes?

I returned to America to join the "tourist group" that was going to take the crown to Russia. I arranged matters so that we would forfeit part of the plane ticket and travel by hydrofoil from Vienna to Budapest, there to deliver the crown for Hungary to a wonderful lay woman (whose story and identity must, for the moment, remain anonymous) who would, in turn, deliver it to the Archbishop in Esztergom the following day.

Our itinerary, of course, included Fatima. Before leaving the Shrine, I went to see Bishop Venancio once again to get his blessing and to say goodbye as we were about to leave for Hungary and Moscow. The Bishop was smiling when I entered the room.

"John, I have wonderful news."

I had already given up hope of receiving a message from the Pope regarding the simultaneous coronations at this late hour and thought only of the crown for Hungary which Fr. Kondor had originally promised to get into that imprisoned country.

"Fr. Kondor is going to get the crown into Hungary?" I asked, expecting an affirmative reply.

"No," the Bishop said, as his smile became broader. "It is something much, much better than that."

There was a moment of impatient silence. And then His Excellency added: "I have just this moment received a telephone call from the Nunciature in Lisbon that *the Holy Father has given the message,* and has sent tapes not only for radio, but also for television."

I could hardly believe my ears. Whether it was from the emotion of the moment, or the strain of so much travel and trying frustration, I shall never know, but I buried my head in my hands and wept unashamedly....

Below: Bishop Ahr at blessing of the cornerstone of the Shrine of the Immaculate Heart of Mary at the Blue Army's U. S. National Center. Assisting His Excellency is Msgr. Edward U. Kmiec.

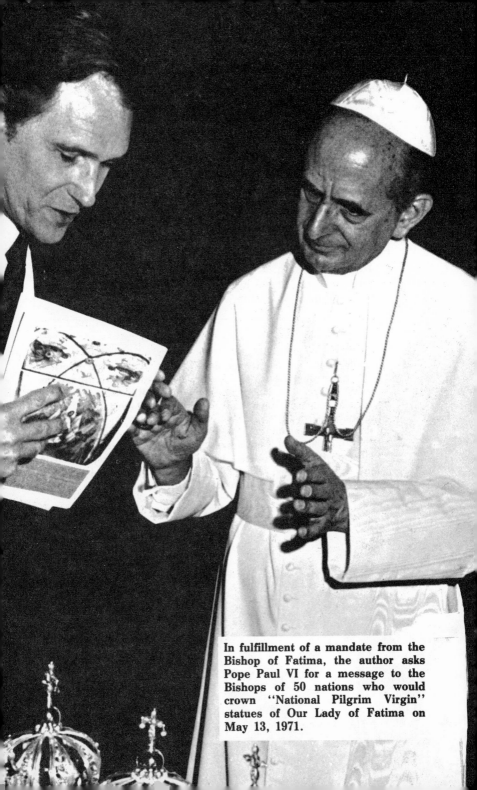

In fulfillment of a mandate from the Bishop of Fatima, the author asks Pope Paul VI for a message to the Bishops of 50 nations who would crown "National Pilgrim Virgin" statues of Our Lady of Fatima on May 13, 1971.

Chapter Eighteen

1) Blue Army builds Byzantine (Russian) Chapel at Fatima - 2) Major theologians come to Fatima to examine Message of Fatima in relation to Russia - 3) By 1951, conversion of Russia already begun, according to Archbishop Fulton J. Sheen

On the steps of the International Center of the Blue Army at Fatima the Most Rev. John Venancio (Bishop of Fatima) and the Most Rev. Andrew Katkoff (Rector of the Russicum in Rome) hold the Icon of Kazan. Left to right are Albert Setz-Degen, International Secretary of the Blue Army, Basle, Switzerland; John Haffert, International Lay Delegate; Msgr. John Mowatt, Byzantine Chaplain. Center are the two Bishops, then Dr. Angel Palacios, Blue Army Lay Delegate of Spain; Archimandrite Januarius Izzo; Rev. Dr. Andre Richard, President of the Blue Army of France and International Vice President.

THE BLUE ARMY AND RUSSIA

"Russia will be converted." — *Our Lady of Fatima*

There is no question about the close connection between Fatima and Russia, because in Her apparitions Our Lady specifically mentioned Russia, and made the triumph of Her Immaculate Heart and an era of peace to mankind contingent upon Russia's conversion, which in turn depended upon a sufficient number complying with Her message.

I had never thought of our Apostolate being identified in any other way with Russia. But in the early 1960's, I became conscious of other important connections, and these developed apace.

Initially, I felt the growing need for a Byzantine Chapel and a small Latin Chapel in our International Center as symbols of the essential unity between East and West. I am sure it was an inspiration developed by Our Lady Herself through Cardinal Tisserant, who had sent Fr. Pavel Bliznetsov—that daring ex-Soviet flier, who decided that such a "grand plan" had to have a *grand* reality.

It may well be that during the coming era of peace promised by Our Lady, history will judge that Russia played a very important role in the salvation of the world, and that during the years of communism, it was far more a victim than a scourge—far more an instrument of Our Lady's triumph than an enemy of that triumph.

I was only a small instrument, preoccupied with many personal problems and doing many useless and thoughtless things, but at the same time consumed by the compulsive necessity of shaking the world by the shoulders and telling everyone that Our Lady had appeared at

Fatima and predicted the annihilation of nations unless they woke up and heeded Her special message.

2   I had never paused to analyze the Message of Fatima in depth, as was done, for example, in that marvelous seminar in 1971 at Fatima. That was when we went to the Marian Congress in Zagreb and brought back some of the top Mariologists of the world in a chartered plane so that they could climax the first Marian Congress in history under a communist (red star) government, with a seminar at the very place where Our Lady promised the conversion of Russia and world peace—a seminar to study in depth the meaning of the Message of Fatima and devotion to Her Immaculate Heart.

One of the six experts who spoke at that seminar—and whose discourse was recorded in a book of that memorable meeting,[1] which was translated into five languages and sent to all the bishops of the world—was Msgr. John J. Mowatt. He was a mitred Archpriest of the Byzantine Rite, who served for several years as Chaplain of our House at Fatima, and who celebrated daily Mass in the Byzantine Rite in our "Russian" Chapel.

Oddly enough, almost every speaker at that seminar seemed preoccupied with the subject of Russia. Although the conference by Luigi Cardinal Ciappi, O.P. (then Fr. Ciappi), the papal theologian, was of major importance, since it treated of the doctrine of devotion to the Immaculate Heart of Mary, perhaps the most significant contribution at that seminar was Msgr. Mowatt's explanation of the Russian people's devotion to Our Lady, and the *mystery* of Russia's involvement in this climactic moment in world history, which is going to end in the triumph of the Immaculate Heart of Mary and "an era of peace for mankind."

I cannot recall telling Your Excellency about our plans for a Byzantine Chapel when I first broached the subject of a Blue Army International Center at Fatima to you in the early 1950's, since I considered the idea of secondary importance. But then Cardinal Tisserant sent Fr. Pavel, the plans where changed, and ultimately the Byzantine Chapel assumed an importance beyond anything we had imagined.

A former Russian prince who had emigrated to America and became a priest in the Byzantine Eparchy of Passaic offered to go to Fatima to supervise the construction of the Byzantine Chapel. His name was Msgr. Bonetzky, and he became the first chaplain of our International Center.

He had special qualifications for building, having already been responsible for the erection of an important church here in America. With diligent and dedicated efforts, he greatly improved on the plans of Fr. Pavel, and soon *the whole center of our building was taking on the aspect of a stylized version of the Chapel of the Assumption in the Kremlin*. The giant Byzantine dome was rising to become the highest building in Fatima after the tower of the Basilica itself. Indeed, if you look at Fatima today from the Castle of Ourem, the only two buildings you can see at the Cova are the tower of the Basilica and the Byzantine dome atop the Blue Army's International Center.

Msgr. Bonetzky personally raised the funds for the iconostasis, which is said to be one of the most beautiful in the western world. A celebrated Russian artist, an emigre from the Soviet Union, was the iconographer.

The chapel was solemnly dedicated by Cardinal Tisserant, seven years after he, as legate of Pope Pius XII, had dedicated the main building.

Msgr. Bonetzky was succeeded at Fatima by Msgr. Mowatt, whom we previously mentioned. The latter saw his role at Fatima not merely as chaplain for the few persons who might come to assist at the Byzantine Rite services, but as a special apostolic mission to Russia, and also of helping the people of the Western Church understand the beauty of the Byzantine Rite and the mystical role of Russia in the triumph of Mary's Immaculate Heart. This would help to prepare the way for the union of East and West which was implied in the message and promise of Our Lady at Fatima.

I had first come in contact with Msgr. Mowatt in 1951, when he wrote to me from Rome that the choir of the Russicum ought to come to Fatima when a Russian Archbishop had been invited to celebrate the principal Mass there for the closing of the Holy Year for "all the world outside of Rome."

This was that important occasion after which Archbishop Sheen sent a news release through the news service of the National Catholic Welfare Conference (now known as

3

the National Catholic Conference) prophesying that from that day (October 13, 1951) Russia had been converted but "the news has not leaked out yet." He then added the historic prophecy that "by 1985 Our Lady would be reviewing Her troops in Red Square," provided there had been an adequate response to Her Fatima Message. Archbishop Sheen stressed the compelling need for All-Night Vigils, which were eventually to be developed and propagated throughout the world by the Blue Army.

This was the only time that I recall a Byzantine Mass celebrated as the principal Mass on one of the "big days" at Fatima, and perhaps it was the biggest day in the history of Fatima outside of May 13, 1967, when Pope Paul VI was there in person, together with Sr. Lucia.

Certainly there were over a million people present on that day and by coincidence, it was through Msgr. Mowatt and the Byzantine group which dominated the altar in front of the Basilica for the major ceremonies, that I was invited to speak the only words of English before that immense multitude on that important occasion. I remember saying, as I am sure hundreds of thousands felt, that we seemed to have on this great occasion a foretaste, an augury, of the fulfillment of Our Lady's promise of the conversion of Russia and world peace.

Msgr. Mowatt began his work at our International Center by publishing an excellent bulletin titled "Looking East." This, however, was an unexpected surprise. I thought he would devote himself to the reception of pilgrims at the Center, lecturing to them about the Blue Army, the Byzantine Rite, and so on. But Msgr. Mowatt became increasingly preoccupied with his special vocation and this, I now realize, will bear lasting fruit in the many writings he produced during his solitary and often difficult days in our International Center.

There was, for example, the mysterious and yet wonderful visit of Metropolitan Nicodim of Moscow to Fatima the year before Msgr. Mowatt left.

Msgr. Mowatt recalls with emotion the sincerity with which the great Russian Metropolitan, perhaps the most influential Russian religious leader under the Soviets, fell on his knees at the spot where Our Lady had appeared in 1917—just days before Lenin's followers stormed the Winter Palace in Petrograd—and spoke of his beloved nation which for centuries had been so devoted to Her!

With what joy he saw the little side chapel at our Byzantine "church" at the Blue Army's International Center reserved for the original Icon of Kazan, *Liberatrix and Protectress of Holy Mother Russia!*

Moved with gratitude, he gave Msgr. Mowatt a precious remembrance of his visit. My memory fails me, but it was either a ring or a pectoral cross.

And has the world paid sufficient attention to the mysterious fact that Metropolitan Nicodim *had confided a secret* to Pope John Paul I when he collapsed in the Pope's office? Moments later, he died in the Pope's arms as the Pontiff was giving him his blessing!

I had the privilege of attending one of the very few audiences given by Pope John Paul I during his tragically brief reign. I thought he was the most extraordinary Pope of our age (not excluding his successor, John Paul II). Perhaps I understand why God willed that he be taken from us so soon. He was so gentle...so frank...he must have been meant to prepare the way for a similar Pope who would have the broad shoulders to bear the constant dealings with communism and the extension of its evil power into the lives of all whom it grasped in its godless embrace.

Shortly before he had been elected Pope, a powerful, trenchant article on Fatima, written by him as Cardinal Archbishop of Venice, had appeared in the Blue Army magazine of Italy. In it he described his meeting with Sr. Lucia a few months earlier in which the seer had stressed that "we must be as radical as the saints" in these sin-drenched days "if we wish to belong seriously to God."

And what secret did the Metropolitan Archbishop of Russia whisper in the ears of Pope John Paul I? We only know that the Pope said afterwards that he felt that he had assisted at the death of a saint.

And of what else would Nicodim have spoken to the Pope of Rome than the fulfillment of the promise of Our Lady of Fatima—the spiritual rebirth of a new and glorious Russia under the radiant blue banner of Mary?

FOOTNOTES

1. **A Heart for All**, 1972, AMI Press, Washington, N.J. 07882. While not an easy book to read, it is worth the purchasing because of the wealth of information and understanding concerning the importance of Russia in the Fatima Message.

Below: Modeled and named after the Basilica of the Assumption in Moscow is this Byzantine Chapel at the Blue Army's International Center at Fatima. This picture was taken during the blessing of the bells, which are rung during the Byzantine liturgy. His Eminence, Eugene Cardinal Tisserant, came from Rome to dedicate this chapel in 1963, seven years after he had blessed the main part of the Blue Army building as Legate of Pope Pius XII.

Below: The interior of the Byzantine (Russian) Chapel at Fatima, showing the iconostasis (altar screen).

Chapter Nineteen

1) Is it God's will for Blue Army to undertake great financial burden of redeeming the Icon of Kazan? - 2) Unmistakable proof of God's Will - 3) Blue Army takes leap forward - 4) After two famous images meet at Fatima, Bishop goes to Russia! - 5) Joy of Patriarch Athenagoras - 6) Cardinal Tisserant lives to see evidence of Our Lady's triumph in the world

Below: The "original" or "principal" Icon of Kazan, which the Blue Army will return to the people of Russia.

LIBERATRIX OF RUSSIA

─────────────────────────────

"It is priceless...priceless." — *Orthodox Archbishop of San Francisco concerning Icon of Kazan*

S ince Your Excellency was the only person apart from our Trustees who received copies of our financial reports, there is hardly need for me to repeat here the parlous state of our funds. We rarely had sufficient funds other than what might be needed to meet our current expenses and payroll (sometimes for as many as 40 employees, and currently 45). And feeling that the major responsibility of raising funds rested with me (although of course it was always the Providence of God and the intercession of St. Joseph), I invariably hesitated before embarking on any new project which required financing.

Thus when Fr. Karl Patzelt, S.J., a Byzantine priest and chaplain of the Blue Army center in the Archdiocese of San Francisco, wrote and said that the Blue Army would have "to redeem the Icon of Kazan," my first impulse was to write back and say that we were not a Russian apostolate, that we had nothing to do with icons, and to end matters, we did not have the money for even the smallest down payment on such a valuable object.

But then (and I thank God that I developed this holy habit), I asked myself, as I always do before any new project: "Is it God's Will for the Blue Army to undertake the great financial burden of 'redeeming' the Icon of Kazan?"

So before sharing the question about the Icon with anyone, I wrote at once to Msgr. Mowatt at Fatima to ask his opinion. And while awaiting his answer, I called the Orthodox Archbishop of San Francisco to ask about the authenticity of the Icon, and its real value.

"Of course it is authentic," the Archbishop replied. In answer to my question of its value, his voice fell almost to a whisper: *"It is priceless...priceless..."*

An official and certified estimate of the value of the Icon was three million dollars—not only because of its antiquity and the jewels donated to it by Catherine the Great and Ivan the Terrible, but because it had a history rarely equalled by any religious image in the history of the world, and certainly, of course, in the history of Russia. Our Lady of Kazan had, for centuries, been acclaimed as the "Liberatrix and Protectress" of that great country. Furthermore, there was an undoubted sense of "presence" about the Icon that inspired awe in most of those who saw it.

I had seen it in a special display at the New York World's Fair in 1964 when we were in the Vatican Pavilion for the first major All-Night Vigil held here in the United States under the Blue Army's auspices. The Russian Orthodox Church had a reconstruction of one of their early chapels in Alaska at the Fair, in which the Icon was exhibited, since they were trying to raise a million dollars to buy the Icon from a private owner and enshrine it in a church in San Francisco. For security, the Icon was brought to the safe of the Vatican Pavilion each night, and was therefore under the same roof when we made that memorable first Vigil, with the Honorable Henrietta Bower from England and Bishop Venancio from Fatima participating.

Who would have dreamed that barely five years later theives would have twice absconded with hundreds of thousands of dollars that had been collected by the Orthodox Church in America to redeem the Icon? Although they had a prior commitment from the owner to sell the Icon to them, they felt too embarrassed to solicit funds any further and had notified the owner that they were giving up their efforts.

The ways of God are sometimes very mysterious, but from the benefit of hindsight, it does seem that Our Lady did not want the Icon enshrined in San Francisco, but returned to Russia after that country's conversion.

The letter from Msgr. Mowatt was quick and to the point. Only a few days before he had received my letter, he had established a "Guild of Our Lady of Kazan" at our Byzantine Chapel in Fatima, with the intention of promoting membership in the Guild among his friends in America in order to finance his apostolate *Looking East.* "What could be more wonderful," he exclaimed, "than to have two of the most important images of Our Lady in the world meeting here together at Fatima—the miraculous statue of Our Lady of Fatima, and the miraculous Icon of Kazan?"

"So," I thought with a feeling of heavy responsibility, "it must be God's Will that we purchase it."

Yet I felt the imperative need to be absolutely certain of this. At the back of my mind there lurked the shadowy possibility that Msgr. Mowatt was merely giving expression to the understandable enthusiasm of a person of Russian descent who greatly loved Our Lady of Kazan as the Liberatrix and Protectress of his ancestral country. After all, what Russian who believed in God and Our Lady would not want to have that miraculous Icon?

These suspicions seemed to be confirmed by another letter from Fatima: Msgr. Mowatt had second thoughts. He was beginning to think of all the good that could be done with so much money—so many publications—so much promotion of unity between East and West—so much greater impulse to the Apostolate.

Days later, however, he sent me a second, very different letter. Because of his fear of making the decision himself, he had written to Bishop Katkoff in Rome (the Apostolic Visitor of the Eastern Churches in the western world) to ask his advice. And Bishop Katkoff answered with just two questions:

"Why do you hesitate? Is this not obviously the Will of God?"

There could now be no doubt. The Blue Army was being chosen by Our Lady to "redeem" Her miraculous Russian Icon, even though we were simply an apostolate of holiness, with no dues, whose members were only asked to sign a pledge to fulfill the spiritual requests of Our Lady of Fatima. And since their names were buried at Fatima without a record kept of their identity and location, they could never be solicited in any way. We could call upon only our few "crusaders" who received SOUL Magazine and upon whose shoulders rested the entire financial responsibility of the Apostolate—at least here in the United States.

To compound our problems, Msgr. Colgan was now quite ill, and had been compelled to retire as pastor of St. Mary's, Plainfield. It was enough for him to read the letter from Bishop Katkoff, but the Trustees of the Institute included some very practical businessmen, and they were more skeptical of agreeing to the purchase. However, when they saw that the evaluation of the Icon was so much more than we would have to pay for it, they agreed to signing a contract of purchase.

3   As you know, Your Excellency, it really was an act of faith. In order not to have to pay a very large sum at once, we agreed to pay a considerable sum each month for five years, and if we should once fail in the payments, we would forfeit all that we had paid and also forfeit the contract of purchase.

The letter was signed on July 21, 1970 (Feast of Our Lady of Kazan), and after that the Apostolate of the Blue Army—especially on the international level—seemed to leap ahead.

It was just two months later that *the Bishop of Fatima* (after considerable hesitation) *accepted the official position of International President of the Blue Army* in the place of the ailing 76-year-old Msgr. Colgan.

But what greater favor could the Blue Army have received from Our Lady—what greater act of confidence from Her—*than that She should have entrusted this precious image to us and ensured that the heavy monthly payments would be met?*

Long before the Communist revolution, the Russians had a special liturgy honoring the Icon of Our Lady of Kazan as *"Thou who destroyest atheism."* And the atheists destroyed the Kazan Basilica in Moscow to "prove" atheism! Was not, therefore, the acquisition of this inestimable relic a wondrous and prophetic sign to underscore the Blue Army's role in Our Lady's plan to bring about the conversion of Russia?

As though in acknowledgement of our readiness and confidence in Our Lady to accept this trust—not for ourselves but to ensure that Her precious Icon would be returned in due time to the Russian people—She gave us an even greater favor, an even greater trust:

On the following May 23, we were given the privilege of purchasing *the actual convent* of the apparitions of the Immaculate Heart of Mary in Pontevedra, Spain!

Dr. Joaquin M. Alonso, C.M.F., official documentarian of Fatima and editor of *Ephemerides Mariologicae*, has emphatically declared that this was one of the greatest signs of Heaven's approval of the Blue Army.

This new acquisition (Sr. Lucia's former convent in Spain) was so important that we must speak of it at greater length. Yet, it was only one of several marvelous developments that followed the purchase of the Icon of Kazan.

The following July, the Icon was taken to Fatima to be enshrined in our Byzantine Center, where the two great images of Our Lady of Fatima and Our Lady of Kazan were to meet.

Bishop Katkoff came from Rome for this great occasion. He and Bishop Venancio together carried the Icon of Our Lady from our Byzantine Chapel to the actual spot where Our Lady had stood in 1917—at the moment of the Bolshevik Revolution—and foretold that an atheist-controlled Russia would spread error, war and havoc throughout the world, but that She would bring about the conversion of Russia and an era of peace.

Shortly before we had left the Blue Army Center to go to the Capelinha, Bishop Venancio said to me with great faith and earnestness: "We have a tradition that whenever two famous images of Our Lady meet, great results are to be expected."

We had chosen the Feast of Our Lady's Queenship, August 22, for that great event as a fitting climax to the success of the worldwide coronation of Our Lady by bishops all around the globe the previous May 13. And meanwhile the somewhat wild idea had come to me to charter a ship so that *we could take the Bishop of Fatima and Our Lady's statue to Russia itself!*

I managed to hire the ship in Yugoslavia, and after the ceremonies at Fatima the following October 13, we set sail from Venice, having attended the beatification of Bl. Maximilian Kolbe in Rome.

It will be recalled that Bl. Maximilian said that one day Our Lady's statue would be enshrined in the Kremlin and that peace would come to the world.

We had two main objects in this trip—which was paid for by the 238 pilgrims who had the good fortune to participate in it. They were:

1. To have Holy Mass in the presence of Our Lady's statue at the foot of the Odessa Steps, the very place where the first blood was shed in the Soviet uprising—in which 700 persons died in 1905, just twelve years before Lenin seized power in 1917 and Our Lady appeared at Fatima

4

foretelling the ultimate doom of his revolution.

2. To enable the Bishop of Fatima to visit personally the saintly Patriarch Athenagoras I, leader of all the Orthodox Christians (the predominant religion of all Russia), who had previously gone to Jerusalem to meet with Pope Paul VI in a great ecumenical embrace. It was the Bishop's hope to present the Patriarch with a Pilgrim Virgin statue, identical to those which had been crowned around the world the previous May 13, for all the world's Orthodox Christians.

5

The historic meeting between the holy Patriarch Athenagoras and the Bishop of Fatima was, for us, a moment of supreme joy—a foretaste of the great triumph of the Immaculate Heart of Mary.

The holy Patriarch of Constantinople (now called Istanbul) was the 262nd successor of St. Andrew and spiritual leader of over 160 million members of the Orthodox Church. He spoke fluent English because for eighteen years he had lived in the United States as Archbishop of the Orthodox Church in North and South America. And in 1967, when the Pope went to Fatima, the Venerable Patriarch told a reporter:

"I often see a beautiful hand holding the Chalice of Our Lord over a nearby hill, and I hear secret voices that speak of love between humanity and peace among men."

I could never describe the look of almost ecstatic joy with which the Patriarch greeted Our Lady's statue. After a long moment of reverent silence, he turned to us with tear-filled eyes and said: "What a great blessing you have brought us!"

Then as we sat down, the Patriarch looked at the Bishop of Fatima with fraternal regard and said: "*I was at Fatima with Pope Paul VI.*"

I was nonplussed and I presume Bishop Venancio was too. We knew, of course, that the Patriarch had never left Constantinople at that time. He had wanted to do so, but political pressures made it impossible. And then with a little twinkle, he explained: "*I was there in spirit.*"

Bishop Venancio knelt for the holy Patriarch's blessing, but the latter insisted on being blessed himself, and kissed the head of Bishop Venancio when he knelt for the blessing, and then embraced him.

Upon learning our itinerary, he seemed amazed that we

were daring to take a ship to Russia and he wondered how it would be possible for us to arrive at Odessa with Our Lady's statue, and have Mass celebrated there.

We not only did this, in a ship flying the Red Star, but the Soviets supplied a special plane to carry almost 100 of our pilgrims to Moscow, and a duplicate statue (although wrapped) was carried through Red Square and now is enshrined in our National Center of the Blue Army in the United States.

These triumphant milestones in our Apostolate were inevitably marked with crosses. Cardinal Tisserant died only a few months later. I had just had an audience shortly before his death and asked what he thought Our Lady had really meant by the words "Russia will be converted."

And this great Cardinal—perhaps the greatest of this century—spoke with love and longing of the Christian unity that was certain to come through the triumph of Mary's Immaculate Heart. When I asked if he felt that there might be a third world war before the conversion of Russia, he admitted that he personally felt the likelihood of some awful cataclysm or punishment before this great favor was obtained—due to the relatively small number who were complying with the Message of Fatima.

Your Excellency will recall our recent conversation about some of the *great men in the Church*—many of them unknown to the public and many of whom you knew in Rome. And I told you of my own deep edification when Cardinal Tisserant showed me through his apartment in Rome—which included a magnificent "throne room" where he presided as the President of the Congregation of the Oriental Church.

6

But the rest of the apartment was filled with books, and his own room had only two pieces of furniture: a simple iron bed, and a canvas beach chair! Around the walls were cabinets with shelves and drawers in which were his various robes and liturgical vestments. The room opened onto a small balcony, where he took his daily exercise walking up and down reciting the Office or praying the Rosary. For many years he had lived the act of *total consecration* to Our Lady according to St. Grignon de Montfort!

His Eminence had confided to me years before, when he first came to Fatima, that the reason he had been able to endorse the Blue Army so completely was because he had read my book *Russia Will Be Converted* (which was the first book I wrote after I left the Scapular Apostolate in 1948). He told me in a low, confidential tone:

"I kept that book by my bed, and read a few pages every night before going to sleep."

I never told this to anyone until after the Cardinal died. Even though he did not tell me that it was confidential, I gathered this from his tone of voice and kept the secret.

I had never thought the book was very worthwhile, and had never had it reprinted. Perhaps it served its main purpose there on the table, in that austere room of the Dean of the Sacred College of Cardinals of the Roman Catholic Church....

Below: The Bishop of Fatima chats with His Holiness, Athena-goras I, just after delivering the Pilgrim Virgin statue blessed by Pope Paul VI seen in the background. Above the Patriarch's head can be seen the famous photograph of his meeting with Pope Paul VI in the Holy Land. "What a great blessing you have brought us!" the head of millions of Orthodox Christians throughout the world exclaimed to the Bishop of Fatima. And then with a long glance of emotion at the statue, the Patriarch said: "What a joy, dear Mother, to receive you!" His Holiness prayed for the speedy unification of all Christians, of all men.

The historic picture below was taken on October 13, 1956, when the first international statutes of the Blue Army were adopted. Left to right, facing camera, are Bishop Rupp, auxiliary of Paris; Bishop da Silva, first Bishop of Fatima; Cardinal Tisserant; Bishop Venancio (then Auxiliary to Bishop da Silva) and Msgr. Colgan (speaking).

The statutes, or rules, to govern the Blue Army had been drafted by a Canon lawyer appointed by Bishop da Silva in cooperation with several Blue Army leaders from Europe and America.

Approved at this meeting, the statues were taken to Rome by Cardinal Tisserant and approved by the Holy See AD EXPERIMENTUM.

Chapter *Twenty*

1) Prayer community comes to our National Center -
2) Special vocation of Sister Mary Miranda, C.SS.F. -
3) We prayed for a sign from God - 4) The sign is given -
5) Blessed Maximilian and Padre Pio! - 6) As usual we
turn to Saint Joseph - 7) Wonderful atmosphere of holiness comes to our National Center - 8) Shrine at our National Center proposed - 9) Bishop decides it should be
built now

Below: On October 13, 1978, the Most Rev. George W. Ahr dedicated the Shrine of the Immaculate Heart of Mary on the grounds of the U.S. Blue Army's National Center.

THE U.S. NATIONAL CENTER

"It is a beautiful concept." — *Most Rev. George W. Ahr, seventh Bishop of Trenton, on proposal to build a shrine at Blue Army National Center*

Two months after Cardinal Tisserant passed away, Msgr. Colgan also passed away, and the following July the Pope accepted Bishop Venancio's resignation as the Bishop of Leiria. On this occasion, the Bishop gave a wonderful talk at Fatima concerning the Blue Army. Despite repeated severe warnings from his doctors that any kind of stress was now dangerous, he continued for some time to dedicate his energies to this Apostolate as its active president.

It was shortly after this that the Pilgrim Virgin statue, which had been traveling in the United States, was seen to shed tears. Newspapers all over the world covered the phenomenon, many of them displaying poignant photographs of the weeping statue.

Even though much had been done to promote the cause of Our Lady, and there was so much good will on the part of the Holy Father and so many bishops, the faithful in general did not seem to be responding with the depth and fervor one would expect from a divine message to this nuclear-threatened world.

On the Feast of the Holy Rosary, October 7, 1970, Your Excellency came to our Center in Washington, N.J., to lay the cornerstone of our new convent—a major turning point in the history of our National Center, and perhaps of the Apostolate in our nation.

As mentioned in an earlier chapter, we must have seemed particularly vulnerable to the United Steelworkers Union back in the late 1950's when we had only lay workers here at the National Center of the Blue Army. We did not even possess an Oratory. All we had was the Pilgrim Virgin statue which the Bishop of Fatima had sent to us in 1950, which now stood in my little office in the center of that converted barn housing our printing press, supply shop, mailing and shipping department, and personnel answering up to 1,000 letters a week.

And then Your Excellency kindly gave permission for the Felician Sisters to take up residence in the Institute until their own convent on the grounds would be finished. The top floor was converted into a temporary convent with a small chapel at the far end where, for the first time, we were blessed with the presence of the Blessed Sacrament.

1 Sister Mary Miranda, a Felician Sister of the Province of Lodi, had come to the Institute many years before and, on August 22 (then the Feast of the Immaculate Heart of Mary), she had symbolically buried a wax heart and a little statue of St. Joseph at the Institute with the fervent prayer that one day she would be able to come with some of her Sisters to be a "heart of prayer" at the Blue Army's National Center.

She had been one of the first and most successful apostles of the Blue Army way back in 1950, when we first began to make the Blue Army known through SOUL Magazine. She was a nurse who also taught in school; she had even written a book about Catholic nursing. Sr. Miranda used all of her contacts to get Blue Army pledges and sent in over a thousand pledges—an amazing achievement for a single person. As a result, I went to Lodi and presented her with a statue of Our Lady of Fatima, naming her one of the most outstanding apostles of that year.

2 It was about twenty years later that Sr. Miranda came and told me that during those years she had felt an inspiration to come to our National Center with some of her Sisters to establish a "house of prayer." She disclosed that she had been preparing for this by visiting various cloistered communities and studying their life. She was now seeking permission from her major superiors and was wondering whether, if the permission were granted, we would welcome them.

Your Excellency can imagine how warmly and enthusiastically I responded—subject of course to your approval. But even so, I wanted to be sure that this was indeed the will of God. And so, after the coronation of Our Lady's statues around the world on May 13, 1971 (for which I was present in Moscow), I decided to return to the United States via Warsaw (where the Felician Sisters had been founded), in the hope that Our Lady would give me some sign that this was God's Will.

(I must explain here, Your Excellency, that I harbored certain misgivings since a community like the Felicians, established over a hundred years, had its own specific goals, its own particular apostolate, and if we admitted them to the Institute, there was a possibility that with a change of Superior, the direction or emphasis of our Apostolate might also be changed. I always had a deep conviction that we needed a religious community at the National Center for the continuity of the Apostolate, but I felt strongly that this had to be a community founded and dedicated exclusively to the aims of the Blue Army.)

I have already mentioned to Your Excellency that I had some difficulty getting out of Moscow and believe that I should never have done so but for some extraordinary and daring help. And I was still very nervous even in Warsaw because I was not yet outside the Iron Curtain.

The airport officials ordered me to stay at the airport for about 24 hours until a connecting flight arrived, which would take me to Berlin. But about 2 o'clock in the morning I somehow persuaded them to let me go to a hotel in the city.

It was raining. I was the only passenger on the bus which discharged me on an empty street in front of a small hotel, the doors of which were locked. Unable to get a response to my knocking, I turned away from the barred doors and by then the bus had disappeared. I stood alone in the dark, the chilling rain lashing my face, adding to the sense of loneliness and fear.

I did not usually pray to Padre Pio, but at that moment, there rose instinctively to my lips the words: "Padre Pio, you know why I am here. I am hoping to see the statue of Our Lady which was crowned here in Poland yesterday while we were crowning Our Lady's statue in Moscow, and to have some sign that Our Lady wants the Felician Sisters at our National Center in Washington. Are you leaving me standing here in the rain?"

My mind had hardly finished forming the words when I

saw the lights of a car coming from a distance. It was a taxi that came, circled, and picked me up.

Did someone see me knock at the door of the locked hotel—or had Padre Pio really "heard" my plea for help? The latter explanation cannot be ruled out.

I did not speak Polish, but the driver understood "hotel" and within a few minutes I was safe and dry under a roof. I slept only two hours because I had made up my mind next morning to go to the Cathedral—which I was sure would be in the old part of the city—and find a priest to whom I could explain in Latin that I wanted to get to Niepokalanow (since I had not the remotest idea where it was!) where the crowning had taken place yesterday, and also to the headquarters of the Felician Sisters. (It is amazing how much Latin one can remember in an emergency. It is not nearly so dead a language as one would suppose!)

I boarded a bus going to the old part of the city (about two miles away) and realized that I had no Polish money, and of course did not speak a word of the language. Perhaps my gesture explained this to the driver because he only shrugged his shoulders, and I sat down.

As we approached the old city, the bus suddenly turned in a different direction. I had only so many hours before I had to be back at the airport, and with concern I tugged at the cord. The bus ground to a halt and as I descended, I tried in vain to determine what number it might be, or where I was, so that I might find my way back.

As I watched the bus pull away, I suddenly saw to my amazement just across the street, a life-sized statue of Our Lady of Grace in front of a church.

It was still very early in the morning, and I went over to visit the Blessed Sacrament. Since my mind was slightly dazed, after so little sleep, I resolved to continue the search for the Cathedral afterwards. I left the Church and started to cross a little bridge on which I saw a fresh lilac. As I picked it up, I remembered seeing a picture of Our Lady of Czestochowa at the communion rail of the church I had just left and I recalled how, years earlier, a Polish woman had said to me: "Whenever you need anything, go to the Black Madonna."

I picked up the flower and retraced my steps.

I had hardly finished my prayer to Our Lady, after placing the flower before Her picture, when I noticed that the priests in the church seemed to be Franciscans, and they were also wearing beards. And then I thought: "Well, I might as well approach a priest here."

So I went into the sacristy, and gave my little Latin speech to the first priest I met. His reaction could be imagined! An American layman speaking Latin, claiming he had just been in Moscow for the crowning of a statue of Our Lady of Fatima!

With an excuse that he was quite busy, the priest disappeared in a flash. I felt momentarily helpless, but then I noticed another priest walking across the sacristy, so I decided to try again.

Obviously I was laboring to explain myself in Latin, and I asked if he knew any other language. To my joy he was fluent in French! I poured out my heart!

"Concerning your question about Niepokalanow," he said, "I will call the Prior and make arrangements for you to visit there. And regarding your question about the Felicians, *you are in the very place where they were founded!*"

I was completely overwhelmed!

He arranged for a car to take me to Niepokalanow, where I was received like royalty. The Fathers knew my name because I had previously arranged to get the statue there, then the crown, and finally (through some Felician Sisters) some gold and jewels to decorate the crown. To my astonishment and delight, they had renovated the entire main chapel of the community (where in Bl. Maximilian's time there had been 700 Franciscans!) and made the statue of Our Lady of Fatima the center of the chapel. And there the coronation of Our Lady's statue had taken place for all Poland on May 13.

He seemed to want to keep me there, but he said that he had "strict instructions" from the Capuchins that I was to be back at their place by noon.

When I arrived back, I was treated as a most honored guest and I answered questions given by the priest who spoke French, and during the meal he translated the answers for the entire community. I sensed that some of the priests felt he was being rather careless, for they looked at me with ill-disguised suspicion. I thought—and with little wonder!

All during the meal, I was moved by the sight of two pictures peering steadily down from the walls—those of

Bl. Maximilian and Padre Pio!

The Sisters of St. Felix had actually acquired their name because the foundress and her companion used to bring orphans to pray at the statue of St. Felix at the entrance to that particular church, and a Capuchin Father there had been their spiritual director. (St. Felix was a Capuchin lay brother in Rome, a contemporary of St. Philip Neri.)

I returned from Poland in a surer frame of mind. I had been given my "sign," though as it turned out, the installation of the Sisters at the Institute did not go as smoothly as I had hoped.

One day the Mother Provincial, together with her entire council, arrived at the Institute and was shown into my little office. Of course, I thought they had come to discuss the contract. Before the Mother Provincial could speak, I told her with enthusiasm how much we welcomed having the Sisters come here, I explained that we could hire typists, printers, artists, writers—but we could never hire "a heart," and that we desperately needed holiness and prayer at this National Center of our Apostolate.

While I was still speaking, my secretary interrupted me to say that there were two priests outside waiting to see me who had come from Italy and who could not speak English. (She normally would never have interrupted a meeting such as this.)

So I excused myself for a moment to go out and welcome the priests and to explain that I would be with them as soon as possible.

When I returned, the Mother Provincial amazed me with these words: "Mr. Haffert, we had come here today to tell you that we had decided that we could not possibly spare the Sisters. But while you were out, since the entire council is here, we were able to reconsider our position after you spoke to us and we have decided that regardless of the sacrifice, we will send the Sisters."

I genuinely praised and thanked God, and at once asked if they would join me in going out to place a statue of St. Joseph on the grounds so that we could place the building of the convent in his hands.

All the extraordinary details which followed could probably fill several chapters, but perhaps they are not really essential to a "history" of the Blue Army.

Further obstacles presented themselves—and to such

6

an extent that there came a point *when it seemed an absolute impossibility for the convent to be built.* A partner,
who felt that I had already given too much of everything to
the Apostolate, refused to co-sign any deed for even the
smallest piece of property for the building of the convent.

Eventually, under circumstances which I would
describe as little short of miraculous, twenty acres were
acquired *directly behind the spot where we had placed the
statue of St. Joseph* that afternoon. By the Feast of the
Holy Rosary a year later, the building was under way. On
that blessed day Your Excellency was here to lay the cornerstone of the "Holy House, U.S.A.."

And this was the beginning of something you and I had
never foreseen: A great American Shrine to the Immaculate Heart of Mary.

We had wanted to create as great an atmosphere of holiness as possible, and since the Holy House of Nazareth is
the "holiest place on earth," we solicited some stone from
the original Holy House to be used in an exact replica as
the chapel of this "house of prayer."

As it turned out the Holy House proved to have an at-   7
mosphere of holiness not only for the Felician Sisters who
dwell there in an almost semi-cloistered life, but for the
visitors which it attracted in ever greater numbers. Some
favors—perhaps even "miracles"—were claimed. And
the Sisters themselves reported hearing angelic voices
during the night coming from the area of the chapel.

I thought beyond doubt that this was a hallucination, or
the sound of wind, and the Sisters never tried to convince
me. But after a few years when Mother Mary Antoinette,
the former Provincial, came as Superioress, she told me
that shortly after she was in the convent, she had been
amazed to hear a beautiful choir in the chapel, and she
marvelled that the Sisters there had such beautiful voices,
and wondered what they were doing in the chapel at that
hour.

I then wrote to Father James Cholewka, O.F.M. Conv.,
who had been Chaplain there for four years, to ask him if
he had heard any such voices. To my surprise, he gave us
a written testimony specifying the exact times, the quality
of the voices, and the fact that even some of the melodies
had lingered with him so that he was singing them the
following morning.

There seemed to be no doubt then that this mountain,

where the Pilgrim Virgin statue had been enshrined for almost two years before "flying off" to Moscow, was in some mysterious way very precious to Our Lady. To me it had always been simply a place of work where we rarely had place or time for visitors. And I must confess that I was dismayed to think that there would be an attraction here which might bring crowds of people to disrupt our exceptionally heavy work load. The volume of mail alone would frequently exceed a thousand letters daily.

The next thing we knew was that Sr. Miranda—who at the very beginning had prophesied that one day there would be a shrine on this mountain to the Immaculate Heart of Mary—was proposing to Your Excellency that due to the continuing increase of visitors, the shrine should no longer be delayed. I was relieved when I heard that Your Excellency replied: "Over my dead body."

I must confess that I felt the same. If it had to come, let it happen after we had finished our strenuous burden of work here.

But on the 50th anniversary of the apparition of Our Lord to Lucia at Pontevedra (the convent which had now become the property of the Blue Army), Msgr. Connell, who had succeeded Msgr. Colgan as President of the U.S. Blue Army, began to urge that some kind of monument to the Immaculate Heart of Mary be built in response to those poignant words spoken by Our Lord to Lucia at Pontevedra: *"What is being done to establish devotion to the Immaculate Heart of My Mother in the world?"*

As a compromise, I suggested a tower with a statue on top, around which *some day a shrine could be built.* It was discussed with an architect, who explained that for little more than the cost of the tower, we could have an open shrine. The next stage was a suggestion that there should be a crypt, and before we knew it, we were in Your Excellency's office with a set of plans which would involve the commitment of one million dollars!

While I would have preferred not to have had a shrine at this difficult time, my ultimate concern was, as usual, whether or not *God willed it.* I was perfectly willing to accept what you were going to say, although I expected and hoped that it would be a cautious suggestion that we postpone it for the moment—at least until some funds were available.

When you began to ask questions about the

engineering, my heart sank somewhat.

"Do you realize how much this would cost, Excellency?" I asked.

You looked up with a smile and said that the diocese would not have to pay for it!

I hesitated and then said: "Are you sure, Excellency, that we should build this?"

You looked up from the plans and said simply: "It is a beautiful concept."

At that time, we were just about to celebrate the bicentennial of the United States. In 1776 George Washington had marched with his retreating troops from New York down the very valley at the foot of our mountain, a few months after the Declaration of Independence. So having finally made a decision in favor of the shrine, we planned a ground-breaking ceremony following the Eucharistic Congress in Philadelphia. Our dear Bishop Venancio, still the International President of the Blue Army, flew over from Portugal, and there were about thirty Portuguese priests and many Blue Army leaders of the United States, as well as the Rector of the Shrine of Fatima, present at the ceremony. We have some wonderful memories and happily, beautiful pictures of that historic moment.

Two years later the Shrine was complete and again Your Excellency kindly came for the laying of the cornerstone and the blessing of another building: A major Marian shrine!

I realize now how shortsighted I had been. This noble shrine, with its soaring beauty and inspiration, has done more than any television program, or any other project we have undertaken, possibly including even the World Peace Flight in 1978, to make known the reality of Fatima. *In a sense, it has brought Fatima to America.*

For so many years I had been trying to get people to go to Fatima so that they could *realize* for themselves its immense significance. And now the realization is here in our midst, in the heart of the great megalopolis which extends from Boston to Washington, D.C. The Shrine is within a two-hour driving distance for perhaps as many as *ten million* American Catholics! And it is a symbol of the entire nation's warm response to those moving words of Our Lord: "What is being done to establish devotion to the Immaculate Heart of My Mother in the world?"

Chapter Twenty-One

1) First Daughters of the Immaculate Heart of Mary -
2) Carmelite Brothers of the Holy Eucharist - 3) Hand-
maids of Mary Immaculate - 4) Handmaids of Mary
Immaculate established at our National Center by Bishop
Ahr - 5) Handmaids of Mary Immaculate administer U.S.
Blue Army National Center - 6) Increasing participation
of Felicians - 7) Significance of habit of the Handmaids of
Mary Immaculate - 8) They wear the Miraculous Medal

Below: Rev. Charles F. Kelly, Vicar of Religious Communities
for Diocese of Trenton looks on, with Msgr. Edward U. Kmiec in
background, as Bishop Ahr signs decree of foundation for
Handmaids of Mary Immaculate, in the convent chapel, October
13, 1977. On this same date, the Bishop received the first
candidates for the postulancy.

21

DEDICATED SOULS

"God wishes to use you to make me known and loved." — *Our Lady of Fatima*

It is difficult to evaluate the contribution made by three different religious communities to the development of the Blue Army in the United States, and of other religious communities which have undertaken the work in other parts of the world, especially in Spain and in Italy.

I do not expect to live to see it, but I would presume that in the days to come—as we approach even closer to the triumph of the Immaculate Heart of Mary—these communities will play an ever more important role.

We came to believe that we must have these totally dedicated, consecrated souls at the center of the Apostolate in the United States.

This is evident for many reasons, but perhaps the most important is the fact that we are engaged in a colossal spiritual struggle between Our Lady and Satan, between Her seed and his seed. And the person of "average" sanctity could not stand up *at the center of this conflict* without not only great personal sanctity, but also without the prayer support and companionship of similarly dedicated souls.

That special vocation of Sr. Mary Miranda, of the Felician Province of Lodi, New Jersey, began (as I mentioned in the last chapter) in 1950, the year in which the Blue Army effectively began as a national movement. The special calling she felt within herself to pray and to sacrifice herself for the Apostolate in general, and finally to found at the National Center of the Blue Army a "House of Prayer" (to be a "spiritual heart" of the Apostolate in the United States) is such an important element in our development that it could probably never be overemphasized. And yet it is not something so tangible that one can adequately verbalize its true value, its true importance.

1 The Felicians (founded as "the Daughters of the Immaculate Heart of Mary") numbered over 5,000 in the world when our Holy House convent was opened.

Mother Virginette (the Provincial who had come with her Council to tell us that the Sisters could not be spared and then decided on the spot to make whatever sacrifice was needed) shortly afterwards became the General of the entire order. She was succeeded in Rome by Mother Mary Amadeus, also of the New Jersey Province.

In appreciation for the great sacrifice the Felician Sisters had made on behalf of the Blue Army, the Bishop of Fatima presented a special and beautiful wood carving of the Immaculate Heart of Mary to Mother Virginette (in St. Mary Major's in Rome) on the occasion of the anniversary of the founding of the Felician Sisters. It was my joy to be present on this glorious occasion.

Naturally this Polish-born community is well known to the Polish Pope, John Paul II. Before Mother Virginette left Rome to return to America, she was invited to the Pope's apartment and attended Mass in the private chapel of His Holiness.

Subsequently the Felicians were invited to staff the International Center of the Blue Army at Fatima. It seemed only fitting that this great community of "Daughters of the Immaculate Heart of Mary" should have a special place at Fatima itself, where Our Lady had revealed Her Immaculate Heart and had made known that now God wishes "to establish devotion to my Immaculate Heart in the world."

2 Another community which played a mysterious yet important role is the Carmelite Brothers of the Holy Eucharist, founded by Br. Aloysius Scafidi, the same Brother featured in my book *The Brother and I*.

Those who have read this book will know that I have always considered myself a sort of surrogate of Br. Aloysius, the founder of the Carmelite Brothers of the Holy Eucharist. At the time that he received the message of my own vocation, he felt called to found a community of brothers which combined devotion to Our Lady and to the Most Blessed Sacrament. And he had hoped that ultimately these very brothers would serve in Blue Army centers to complement the work of communities like the Felicians and the Handmaids of Mary Immaculate, while at the same time fulfilling their own special mission of promoting devotion to the Most Blessed Sacrament in and through the Immaculate Heart of Mary.

Like most communities in history, this one—although founded with the permission of Brother's Carmelite superiors and always following the path of love and obedience, has gone through untold hardships. And similarly the Handmaids of Mary Immaculate, which had been founded shortly after 1950 *specifically* to live and to spread the Message of Fatima, has had the extremely difficult path typical of those followed by St. Alphonsus de Liguori, St. Peter Julian Eymard, St. Grignon de Montfort, and so many, many others who founded new communities to serve special needs in the Church at special moments of historical need.

3

Satan seems to know the harm that he is bound to suffer in the future from these chosen, totally dedicated, "special vocations" and does everything in his power, from the very beginning, to prevent their foundation, and then their development.

The history of the Felician Sisters is amply recorded but it might be well to recall here the beginning of the Handmaids of Mary Immaculate in which Your Excellency played a *most* important role.

This community was founded in 1952 by an Ursuline nun, Mother Stanislaus, from Helena, Montana, who had obtained permission to live outside her convent temporarily in order to care for an invalid father. Like Sr. Miranda, she had read about the Blue Army in SOUL Magazine, and felt inspired to found a community to serve this Apostolate. She and a companion came to Plainfield, New Jersey, in 1953 to speak to Msgr. Colgan. He and I warmly and enthusiastically welcomed the idea of a community for the Blue Army, which was then beginning to grow.

But we were so new—so unproved! And Your Excellency wisely judged that we would have enough problems without taking on the formation of a new community. Moreover, you had adopted a policy of not accepting into the diocese any community not already established. (Incidentally, Bishop Venancio had this same policy at Fatima.)

You suggested that Mother Stanislaus return to Helena where her own Bishop knew her and establish the community there' first. Once their roots had been firmly planted there, the community could apply to come here.

The day finally came, however, when they did receive permission from the Bishop of Helena to participate in the Blue Army Apostolate for a trial period of one year.

The Sisters spent that year inaugurating a Blue Army School of Apostolic Formation in Detroit, Michigan. At the conclusion of the year, the Sisters were so enthusiastic about their new work that they petitioned the Bishop of Helena for a three-year extension and also for permission to establish a Novitiate for candidates to the Community.

The Bishop told the Sisters that in order to establish a Motherhouse and Novititate in the diocese of major work, the Community would have to be refounded in the Diocese of Trenton.

During these early years, the community sustained incredible trials. The holy foundress, Mother Stanislaus, suffered spiritually and physically to an almost unimaginable degree. But she had a lifelong, in-depth understanding of true devotion to the Blessed Virgin of St. Grignon de Montfort. She imparted this to her Sisters by total reliance on Divine Providence and a high esteem for the evangelical virtues. My discovery of this within the community has rarely ceased to amaze me.

From time to time I would send out "feelers" to see if there was a possibility that the Bishop might release them from his diocese and that I might therefore ask Your Excellency to let them come here, but they were apparently too much needed—and too much appreciated—where they were...even though they were unable to attract candidates.

To my great joy, Your Excellency agreed to establish the Community, making the first exception in more than a quarter century to your own rule of not accepting a new foundation in the diocese.

Despite the fact that they had existed for twenty-five years, they were "new" in the sense that they had been established only as a pious union in another diocese, and would have to be completely re-established here.

I am sure that as a Bishop who feels that he did nothing but his duty for thirty years, there will nevertheless be many monuments to you. But this is a *living* one. These Sisters, and all who come after them, will cherish the memory, captured in beautiful photographs, of Your Excellency standing in their poor little chapel in the Institute, signing the documents of their foundation in the Diocese, and receiving the first postulants.

They are a humble little community founded by Our Lady for this Apostolate, to bring about the triumph of Her Immaculate Heart in the world: a special vocation for a special purpose. Through the saintly Mother Stanislaus, they have been formed to form others, and have been sanctified to sanctify others. If the Blue Army Crusaders are the active limbs of the Apostolate, the Handmaids of Mary Immaculate are its ever-beating heart.

Sr. Mary Joseph (formerly Valentina Brech) was sent by Mother Stanislaus to make her novitiate at Fatima with the Reparation Sisters of Our Lady of Sorrows of Fatima. Later, her profession was made in the Chapel of the Apparitions to Bishop Venancio, then Bishop of Fatima.

I often marvel how these "Handmaids of the Handmaid of the Lord" sustain the burden that has been laid upon them. I am sure it can only be because they are indeed the Handmaids of Mary Immaculate, strengthened by the Blessed Virgin Herself, and hence almost all the responsibility that I had borne in the National Center, and had learned to shoulder over a period of many years, suddenly fell upon them: all the personnel problems, and many new projects such as the development of the Blue Army Cadets, the National Blue Army organization, the ever increasing personnel, the Shrine and other building projects constantly looming ahead, and so on. Yet they carry all this burden with great ability and efficiency while fulfilling at the same time a prayer schedule almost as heavy as that of a cloistered community!

5

The authority of the National Blue Army of the United States now rests with the elected officers of the Blue Army throughout the country—specifically at the present time in ninety dioceses, but ultimately I would presume in all.

This National Council meets once a year and elects a National Executive Committee which meets four times a year, composed of members who live within a reasonable traveling distance of the National Center. And the "power" of the U.S. National Blue Army rests with this

205

Executive Committee.

The National Center is administered by an "administrative board," composed also of legal trustees. The core of this board is the Handmaids of Mary Immaculate.

Meanwhile the role of the Felicians increased greatly.
6 Not only do they continue their prayer life for the Apostolate but they open all the mail (average of one thousand pieces daily!) and receive an ever-increasing flow of pilgrims.

Hence there is great dedication and holiness at our National Center. There is the "Holy House Convent," with the Felician Sisters. Then there is the complex work of our National Center, with the Supply Shop, Printery, its Art and Typesetting Departments, its computerized Addressing and Mailing Department, its Book Publication and Supply Shop Departments, Accounting, Editing, Stenography, etc.

I hope our Blue Army membership throughout the nation (and the world!) realize how much the totally dedicated and consecrated nuns and priests at our National Center and Shrine need prayers! I know—because "I have been there." I know how unceasingly the devil works to sow dissension, to create doubts, to block the way at every turn. To the complex problems necessarily associated with so complex a work is added the constant scheming and interference of an infernal enemy, infuriated with despair by the very words which comprise our hope:

"In the end, my Immaculate Heart shall triumph, Russia will be converted and an era of peace will be granted to mankind."

In conclusion, I feel impelled to record, Your
7 Excellency, the meaningful habit of the Handmaids of Mary Immaculate. When it was adopted almost thirty years ago, it seemed somewhat modern, and certainly different from the traditional garb worn by nuns at the time. But today, without having been substantially changed on their part, it is similar to the habits now being worn by *most communities*.

The three colors of this habit, however, are very different from that of any other community and signify the various apparitions of Our Lady at Fatima. The tunic is blue, because in one of the apparitions, Our Lady

appeared dressed in blue, seemingly emphasizing the
Sorrowful Mysteries of the Rosary and the sanctification of
daily duty. They wear the full Brown Scapular of Our Lady
of Mt. Carmel, which Our Lady wore in the last vision.
And they wear white on their veil, signifying both purity
and the white garment which Our Lady wore in most of
Her apparitions at Fatima. Around their neck they wear
Our Lady's "miraculous medal."

8

As we speak of the tremendous contributions of these
"special vocations" raised up by Our Lady Herself to lead
Her Apostolate in the world, one's thoughts run also to
that wonderful Italian nun, Mother Ludovica, who
founded a community in Turin also dedicated to the Immaculate Heart of Mary and took upon herself the responsibility of the Blue Army for all of Italy after the death of
Msgr. Giovanni Strazzacappa, mentioned elsewhere in
these pages as one of the international "giants" in the
development of the worldwide Apostolate of Fatima.

I feel that I must confine myself to reminiscences about
those events particularly known to me, especially about
the beginnings of the Blue Army in the United States. But
it is to be hoped that someone else will write a more
objective and far more complete overview of the
development of the Apostolate throughout the world.

One thing above all is evident: this is an army which
was raised up by Our Lady Herself, and She Herself
called special and capable children to respond as did
Lucia, Francisco and Jacinta to Her first words addressed
to them on May 13, 1917:

"Will you be willing to accept whatever God will send
you?" and Her subsequent words in the second apparition
on June 13: *"God wishes to use you to make me known
and loved."*

Chapter Twenty-Two

1) Center in Portugal assailed by Communist propaganda 2) Secretariat opens in Switzerland - 3) Fribourg Shrine considered for future - 4) Significance of Bourguillon, main Scapular Shrine on European continent - 5) Task of the International Secretariat - 6) Centers arise throughout the world - 7) Spirituality of the Apostolate deepens - 8) Major leader rises in Germany - 9) International motto adopted

The tree shown below is preserved as a replica of the one beneath which the children of Fatima waited for the coming of Our Lady [the original tree no longer exists, having long since become "relics" for the faithful.] Millions of signatures to the Blue Army pledge were buried under the tree pictured here.

22

SECRETARIAT
IN SWITZERLAND

"An era of peace to mankind."   — *Our Lady of*
Fatima, July 13, 1917

During our early years, as I have already related, the International Secretariat of the Blue Army was in Fatima and its correspondence was answered by the indefatigable Dona Maria de Freitas, with the assistance of a typist-secretary.

We had been hoping that a dedicated community, like the Felicians or the Handmaids of Mary Immaculate, would come to serve our Apostolate not only in America, but also in Fatima, in Pontevedra, and eventually in other important centers of the Apostolate throughout the world.

As Your Excellency is aware, it was twenty-five years before the Handmaids of Mary Immaculate came to our Center in America, and then the work had developed to such an extent that my major concern was that it might overwhelm them. When Maria de Freitas could no longer continue as International Secretary due to ill health, we had no one sufficiently multi-lingual to handle the heavy correspondence at Fatima. It was decided, at least temporarily, to transfer the Secretariat to Switzerland.

Again the Queen of the World was showing Her power, Her own personal direction to Her "Army."

The Apostolate began to develop on a world scale, wider than ever before, despite the increasing effectiveness of Soviet propaganda directed against it. Foremost among their numerous counterthrusts were the insidious charges that the Apostolate of Fatima was a weapon of the CIA and a political "export" of Portugal...a "colonial" power ruled by fascists, which held millions in slavery in Angola and Mozambique.

But Our Lady raised up and carefully prepared an extraordinary man who had been a director of one of the world's major forwarding firms—a company which used fleets of ships, trucks, railroad cars, planes—every means of transportation—to distribute heavy goods of major manufacturers, such as Ford Motor Company, Bethlehem Steel, and many others, to the four corners of the world.

His name is Albert Setz-Degen and he is completely fluent in English, French, German and Italian. He had long since been devoted to Our Lady of Fatima and had been a leader of the Blue Army in Switzerland. He had undertaken a personal apostolate of distributing statues of Our Lady of Fatima all over the world as gifts to bishops for their parishes. He had the simple telegraphic address: Fatima, Basle.

Having retired from his directorship of the forwarding company at the age of 70, Albert volunteered to handle the international correspondence of the Blue Army from Basle, expecting it to be on a temporary basis.

He was soon employing three secretaries (each conversant in a different language), working in offices he provided in his beautiful home, overlooking the port of Basle on the Rhine and the corners of three countries: Switzerland, France and Germany.

By 1980 he was working on a budget of over fifty thousand dollars a year, without any renumeration whatever—and laboring more intensely, and for longer hours, than he had ever worked as director of a multi-million-dollar forwarding firm!

Being in the center of Europe, he was able to reach numerous leaders in different countries easily by telephone, and his house in Basle became a sort of crossroads for leaders not only of Europe, but of Africa, America and even the Orient.

It soon became evident that this Secretariat in Switzerland was a tremendous asset. Even though we had our International Center at Fatima where we had our international meetings, there was a great advantage in having the Secretariat centered in a country whose neutrality was recognized all over the world, and where multiple languages were spoken as fluently and easily as a single language is spoken in most other countries.

But now Albert, although in excellent health and still working to capacity, was past his 80th birthday. There was not a line in his cherubic, round face, and his intelligent blue eyes sparkled with greater vivacity than those of much younger men.

He set his eyes on Fribourg as the most logical place for a permanent International Secretariat of the Blue Army. It was not only the center of Catholicism in Switzerland, but under the most extraordinary circumstances had become one of the greatest centers of Catholic learning in the world outside of Rome. And a global service of Catholic missions was already established in the city, whose secretary was a member of the Blue Army: Madame Aeby-Schwaller.

Because of Madame Aeby's knowledge of languages and her experience in communicating on behalf of the Committee of Bishops to all corners of the world, Albert persuaded her to join the staff of the Blue Army's International Secretariat, doing her work in Fribourg while communicating with him once or twice a week in Basle.

Fribourg has an extraordinary location. It is surrounded by a deep ravine, very much like the geographical situation of Luxembourg, which enabled that Duchy to remain independent and free for centuries. Fribourg means "free city."

You must leave the city along the lines of the medieval defense wall, to cross the ravine on a bridge and then come back to a point on the hill opposite the center of the city, where there is a shrine known as Our Lady of Bourguillon. There is a most interesting story about this shrine which I feel is important to tell, perhaps not so much for the past of the Blue Army, but for its future.

In medieval times there was a leper colony on that hill and one of the lepers had carved a statue of Our Lady out of wood. He was cured, and other lepers invoking Our Lady were also cured of their diseases. The wonder of the cleansing of the entire leper colony attracted the attention of persons far and wide. A chapel was built to house the statue, and in time it became a center of European pilgrimage.

Not long after the apparition of Our Lady to St. Simon Stock with the gift of the Scapular in 1251, Our Lady appeared to the Cistercian abbot of Fribourg exactly as She had appeared to St. Simon Stock (and as She appeared in the final vision of Fatima) dressed as Our Lady of Mt. Carmel and holding the small scapular in Her hands. She told the abbot that She wanted the wooden statue in Bourguillon clothed as She was appearing to him.

Even though the abbot was one of the most revered men of Fribourg, one can imagine the difficulty he had in persuading the citizens of Fribourg to change the vesture and appearance of the miraculous image. It was only after two years—during which time we can imagine that this was through various signs and proofs—that the abbot was finally able to do as Our Lady had asked. (Unfortunately, we only know these essential facts from a former professor of Fribourg University. Many of the details have been lost.)

4 From that time, Our Lady of Bourguillon was known as Our Lady of Mt. Carmel, and when one visits that chapel today—as thousands have done from all over Europe— one sees the walls entirely covered with ex-votos testifying to the favors granted by Our Lady there. But perhaps there was no favor more wonderful, or more significant for the Church, than the manner in which Our Lady answered the prayers of St. Peter Canisius.

When the Protestant Reformation began to spread like a raging fire through Switzerland, the saint used to make a pilgrimage on foot down the steep ravine and up the other side (a truly fatiguing pilgrimage!) to pray before the statue of Our Lady and implore Her to safeguard the Faith in Fribourg.

Every day the saint made this pilgrimage which must have taken him two or three hours to accomplish.

It was as though he were asking Our Lady, who had appeared in this free city, offering to take it under Her Mantle through the devotion of the Scapular, *to extend Her protecting mantle over the Church.* And O wonder of history! Fribourg became an island of Faith in an ocean of Protestantism.

After the storm of the Reformation had abated, from that island of Faith, Catholicism began to spread again throughout the Cantons, and beyond Switzerland, and students came to the Catholic University of Fribourg from all over the world, especially to be trained in its great seminary. How many priests, how many bishops returned from Fribourg to their native lands, strengthened in the supernatural and intellectual basis of the Faith to enable them to sow the seed more effectively among their fellow countrymen!

Madame Aeby-Schwaller's husband, now deceased,

was one of the prime supporters of the Shrine of Bourguillon, and the Blue Army eventually hopes to acquire
property near the shrine as its permanent International
Secretariat. It would please me greatly if I could live to see
that day.

Perhaps a word should be said about the work of the 5
International Secretariat.

One major task is to evaluate the leaders of the Blue
Army in more than 100 countries in which the Blue Army is
established. These reports help ensure that the leaders are
well informed and working only with permission of the
bishops.

In some areas of the world financial help is necessary
and, even though Blue Army centers in most countries of
the world have need of whatever funds are available for
their work, all who can do so send two percent of their
annual gross income to support the International Secretariat. From this, help is given to areas where the Blue
Army is just starting and where it could hardly make
progress without external assistance.

Most financial help, of course, has come from the
United States, but an increasing amount in recent years 6
has also been coming from Switzerland and Germany.

Looking at this "Army of the Queen" with faith, one
can only marvel at the work Our Lady has done over the
years in drawing Her special children, many of them
eminently capable persons, to serve in Her army.
Consider, for example, how She used the many talents of
Msgr. Giovanni Strazzacappa in Italy.

While the establishment of important centers of the
Apostolate in France and Germany were largely the result
of our direct efforts, we were amazed when we saw a
booklet printed in Italy about the Blue Army, and that
centers were being established in Padua, Rome, and
Naples by Msgr. Strazzacappa, who was the publisher of
no less than sixteen Catholic magazines in Italy!

This brilliant priest also had centers for secular priests
in Padua, Rome and Naples, although Padua was his
diocese. He became one of the most influential and
capable of all our international leaders, and made
important contributions to the final version of our international statutes and the many resolutions passed, year after
year, by the International Council, of which he was a prominent member.

Like Msgr. Connell (second president of the Blue Army in the United States), Msgr. Strazzacappa died very suddenly in the prime of his life when it seemed that he was in perfect health. Shortly before this unexpected sorrow, I witnessed an unusual exchange between himself and Padre Pio.

As Your Excellency knows, Padre Pio had become mysteriously ill when the Pilgrim Virgin first arrived in Italy under the auspices of the Blue Army. During the many weeks that the statue was traveling through the country, where it was received by hundreds of thousands of people, with white doves frequently accompanying it, and many miracles along the way, Padre Pio remained ill, and often seemed to hover at the point of death. During this period he was unable to celebrate Mass once—a clear indication of his critical condition, for the Holy Sacrifice was the center of his life.

When the statue arrived at San Giovanni Rotondo, thousands upon thousands of people were there to greet the Pilgrim Virgin. But Padre Pio could not leave his sickbed. After the visit, the helicopter carrying the statue took off from the plaza in front of the Church of Our Lady of Graces.

"Suddenly," Msgr. Strazzacappa told me, "the helicopter lurched back so that I had to quickly reach for my balance. The pilot himself said it was simply a sudden instinct to turn back and to bring the helicopter close to the monastery one last time."

At that very moment Padre Pio was heard to exclaim to Our Lady: "Madonnina, when you came to Italy, I became like this. Do you leave me this way?"

And even as those around Padre Pio's bed heard the roar of the helicopter coming close to where Padre Pio had been bedridden, the saintly stigmatist rose from his bed, went to the window, and waved to Our Lady—completely cured! He was able to say Mass from that day on until the day of his death, when he had borne the stigmata for exactly fifty years.

In thanksgiving, Padre Pio sent a crucifix to the Bishop of Fatima, and in return the Bishop decided to send a very beautiful statue of Our Lady as a gift from Fatima to Padre Pio. Msgr. Strazzacappa wrote and told me about it, and said that if I would like to come with a group of pilgrims to Naples, he would organize some members of the Blue

Army of Italy, and together we could take the statue to present it to Padre Pio. I was privileged to share in this undertaking for the venerable stigmatist.

On the drive from Naples (where the statue had arrived by ship), we took turns carrying the statue of Our Lady in the front of the coach, praying the Rosary.

Padre Pio received us with his habitual graciousness and when we presented the beautiful statue, he asked Msgr. Strazzacappa:

"Where are you from, Monsignor?"

"Padua, Rome, and Naples," answered the good priest.

Padre Pio asked again with slightly greater emphasis: "But where are you from?"

Msgr. Strazzacappa repeated the same answer.

The third time Padre Pio asked, now with greater emphasis: "But where are you *from*?"

This time Monsignor named his diocese, Padua. And Padre Pio asked quietly: "And why did you not say that the first time, Monsignor?"

And Msgr. Strazzacappa suddenly realized that Padre Pio had looked into his heart and revealed to him a remnant of pride. With great humility he thanked the saintly stigmatist for his spiritual kindness.

This was the special mission of Padre Pio—to make holy persons holier. And the special grace mentioned above was given to Msgr. Strazzacappa only weeks before his unexpected and sudden death.

Padre Pio subsequently placed the statue in the sacristy over his vesting table, so that he saw it before and after each of his liturgical services. It remains there to this day.

In the early days of the Apostolate, we felt that the primary goal of the Blue Army was to obtain ever-increasing numbers of pledges. But over the years, we gradually came to realize that multitudes doing the minimal which Our Lady asked, from which many would be certain to fall away, might not hasten Our Lady's victory so much as a few, like the children of Fatima, helping each other to penetrate ever more deeply into that sublime formula of holiness by which we enter, through the Immaculate Heart of Mary, into the secrets of the Sacred Heart of Jesus, causing ever greater floods of grace and mercy to flow upon the world.

After the death of Msgr. Strazzacappa, a religious community dedicated to the Immaculate Heart of Mary and with a motherhouse in Turin, decided to direct its spiritual energies to the support of the Italian Blue Army. Under its charismatic foundress, Mother Mary Ludovica, this dedicated community fulfilled the same role in Italy that the Handmaids of Mary Immaculate were fulfilling in America. They had the warm and intimate support of Bishop Hnilica, who was mentioned previously in this "history." One of the most outstanding Catholic laymen of Italy became the Blue Army's national president: The Honorable Oscar Luigi Scalfaro, a member of the Italian Parliament and with close ties in the Vatican.

Rather than resist the pressures of the *Ostpolitik*, Italy used the Blue Army's second official name: "World Apostolate of Our Lady of Fatima" with the title of Blue Army in small letters beneath. The greatest evidence of their effectiveness came in May, 1978, when the Queen of the World flight brought the International Pilgrim Virgin to Rome *and more than a million people turned out to honor Our Lady on the Communist May Day (May 1).*

Shortly after that the National Pilgrim Virgin of Italy was carried from diocese to diocese to obtain the consecration of each one to the Immaculate Heart of Mary. Padre Pio's prayer groups took an active role in this Apostolate, calling upon all Italian Catholics to turn to Our Lady and to follow Her formula for holiness and reparation.

However, Your Excellency, I am sure you would not want me to go into the detailed history of the Blue Army in every nation, and perhaps not even in our own nation. Such a comprehensive survey would take volumes to record. For example, in the United States alone, long individual stories could be told of all the ninety different diocesan centers of the Apostolate already established, such as the large center in Detroit, formerly a Franciscan monastery and print shop, which would need a chapter to itself. Abroad, too, the story is the same, with the many vicissitudes of the Blue Army's progress in some one hundred countries, especially in England where the Apostolate had been established in the mid 1950's by that great Marian apostle, Laurence Harvey.

Before closing these brief recollections of some of the highlights of our international history, I think it both fitting and necessary to remember one most outstanding Blue Army leader, whom we have only briefly mentioned earlier: Fr. Andreas Fuhs of Germany.

Father Fuhs had learned of the Blue Army while visiting **8**
Canada, and had begun to speak of it on a radio program
from a powerful station at Saarbrucken in central Europe.
He was a virtual "Bishop Sheen of Europe."

When Msgr. Colgan and I went to Europe in 1951 in the
hope of establishing some centers of the Apostolate in
leading countries, I advised Fr. Fuhs in advance that we
were coming. He met us in Paris and took us in his car to
Saarbrucken, and then to Cologne where arrangements
had been made for me to speak to a large crowd in
Cologne Cathedral.

While I knew German, by the time we left France I was
both physically and mentally exhausted—having spoken
day after day. And to my consternation I found that
German words would not come to me. But even more
concerned was Fr. Fuhs, who had broadcast my coming all
over Germany, and was expecting an enormous crowd. It
was the first time an American Catholic had been invited
to give a major lecture in Germany after the war, and I
suppose many came out of curiosity.

In desperation, I had to do something which I had never
done before: write out my talk and read it. It was
fortunate that I did so, for a huge crowd turned up. But
when the question period came, that mental block
disappeared and I found myself at ease, greatly to Fr.
Fuhs' relief!

It was during this trip in Germany that we developed **9**
the international motto of the Blue Army: *Orbis Unus
Orans*. It can mean "one world praying," or in a
paraphrase of Fr. Peyton's famous slogan, "a world that
prays together will remain together."

We look to Our Lady appearing at Fatima with Her
hands folded in prayer, and hearing Her message we try
to unite the world in prayer with Her to bring about the
triumph of Her Immaculate Heart and the fulfillment of
that great promise: "An era of peace to mankind."

Fr. Fuhs eventually took leave of absence from his
parish with the permission of his bishop, to become the
right hand of Bishop Venancio at Fatima in the direction of
the international Blue Army. He directed our International
Center at Fatima and was responsible for the decoration of
the beautiful Latin Chapel. He died there suddenly and
was buried in the cemetery of Fatima, near the spot where

Francisco and Jacinta had been buried, and near the tombs of Maria de Freitas and Dona Maria do Carmo. The latter had been one of the most distinguished women of Portugal, the head of Catholic Action of the nation, who became the first national president of the Blue Army of Portugal. In her last years she supervised the reception and the servants of the International Center, and assisted in the International Secretariat.

O, what precious, wonderful devotees of Our Lady came forth to serve in Her Army! Many of them still serve, and many will serve in the future. But with each passing year, the Queen of Heaven comes to welcome some to their eternal victory.

The Blue Army exists today in 110 countries. When I began this "letter" of reminiscences on the Blue Army history I wrote to the leaders of each nation and asked them to send their own recollections of the development of the Apostolate in their particular corner of the world.

The total will require another volume! Therefore, it is best that I confine my reminiscences here merely to the early stages of the "international" Apostolate.

I have mentioned the important roles played from the very beginning by Father Fuhs in Germany and Msgr. Strazzacappa in Italy, but have only briefly mentioned Abbe Andre Richard in Paris.

These three were the real "giants" in the very early stages of the development of the international Apostolate, together with Maria de Freitas and Father Messias Coelho in Portugal and Father Pablo Baussmann in Spain. Subsequently important roles were played by Canon Galamba de Oliveira (Portugal), assisted by Dona Maria do Carmo who succeeded Father Fuhs in the direction of our International Center at Fatima. Several outstanding laymen also played important roles, such as Dr. Angel Palacios, a notary from Madrid; the Honorable Luigi Scalfaro, for many years a member of the Italian Parliament; Mme. Dauprat-Sevenet of Paris; Margot and Ben O'Riordan of Ireland; Jose Correa from Brazil.

In recent years the list grows and grows as national centers become active and important in one nation after the other.

Several times in these pages will be found references to Dr. Joaquin Alonso of Madrid, who was not only the

official documentarian of Fatima, but also a most
providential person in the development of the Blue Army
as an international Apostolate. In 1981, Fr. John Power,
O.S.A., Spiritual Director of the Blue Army in Ireland,
became the International Vice-President of the Blue Army
with a most important role in the International Council.

As my thoughts turn to other great men whom Our Lady
has directed to serve in Her army, many names leap to
mind. Consider just the case of Father Pietro Leoni, S.J.,
who was ordained in the Byzantine Rite in 1939, and when
the war opened, he went as a chaplain to serve on the
fronts in Albania, Yugoslavia, Greece, and finally Russia.
He was arrested in Odessa in 1945 and condemned to
prison as a "spy of the Vatican." He was condemned
again in 1947 and was sent to work in the mines of Siberia.
To his great surprise, this "dry martyr" was liberated in
1955. He went to serve in a Byzantine church in Montreal,
where he became Chaplain to the Blue Army. In the face of
many difficulties which the Apostolate had experienced in
Canada, he was eventually chosen by the International
Council to unify the Apostolate in all of Canada. He dedicated himself to this great task with the gentleness and
firmness possible only to a man of his spiritual stature and
commitment to the Fatima Message.

I feel it is almost an injustice to single out any of these
great men and women whom Our Lady Herself has raised
up for Her Blue Army. The greatness of Mary is known to
God above.

I was somewhat amazed towards the end of 1981 when
one of the most outstanding leaders of the Apostolate in
the United States asked the question:

"Have you ever wondered why I have persevered in the
Blue Army for so many years?"

This leader had begun work in the Blue Army in 1952,
that is, almost from its beginning! Invariably the thought
came to my mind which I expressed in a counter question:

"Did Our Lady appear to you?"

She looked a little surprised, and then told me:

"In 1952 I had never even heard of the Blue Army. Our
Lady appeared to me and told me that She wanted me to
join this Apostolate and that She was its General. She
then showed me a large building and led me up the steps.
I thought it was some kind of museum. Only many years

later, when I visited Fatima, I was walking up the steps of the International Center of the Blue Army and realized that this was the very building—these were the very steps up which Our Lady had led me in that vision in 1952.''

How presumptuous it would be of me to single out any individual! And how I must tremble before the list of my own omissions and weaknesses in the face of so many great persons whom Our Lady, as the General of this Army, has raised up to lead Her militant children in a spiritual crusade to bring about the triumph of Her Immaculate Heart.

But in conclusion I will dare to mention one other person again: Abbe Andre Richard, D.D., of Paris; perhaps one of the greatest priests France has produced in this generation.

Recently I asked him:

"Father, are you still using the Church of Our Lady of Victories in Paris for the monthly All-Night Vigils?"

"Oh no," he answered, "it is too small. We never have fewer than 1,000 attend our Vigils and we must use *the largest churches in Paris.*"

Far above whatever Abbe Richard has accomplished in France, his concern for the Apostolate and his constant contributions at the international meetings for the past quarter century have been such that Bishop Venancio remarked, when forced to retire from the International Presidency because of ill health:

"If I were to select my successor, or to cast a vote for him, it would be Abbe Richard."

In 1981, when Abbe Richard refused any international office because of his age, he was unanimously elected a permanent counsellor of the Blue Army's international executive committee.

For my part, I don't think I have ever known a greater man, a greater priest.

That Our Lady should draw such men to Her total and dedicated service is one of those evident proofs that She is indeed the Queen of the World.

Above: Mr. and Mrs. Albert Setz-Degen whose home in Basle, Switzerland, became an International Secretariat for the Blue Army.

Below: Monsignor Giovanni Strazzacappa, founder of the Blue Army in Italy, meeting with Monsignor Colgan.

Monsignor Strazzacappa was editor and/or publisher of sixteen periodicals in Italy and founder of homes for priests in Padua, Rome, and Naples. "He was one of our greatest and most effective leaders," said Msgr. Colgan. After his death the work in Italy was taken over primarily by the Oblates of the Immaculate Heart of Mary under the spiritual direction of Bishop Franzi, President of the Marian Apostolate of Italy.

Chapter Twenty-Three

1) Convent of Apparitions available - 2) Would room of apparitions be destroyed? - 3) Termites disappear - 4) Pontevedra becomes pilgrimage center - 5) Intimacy of Our Lady at Pontevedra - 6) Our Lord asked: "What is being done...?" - 7) U.S. Shrine follows as a result - 8) "Final vision" of Fatima asks for Collegial Consecration - 9) Fulfilling Our Lady's requests for Collegial Consecration - 10) Jesus desired that His whole Church should know

Below: The convent in Pontevedra, Spain, where the promise of salvation was made for First Saturday devotion to the Immaculate Heart of Mary, and where Our Lord appeared a year later to ask what was being done to make the devotion known. In 1972 the Blue Army acquired the convent to make it a center of devotion to the Immaculate Heart.

PONTEVEDRA

"What is being done to establish in the world the devotion to the Immaculate Heart of My Mother?"
— *Words of Our Lord spoken at Pontevedra*

An entire book could be written about the Icon of Kazan. What an epic movie that story would make! Perhaps after the conversion of Russia and the return of the Icon to the Russian people, that movie will necessarily be made. I will save some of this extraordinary story for the "climax" of this book!

As I mentioned earlier to Your Excellency, it was after the "meeting" of Our Lady of Fatima and Our Lady of Kazan that the Blue Army acquired what must certainly be its greatest trust, its greatest honor and greatest treasure: the Convent of the Apparitions in Pontevedra, Spain.

I had gone to Madrid to meet with leaders of the Blue Army in Spain to see if we could help them get a Spanish Blue Army magazine published—a venture that ultimately proved successful.

Dr. Joaquin M. Alonso, C.M.F., was present at the meeting and he took me aside to tell me something that he felt was a matter of great importance. It suddenly came into my mind that he was about to tell me that the Convent of the Apparitions in Pontevedra was available for purchase. I volunteered this conviction to him before he even had a chance to speak. He looked at me in amazement, and then nodded and said: "Yes, that is it."

But the building was in a sad state of disrepair. The granite walls concealed an interior infested with termites. And two years before the Dorothean Sisters had abandoned it (although I did not know it at the time), they had written to the Bishop of Fatima with the intention of making the Convent available to him for whatever disposi-

1

tion he deemed fitting, for the greater glory of Our Lady and the spread of the Fatima Message through the world.

The Bishop considered buying it as an "extended part" of the Sanctuary of Fatima, but since it was in a different country and diocese, he did not think the idea fitting. So his thoughts naturally turned to the only World Apostolate of the Fatima Message, the Blue Army. Since Dr. Alonso was the official documentarian at Fatima, and working directly with the Bishop, he conveyed the information to me. Our Trustees in America readily agreed to the purchase, which was at a price far less than the actual value of the building.

But then there was a great disappointment.

Father Pellegrino of the Basilica of St. Mary Major in Pontevedra was appointed by the Archbishop of Santiago to be responsible for the transaction, and he told us that the whole interior of the great stone building would have to be completely demolished...that only the outer walls could be saved. *This meant that we would have to destroy the actual room in which the apparition took place!*

Fr. Pellegrino was not the type of man whom one would expect to change his mind or opinion, and I felt that we would simply have to leave the building standing as it was indefinitely.

Then, on April 16, 1972, which was a Sunday, Msgr. Colgan died. That night, a woman in Chicago had a dream which, for her, seemed to have the force of a vision. She could not sleep after it. She reached me by telephone shortly after I entered my office at 8 o'clock the following morning—which was an hour earlier in Chicago. As I related earlier, she said:

"I dreamed of a convent in Spain falling into ruins and I want to contribute to it."

I did not quite understand her message. I told her that we had already purchased the convent, that it was completely paid for, and in consequence, we were unable to accept her money.

"But I do not want to buy it," she said, "I saw it falling into ruins and I want this money used to *repair it.*"

Could it have been a coincidence that I was scheduled to be in Spain just two days later?

I told her that I would see what could be done and let her know.

When I reached Spain, I told Fr. Pellegrino that we did not have the funds at present to demolish the interior of the whole building, but we would like to spend some money repairing it so that it could be used, *at least for some years,* until such time as major repair would be needed. To my joyous relief, since the money had been offered for this purpose, Fr. Pellegrino agreed.

I was convinced that this was only a very temporary measure because the building had been so badly infested with termites that signs of their destruction were patent everywhere. The sisters had abandoned the convent because they were afraid to walk on the floors.

So I did not bother with an architect. I simply went through the building, marking which walls were to be removed, where toilets were to be placed, how the wall of the room of the apparition was to be opened so that a chapel could be built, and so on.

An American who had been staying at the Blue Army House in Fatima agreed to go up to Pontevedra to supervise the work and a wonderful and capable Dorothean Sister, who had previously lived in the convent, obtained the workmen and helped with the supervision.

To the amazement of everyone, when the floors were torn up to channel the plumbing, *the workmen did not find a single termite in the entire building!*

There was no explanation—it just seemed that the termites had left. And to our intense relief, not one major beam had been touched. All the damage was surface damage on window sills and floors.

When the Chicago lady's contribution had been spent, *it exactly covered the entire cost* of the reconstruction, with sanitary facilities throughout the building, the Chapel of the Apparitions built and furnished, and the entire convent ready for use!

Never will I forget the moment I walked through the finished building with Fr. Pellegrino and said: "How can we explain it, Father?"

"It is as Our Lady wishes," the ebullient little pastor of St. Mary Major said, and then jumping up and down on one of the floors, which had been refinished with a layer of reinforced concrete, he added:

"This building is now forever!"

The International Blue Army put the Convent of Pontevedra under the administration of the Blue Army of Spain, which then bought the building immediately adjacent to the Convent of the Apparitions and converted it into an accommodation center for pilgrims comprising thirty rooms with private baths. Immediately across the street from the Convent stood one of those marvelous government-owned hotels, in a building which had been a baronial mansion and in which at least another fifty rooms were available for pilgrims.

Recently, a very important book about the meaning of Pontevedra in relation to Fatima was written by Dr. Alonso[1] and it would, perhaps, be unnecessary to go into this in detail here. But it is important to recall that the apparition of Pontevedra was foretold by Our Lady during the apparition of July 13, 1917 just after She had foretold the Second World War and that God would punish the world "by war, famine and persecution of the Church..." if men did not stop offending Him. She then added:

"I shall come to ask for the consecration of Russia to my Immaculate Heart, *and the Communion of Reparation on the First Saturdays.* If my requests are heeded Russia will be converted and there will be peace; if not, she will spread her errors throughout the world, causing wars..."

This pre-announced apparition, which took place on December 10, 1925 in the Convent at Pontevedra, was a remarkably intimate visit from Our Lady—perhaps the most intimate of any apparition involving a public message in history. One is reminded how St. Catherine Laboure rested her clasped hands in Our Lady's lap during the apparitions at the Rue du Bac, Paris in 1830.

In her Memoirs, Lucia describes how Our Lady appeared with the Child Jesus elevated on a luminous cloud so that she was able to look into the eyes of both Our Lady and the Child Jesus, and the Blessed Virgin *rested Her hand on Lucia's shoulder,* and with the other hand showed Her heart encircled with thorns as Jesus said:

"Have compassion on the heart of your Most Holy Mother, covered with thorns, with which ungrateful men pierce it at every moment, and there is no one to make an act of reparation to remove them."

Our Lady then said:

"Look, my daughter, at my Heart, surrounded with the thorns with which ungrateful men pierce it at every moment with their blasphemies and ingratitude. You, at

least, try to console me and announce that I promise to
assist at the hour of death, with the graces necessary for
salvation, all those who on the first Saturday of five consecutive months shall confess, receive Holy Communion,
recite five decades of the Rosary, and keep me company
for fifteen minutes while meditating on the fifteen
mysteries of the Rosary, with the intention of making
reparation to me.''

The room in which this apparition took place was so
small that the space beside Lucia's bed was scarcely more
than the width of the door through which she entered. But
next to this little cell was a fairly large dormitory, so I had
the one wall removed, and now the actual space in which
Our Lady and the Child Jesus appeared is the sanctuary of
a chapel formed by the adjacent room. *And one
experiences an extraordinary feeling of intimacy with
Jesus present in the Blessed Sacrament on that spot
where He spoke of the Heart of "your Mother"*—thus
showing the great bond of union which He has with us
through Mary...

Just two months later, in February, 1926, the Child
Jesus came back alone—and under the most interesting
circumstances.

Lucia was given the most menial tasks, and often humili-
ated, as in the case of St. Bernadette of Lourdes. On
this particular day she was carrying waste from the cess-
pool to a sewer just outside the convent gate.

As she was doing this, a small boy passed the gate,
hesitated and looked at her. She spoke to him and he did
not answer. She asked if he knew the Hail Mary. She
repeated it for him, and he did not indicate that he might
not be learning it for the first time. There was an air of
sadness about him, so she added: "Why don't you go
around the corner to the church of St. Mary Major and ask
the Blessed Virgin to give you the Child Jesus to play with
you?"

Suddenly the child was transformed. It was Our Lord.
He asked sadly:

*"What is being done to establish the devotion to the
Immaculate Heart of My Mother in the world?"*

Recovering from her astonishment, Lucia replied that
she had spoken about it to the Mother Superior, but the
latter's confessor had told her that of herself she could do
nothing.

Jesus replied:

"It is true that your superior alone can do nothing, but with My grace she can do all."

Your Excellency will remember the little sister in the Poor Clares of Bordentown who propagated devotion to the Child Jesus and who had those wonderful wood carvings which, with the warm support of Cardinal Cushing, she obtained for various churches in order to propagate devotion to the Holy Child. She gave me one of these precious statues for Pontevedra. I took it to Rome and had it blessed by the Holy Father and it now stands at the very place in the garden where the Holy Child appeared and spoke His poignant words.

On our pilgrimages to Pontevedra we invariably have Mass at the altar which is erected in the garden, as well as in the Chapel of the Apparition of the Five Saturdays. The Convent itself will accommodate about thirty overnight pilgrims, and what a privilege it is to sleep under that blessed roof! And to think that even we lay persons have that privilege!

It has been predicted that this convent of the intimate vision of Our Lady's Immaculate Heart will become to this devotion what the convent in Paray-le-Monial has become to the devotion of the Sacred Heart. Because of this, when the Church recently placed the Feast of the Immaculate Heart of Mary *after* the Feast of the Sacred Heart for the first time, I chartered a plane so that we could attend Mass in the Chapel of the Apparition of the Sacred Heart on the feast day, and be in the Chapel of Pontevedra the following day, which was the Feast of the Immaculate Heart.

As I also mentioned earlier, Msgr. Connell and his sister, who was a nun, were on that trip. I came to know him intimately then and had the occasion to ask if he would assume the position of temporary National President of the Blue Army in the U.S. until such time as we were able to have national elections. I have always thought since that this wonderful priest, so utterly devoted to the Eucharistic Heart of Jesus and the Immaculate Heart of Mary, was a gift from Their Hearts to the Blue Army. He was so impressed by those poignant words of Our Lord spoken in the garden that from then on he longed to see a monument at our National Center in Washington, N.J. in honor of the Immaculate Heart of Mary, declaring to all in our nation that *something* was being done!

But of course I have already spoken about this magnificent Shrine which now rises above the valley down which George Washington marched in 1776 with his defeated troops, only to turn back a few weeks later to win the new nation's first victory in Trenton, Your Excellency's See.

As we mentioned before, Our Lady said on July 13, 1917 that She would come back and ask for two things: the First Saturdays' devotion, and the consecration of Russia to Her Immaculate Heart. The latter was requested during an apparition in the nearby Spanish town of Tuy, on the Portuguese border, where the Dorothean Sisters had their Provincial Motherhouse.

First I will recall that great vision...and then the extraordinary gift of the altar of that vision to the Blue Army. **8**

The apparition took place about midnight, at a time when Lucia had special permission to be praying alone in the chapel before the tabernacle.

It was June 13, 1929.

Suddenly the entire sanctuary was filled with light. She saw Our Lord hanging on the Cross, surrounded by representations of God the Father and of the Holy Spirit. Blood flowed from the crown of thorns of Our Lord and from His Heart, onto a Host suspended at His side, and then dripped from the Host into a Chalice beneath.

Our Lady stood to the side, Her Heart surrounded by thorns as She had appeared in Pontevedra. From the other outstretched hand of Our Lord there flowed like water the words *"grace and mercy"* down *over the altar.*

As Lucia beheld this complex and meaningful vision she received a special insight into the mystery of the Holy Trinity which she remarked was a "secret" and heard Our Lady saying:

"The moment has come when God asks the Holy Father, in union with all the bishops of the world, to make the consecration of Russia to my Heart, promising to save it by this means."

This, as Your Excellency knows, became a special mandate for the Blue Army of Our Lady, to whom the Church itself seemed to confide the responsibility of promoting and bringing about this consecration by the Holy Father together with all the bishops of the world.

Certainly not without having consulted the Holy See, Bishop Venancio (both as Bishop of Fatima and as International President of the Blue Army) instructed us all at an international meeting to promote petitions to the bishops in every nation. As International Lay Delegate, I was designated to find a Cardinal in Rome who would receive these petitions to present them to the Pope.

I first went to a Cardinal recommended by Fr. Balic, president of the Pontifical Marian Academy. His Eminence was very, very well acquainted with the story of Fatima, but said that it was "a very big thing you are asking" and declined because it did not enter within the scope of the Congregation of which he was prefect.

After I left the Cardinal's apartment, I had to pass the door of Cardinal Slipyj, and I suddenly decided to ask this former prisoner of the Soviets if he would receive the petitions.

He readily agreed—and within a few years some two *million* signed petitions had been presented by him to Pope Paul VI and when Bishop Venancio and I went one day to express our appreciation, he told us that he had recently spent an hour with the Holy Father and had told him in no uncertain terms (indeed, in very strong "Russian" terms) that the Holy Father was making a great mistake if he did not command all the bishops of the world to join with him at once in making that consecration.

However, as I have told Your Excellency in a previous chapter, the Holy See indicated to us—when we asked about the possibility of inviting Bishop Hnilica to succeed Bishop Venancio as our International President—that it would be more expedient if these petitions were sent to individual bishops. Bishop Venancio then gave instructions to our leaders throughout the world to continue to seek the petitions, if possible with even greater zeal, and to send them to individual bishops, requesting that they in turn indicate their willingness to the Holy Father to participate in the consecration.

I do not think that I myself realized that the Holy See *expected* the Blue Army to do this until two reporters from Austria asked Cardinal Seper (who succeeded Cardinal Ottaviani in the Sacred Congregation for the Doctrine of the Faith) why he, or some other member of the Curia, did not petition the Holy Father for the Collegial Consecration. The Cardinal answered that it should not be done in this way, but that "*it was up to an organization like the Blue Army*" to have its members throughout the

9

world obtain the consent of their individual bishops, so that the consecration would ultimately be made as a truly collegial act, with the expressed will of the bishops, rather than an act imposed by the Pope alone.

By 1981 there was at least one very evident, beneficial result from the Blue Army's worldwide efforts in this direction. In the previous year, Archbishop Hurley from South Africa had issued a statement to the effect that the Holy Father was pleased with the Blue Army's efforts and this was published by the IDU News Agency in Austria. We then began to communicate anew with all the bishops of the world, sending a summary of the most important statements from the book of the international seminar on the Immaculate Heart of Mary which we had held at Fatima in 1971 after the Marian Congress at Zagreb, and which we had previously sent to all the bishops.[1]

What a serious, what a tragic omission on our part for so many years! Since we *were* the only worldwide Apostolate of Fatima, we should have realized our responsibility concerning the Collegial Consecration much earlier, since Our Lord had "insisted" (as Lucia put it) that even the consecration made by Pope Paul VI at the close of the third session of the Vatican Council was insufficient, and that the consecration had to be made in the manner He had requested (namely collegial) because:

"I want all My Church to know that it is through the Immaculate Heart of My Mother that this favor (the conversion of Russia) *is obtained."* 10

And how could the entire Church ever know if we did not spread the word? The Holy Father had already spoken so many times about Fatima and its message. His Holiness had even made a personal pilgrimage to Fatima. But despite all this the world had not really heard. Perhaps there could be no greater affirmation of the *raison d'etre* of the Blue Army.

FOOTNOTE

1. **The Great Promise of the Immaculate Heart of Mary in Pontevedra**; Dr. Joaquin M. Alonso, C.M.F.; third ed., English translation; AMI Press, Washington, N.J. 07882. (In preparation.)

Chapter Twenty-Four

1) A "force" drew me - 2) Furnishings of Tuy Vision given to Blue Army - 3) Project entrusted to Saint Joseph 4) Again, Saint Joseph! - 5) Pontevedra statue of Saint Joseph now in U.S. Shrine - 6) Saint James plays major role - 7) First Pilgrim Virgin appears among pilgrims to Santiago in Pontevedra - 8) Two saints at the head of Our Lady's army.

Below is statue of "Our Lady of the Blue Army" in front of the International Blue Army Center in Fatima. Above, with the Byzantine dome behind, is the marble statue of St. Joseph as he appeared in the sky at Fatima (on October 13, 1917) blessing the world.

24

SAINT JAMES
AND SAINT JOSEPH

"Blue Army's 'Quartermaster General'"

Few of us in the Apostolate have encountered "mystical" experiences, but one took place in the convent of Tuy when Bishop Venancio and I had gone there to arrange the contract with the Provincial of the Dorotheans for the purchase of the Pontevedra Convent on February 4, 1972.

As was usual with the Bishop, our first thought in coming to the convent in Tuy was a visit to the Blessed Sacrament. The chapel, on the second floor, was the same chapel in which the great vision of the Trinity had taken place on June 13, 1929, in which Our Lady had announced that *now* is the time for the Collegial Consecration of Russia to Her Immaculate Heart.

As we came out of the chapel, since I was the only lay person in the group, I went last. The Provincial and her entourage all turned to the right, but I felt something drawing me down the short length of corridor to the left, at the end of which was a window. The instinct was so strong that I left the Bishop and the nuns going in the opposite direction and, turning, walked down to the window.

At first I could see nothing unusual that would have drawn me there. I peered closer, examining the main street in front of the convent on the right, and a shed to the back, with some large beams protruding from beneath it.

With a few quick steps I rejoined the Bishop and the Mother Provincial, and when there was a lull in the conversation I asked:

"Mother, what are those large beams under the shed at the back of the convent?"

"Those," she answered, "are the pillars and arches that separated the sanctuary of our chapel from the main body of the chapel before we made the changes recommended by Vatican II."

I had been informed about five years previously of the changes in the chapel, when the *altar* of the vision, which is mentioned in Lucia's Memoirs, "over which there flowed like water the words *grace and mercy*" had been removed from the chapel. Others had unsuccessfully tried to obtain it. There were also other furnishings of the sanctuary from that time. So I asked:

"What about the altar and the other furnishings of the sanctuary at the time of Lucia's vision of 1929?"

"We have saved them all," the Mother Provincial answered.

I had a sudden inspiration: "If we conclude the contract to buy the Convent of Pontevedra, *may we also have all the furnishings from the sanctuary of the 1929 vision?*" I asked, holding my breath.

Without hesitation the Reverend Mother agreed that we could. *These are now all in the main chapel of the Pontevedra convent*—with one main exception!

The original altar from Tuy had been quite large and situated against the wall. So we left the central part in Spain and the rest *we brought to America* and it was remade into the main altar in the Holy House chapel of the Shrine at our National Center. The base of the altar will become the base of the altar in the Shrine itself. Furthermore we also brought to America two statues of angels which had been used in the chapel to hold lights before the Blessed Sacrament, and a beautiful statue of St. Joseph holding the Child Jesus.

To our Latin Chapel in Fatima we took from Pontevedra a magnificent statue of Our Lady of Fatima and another of the Sacred Heart.

As a result, the great visions of 1925-26 and 1929 are now commemorated under the same roof in Pontevedra, but there are also some very precious relics of these apparitions at our own Shrine of the Immaculate Heart of Mary in Washington, N.J. The most precious of these is the actual baldacchino from the altar at the time of the vision of the Holy Trinity over the tabernacle. This is now on the lower level of the Shrine, and behind it is an already famous painting by a celebrated Italian artist of that vision which hung for one year in the Chapel of the Apparitions itself in Pontevedra.

I do not know whether all these meaningful details should be included in this "history," but are they not special little signs of Our Lady's smile, of Her favor upon the soldiers of Her Army?

One is reminded of the wondrous apparition of Our Lord to Sister Faustina in Poland after the Trinitarian vision of Tuy in which great rays were seen streaming from His Heart, which symbolized the blood and water draining from that same Sacred Heart when pierced by a lance. And Our Lord revealed to Sr. Faustina that this Heart was *"a fount of grace and mercy"*—the very words Lucia had seen streaming from the pierced hand of Our Lord "down over the altar" during the climactic vision of Fatima, *all the precious "souvenirs" of which have been entrusted to Our Lady's Blue Army!*

I must also tell Your Excellency about the statue of St. Joseph from Pontevedra—and why it is so meaningful to us....

3

Not only did St. Joseph appear at Fatima during the Miracle of the Sun, but Our Lady had said that She would send St. Joseph with the Child Jesus on the day of the miracle *"to bless the world and to bring it peace."*

In order to be quite certain of the description of this vision, I had an artist depict it as best he could from Lucia's Memoirs before I went to see her in 1946. I then showed her the picture, asking if it was like the vision of St. Joseph with the Child Jesus as she remembered it.

The artist had depicted only the upper part of the figures of St. Joseph and the Child and Lucia said that she saw St. Joseph standing, and the Child was also as though standing but held against St. Joseph's side by his left arm, and both the Child and St. Joseph raised their hands three times in blessing.

The Blue Army considers St. Joseph its special patron, not only because of the significance of this vision, but because he is the Patron of the Church, and the one whom God chose to be the provider of natural things for Him who was the Creator of all things.

So in every one of our projects, from the very beginning, we always confide the material things to the care of St. Joseph. For example, when we purchased the land for the International Center of the Blue Army behind the Basilica at Fatima, we had absolutely no funds whatever. It was completely an act of faith. So Msgr. Colgan and a small group of Blue Army members (including myself), took a little plaster statue of St. Joseph in procession from the Basilica of Fatima, where St. Joseph had appeared in the sky, and placed it in the center of the property upon which we hoped to build that world center—which today I suppose would cost about three million dollars or more.

And then we ordered at once *a marble statue of St. Joseph,* exactly as Lucia had described him with the Child Jesus in blessing, which would be *the first structure erected* on the property.

We were grateful that it took the sculptor six months, because it took us that long to raise the funds just to pay for the statue!

4 But when the building was finally completed, we had not borrowed a single penny to pay for it! The statue of St. Joseph was rightly placed on top of the building, in front of the Byzantine dome, overlooking the Cova, with his hand, and that of his Son, raised in perpetual blessing....

(It is interesting to note that this is the only monument in all of Fatima commemorating the apparition of St. Joseph...which we consider another small, but significant, blessing from Our Lady on Her Blue Army.)

When Bishop Venancio and I went up to look at the Convent of Pontevedra for the first time—before we even entered the building—I suggested to the Bishop that we go to some religious store and buy a statue of St. Joseph which he might bless and which we would carry into the Convent with us, so that the project could be placed entirely in the hands of our holy Provider.

The Bishop readily agreed, and our first act upon entering the chapel was to place the statue of St. Joseph near the empty tabernacle.

As I have already recounted, this great building (once the palatial home of the Duke of the Rias Bajas and then a convent and school of the Dorotheans in which Our Lord and the Immaculate Heart of Mary appealed to the world for devotion to that same Immaculate Heart), was acquired (clear of termites), and remodeled without debt. Subsequently, the Blue Army of Spain, which had never possessed any funds, invested a quarter of a million dollars in the adjacent pilgrimage accommodations.

Nor did St. Joseph stop there. Your Excellency will

recall that day in 1976 when you were looking over the plans of the new Shrine in Washington, N.J. and I asked if you realized how much it was going to cost. You were not merely being "offhand" when you replied that the diocese would not have to pay for it. You did not even ask, by this time, whether we had any money towards it! You had complete confidence that St. Joseph would unfailingly provide for his Spouse.

Already our Sisters had nailed a little shrine to St. Joseph on a tree near the spot where the Shrine was to rise, and within two years the million-dollar edifice had been completed, with all the money provided as each bill came due...

As a result, it seemed eminently appropriate for us to take the beautiful statue of St. Joseph, which had been left in the Convent of Pontevedra, to our own Shrine in America where we will proclaim forever our devotion, love and gratitude to this dear spouse of Mary, this foster father of Jesus, this master provider whom Our Lady sends with Her Divine Child to bring peace.

I thought it important to include this all-too-brief reference to St. Joseph so that all Blue Army members will recognize that he is one of the leading "generals" in Our Lady's troops! And he is even more than a Quartermaster General. He is the special patron of the Blue Army throughout the entire world, even as he is the Patron of the Universal Church.

Other saints, too, are involved in the Message of Fatima, and therefore in the Blue Army, in a special way—and have played an important part in our history.

One of these is probably unknown to most members: St. James, brother of St. John, the beloved disciple.

As though to make up for the fact that he had not, like his brother, persevered to the foot of the Cross, St. James went to the ends of the known earth—from Palestine all the way to Finisterre, or Land's End, as it is called to this day, the northwest corner of Iberia.

The first recorded apparition of Our Lady—which was actually a bilocation during Her own lifetime—took place at Zaragoza, in Spain, when She came to St. James at a time when he felt particularly lonely, so far from his own land, so distant from Her, so buffeted by all manner of obstacles and persecutions in a land of pagans. She left him a small stone pillar as evidence that he had not merely dreamed of Her visit, and this is enshrined at Zaragoza in what was perhaps the most magnificent, certainly the largest Marian shrine in the world, until very recent times. During this apparition, Our Lady told St. James that he was soon to return to the Holy Land and that he would have the favor of being the first Apostle to shed his blood for Her Son.

It was near Pontevedra that St. James spent his last months instructing his disciples, before returning to Jerusalem where he was beheaded by Herod.

During the peak of the Moorish persecution, the body was hidden for fear of desecration, since the name of St. James was the rallying battle cry of the Iberian Christians against the Moors.

Those who knew the secret location of the burial place died without revealing it, and for many years extensive searches were made in vain.

One day a shepherd saw a star shining over a field, not far from Pontevedra (which was the nearest important town). When this light persisted, the Bishop concluded that it was either of supernatural or preternatural origin and he ordered prayers to be said for an understanding of the phenomenon. The Bishop then decided that they should dig at the place where the star was seen and to the bewildered joy and amazement of all, they found and identified the tomb of the holy Apostle. On that spot they began the building of a new city which became a major center of Christian pilgrimage in medieval times: Santiago de Compostela.

Since this is a story of the Blue Army rather than that of St. James, I forego the temptation to speak of the Tour St. Jacques in Paris, and of similar towers around Europe whose bells were rung to assemble the pilgrims who traveled "the roads of St. James," which became the first principal highways of medieval times. James Michener speaks of them so well in his book *Iberia*.

But now we come to the special glory of Pontevedra—and perhaps the reason why Our Lady chose this place to be the world center of devotion to Her Immaculate Heart.

7

The main "highway of St. James" from the south of Santiago passed through Pontevedra. One day, in the midst of the pilgrims, a beautiful lady was seen dressed in the typical pilgrim's garb and carrying a child. Suddenly she was *transformed in their midst*. She raised the Child to bless the pilgrims, and then disappeared. The vision was witnessed by many, and had such a profound effect on the pilgrims that they built a beautiful church in the middle of the street where the vision had appeared, redirecting the road (as in the case of the Quo Vadis on the Via Appia in Rome) in honor of the *Pilgrim Virgin*!

Michener remarks that it is Pontevedra's unique privilege to have the only shrine of Our Lady on all the *caminos* of St. James in the world. This Pilgrim Virgin is the Patroness of Pontevedra, and Her feast is celebrated in August as the main festival of the year.

Of course, those of us who had been so deeply involved in the modern "Pilgrim Virgin" knew nothing of this until we first came to Pontevedra. That was during a "Holy Year" of St. James when Bishop Venancio and I went to Pontevedra to look into the question of acquiring the Convent of the Apparitions. (This "Holy Year" is granted whenever the Feast of St. James falls on a Sunday, and the same indulgences can be obtained by going to Santiago during that year as would be obtained by going to Rome in a regular Holy Year, which would only be every twenty-five years.)

I have often been to the Shrine of Zaragoza, where the pillar of St. James still continues to exude a miraculous fragrance. So it was a moving experience for me to assist as the Bishop said Mass at the tomb of the Saint (the brother of St. John, so dear to Our Lady) in Santiago de Compostela.

Was it because of him—to whom Our Lady had come in Her very first "apparition" in history—that She now came to the Iberian Peninsula in perhaps Her most important apparition—the one in which She promised the triumph of Her Immaculate Heart *in the world?*

After all, She had appeared not only at Fatima, perhaps for a special reason of which we will speak later, but also in Spain—both of which countries had been a common part of "Iberia" when St. James had come there to preach the "Good News."

This is perhaps the most beautiful part of Spain, and yet it is remote and visited by few tourists—although Santiago now has a major airport capable of receiving large jets.

I shared my thoughts with the Bishop about St. James—of Our Lady's great love for him, and of his constant intercession in Heaven for the triumph of Our

Lady, in order that Jesus might be known and loved by all.

His Excellency confided that he had been experiencing the same sentiments, the same thoughts.

There is also the fact that St. James is often depicted as a warrior on horseback—as Our Lady's warrior!

All our pilgrims who go to Pontevedra visit, of course, the tomb of St. James. We pray that in returning to the four corners of the world, they will spread renewed devotion to this great Apostle, and see him riding beside St. Joseph at the head of Our Lady's Blue Army!

At right is a picture of the Pilgrim Virgin statue taken in July, 1981. It is the same statue which was brought to America in 1947 and played a major role in the founding of the Blue Army. (See Chapters One and Four.) Shortly before this picture was taken, at the request of Sister Lucia, it was overnight in the Carmel of Coimbra. Lucia said that the expression on the face of the statue resembled the "final" vision of Our Lady of Fatima in Spain.

Chapter Twenty-Five

1) Vietnam begs visit of weeping statue - 2) Pope blesses statue for Vietnam and other nations - 3) Pilgrim Virgin flies across Iron Curtain - 4) Public Rosary in Prague - 5) The statue delivered to Archbishop of Prague - 6) Statues delivered to nations around the world - 7) Importance of Mary's Queenship

Below: The International Pilgrim Virgin statue which, since 1947, has been traveling from nation to nation in the custody of the Blue Army. On various occasions tears were seen in the eyes and flowing down the cheeks.

25

THE PILGRIM VIRGIN

"She set forth as though to claim Her dominion."
— *Pope Pius XII*

We have already remarked that several books have been written about the Pilgrim Virgin alone and that if we started to speak of all the wonders, the crowds, the miracles, there would be room for nothing else in this "history." [1]

As these lines are being written, both of the official International Pilgrim Virgin statues blessed by the first Bishop of Fatima in 1947 are traveling in America. The one blessed on May 13 of that year is traveling in the United States, and the other is journeying throughout South America, both under the direction of the Blue Army, with the special permission of the Bishop of Fatima. But perhaps by the time this is being read, one of the statues will have traveled to a different continent.

They have been on the move for well over a quarter century and have, perhaps, visited every single country of the free world, slowly proceeding from town to town, from diocese to diocese. The Holy Father (Pope Pius XII) himself exclaimed:

"The favors She performs along the way are such that We can hardly believe what We are seeing with Our eyes."

When news of the miracles of the Pilgrim Virgin statue reached Vietnam, they pleaded for us to send the statue there.

So, in 1965, we arranged for a statue of Our Lady of Fatima to be flown to Vietnam for a visit. The effect of the statue's tour was so great that the Vietnamese did not want it to leave their war-torn country. They pleaded

1

that the statue remain until hostilities were over.

Unfortunately, this was not possible, so they asked that a special statue be blessed for their country—and thus was born the idea of the "National Pilgrim Virgin."

2 It was then in 1967 that the Pope came to Fatima, so the first twenty-five statues were taken to the Cova that day to be blessed by His Holiness, and a large Blue Army delegation came from Vietnam, going days without sleep, to be present and to carry that first National Pilgrim Virgin statue back with them at once to their suffering country.

They were signally honored that day among the immense multitude of over one million people who thronged the Cova. In films of the event, the statue borne by the Vietnamese can be seen first at the back of the crowd, and then up by the altar where they had been summoned by the Holy Father. On their return trip to Vietnam, the Pope had invited them to a private audience in Rome during which he encouraged their perseverance in prayer.

The following October, after the major celebrations of the anniversary of the miracle of the sun on the 13th, we set forth on our first around-the-world flight with the Bishop of Fatima to personally deliver "National Pilgrim Virgin" statues to twenty-four different nations.

Your Excellency will recall that in an earlier chapter I told you of Bishop da Silva dozing in his wheel chair, and then suddenly sitting bolt upright and saying to Bishop Venancio: "Bishop, let us go and take Our Lady's statue to Russia!"

And Bishop Venancio smiled to himself as he had a mental image of the old Bishop holding the statue in his wheelchair while Bishop Venancio pushed the chair across Europe towards Russia!

But something almost akin to this actually happened on the flight, which was the first time that a statue of Our Lady of Fatima was to be delivered *publicly* behind the Iron Curtain!

I had chosen the city of Prague for reasons which have not been told before, but may be safely recorded now.

Cardinal Beran, the Archbishop of Prague, had more than once come to Fatima while in exile, and he indicated that he had ways of communicating with his people in Czechoslovakia and would welcome having the statue of Our Lady go there.

But also (and I apologize for intruding any personal motive into something so important!) I always had a great devotion to the Infant Jesus of Prague, and it seemed to me only fitting that "the Mother should visit Her isolated Son behind the Iron Curtain." And had not Bishop Venancio himself said that something wonderful usually happened when two miraculous images "meet?"

We had originally intended, for safety's sake, to carry all twenty-four statues carefully wrapped in an under section of the plane, and then to unwrap them as we arrived at the airport in each country.

But after we delivered the first statue in Berlin, we found this to be awkward. We thought that it would be far more fitting to carry the statue for the next country in the plane itself, in the front of the cabin, where it would be the center of our thoughts and prayers.

So just before leaving Berlin we unwrapped the statue that was to be delivered to Prague and placed it in the front of the plane. Just before takeoff the captain came through and, seeing the statue, said: "It cannot remain there. It must be safely fastened somewhere."

So I picked up the statue and was about to take it to the back of the plane when Bishop Venancio, who was sitting in the front seat and had not understood the words of the captain (which were spoken in English), quickly asked with some anxiety:

"But where are you taking the Pilgrim Virgin statue?"

I explained what the captain had said. The Bishop immediately exclaimed: "Oh, but give it to me!"

And he took the statue, wrapped his arms around it, *and thus in the arms of the Bishop of Fatima the historic statue of Our Lady flew across the Iron Curtain!*

But if I start talking about such revealing incidents concerning the Pilgrim Virgin statue, and the marvels that we experienced, we will run into volumes.

As I am unable to restrain myself from relating that first experience of leading a pilgrimage behind the Iron Curtain, I will make the flight to Prague the only episode to be covered in more detail. We were on the first phase of the delivering of Pilgrim Virgin statues for seventy different countries—with twenty-four stops on this flight.

When we landed at Prague airport, there was not a soul in sight. But *an absolutely perfect and complete rainbow* appeared over the airport...beginning and ending on the tarmac.

I had been a little surprised (because of all the publicity concerning the Pilgrim Virgin and its significance in reference to Russia) that the Soviet-controlled government of Czechoslovakia had not rescinded our landing rights, and that we were actually arriving with the Bishop of Fatima and 107 pilgrims carrying Our Lady's statue openly behind the Iron Curtain!

But I had not counted on the malicious shrewdness of the Communists.

The world "peace flight" had been well publicized. The plane bore the insignia of the Blue Army—of *one world praying*—and on the front of the plane were the words: *"An era of peace"* (the words used by Our Lady Herself in Her Fatima promise).

If the Communists had cancelled our flight, they might have given the impression of being against peace. And since we were scheduled to arrive that afternoon, and to leave next morning, they decided to delay us at the airport, deprive us of transportation within the city, and insist that we leave on schedule—*thus making it impossible for us to take the statue anywhere, or to hold religious ceremonies of any kind.*

I did not suspect that anything was wrong until our visas were being examined one by one, so painstakingly that our people were still standing in line two hours after the plane had landed—even though there was no one else in the air terminal and the visas *were all in order.*

I then began to shout in a loud voice that our buses were waiting, and that if all of our people could not be processed, they should at least allow those who had already cleared the formalities to board the coach.

My shouting made no difference. But since neither did it cause me to be arrested, I kept shouting louder.

Suddenly, a white haired man who was sitting on the sidelines, in civilian clothes, called me over. He pointed to my Blue Army pin and said: "What is that?"

I answered that it was an insignia of our group, which was a group of prayer for peace.

I could tell that he knew very well what it was, and to this day I do not understand why he asked the question and why the gesture. But it turned out that he was a person of high authority. He gave a signal and suddenly all the formalities were over! We were told we could board our coaches immediately!

When we arrived in the center of Prague, our four buses, with all 107 pilgrims and about 200 pieces of luggage, were unloaded in the middle of the square.

I thought we had arrived at our hotel, and would be given our rooms, and then the buses would be back to take us "sightseeing"—a part of the trip which I had carefully planned so we could deliver the statue to the Archbishop of Prague!

To my dismay, the Cedok guides told us we were booked for different hotels. One group would be going two blocks in this direction, another group would be going by trolley car, and so on, to widely scattered hotels in the city.

"But what about our coaches?" I asked.

"Oh, they will be available to take you back to the airport tomorrow," they said tersely.

So that was it!

I immediately went over and explained to the Bishop what was happening and asked his permission to keep our group there all night if necessary.

Then I took my portable microphone and announced to 4 everyone that Cedok had deprived us of transportation, and that we should stay here in the square, luggage and all, until the buses came back. Everyone agreed. I then stood next to the Bishop, and we made a pyramid of luggage on which we placed Our Lady's statue as though on a pedestal, and began a public Rosary.

At the end of each decade, I passed the microphone to the Bishop, and in Portuguese he sang one of the beautiful stanzas of the Fatima hymn.

Can you imagine the picture? Over one hundred Americans, beside a mountain of luggage, with a statue of the Madonna of Fatima, and a Bishop, dressed in his episcopal soutane and wearing his pectoral cross, turning a central square in the capital city of communist Czechoslovakia into a shrine where they were praying the Rosary!

The longer we stayed, the more agitated the Cedok guides became. They kept coming up to me and saying with very threatening authority: "You cannot do this!"

But of course we kept doing it, and they would dash off to a telephone and come back and go off again.

We had just finished the fifteen decades of the Rosary (and certainly, judging by the growing crowds, the entire city of Prague was getting the news!) when our buses came back.

I quickly took the speaker and told everyone to board the buses at once, which they quickly did, taking the statue with them.

Fortunately, the driver of my coach spoke German, and I announced in a loud voice that we wanted to go up to the top of the hill for a view of the city before it got dark.

"But what about the luggage," the four guides cried out, taken by surprise at this quick action.

"That's your responsibility," I retorted. "You are the ones who unloaded it here!"

Apparently the lead driver was a Catholic—otherwise I cannot understand how he could have disregarded the Cedok guides and obeyed me instead! Off we went—into the gathering dusk, up to the top of the hill over the city *where the Archbishop's palace was.*

I unloaded the group in front of the building (the location of which I knew because I had already made a preliminary trip to prepare the way) and while they had a quick view of the city, I went over to the Archbishop's house, which was in total darkness, and tried to determine where the entrance might be. I noticed a large bell—like a school bell—suspended on a post in front of the building, so I decided that was the best way to get attention. I rang it lustily.

In a short time there was a scurrying of feet, the sound of bolts being pulled, and suddenly—right there in front of me—was Archbishop Tomasek (later Cardinal)!

Apparently the upstairs of the Archbishop's House was a sort of "sanctuary" in the old sense because the Archbishop was very noncommittal, almost expressionless, as he led us up the stairs. But the moment we had all gathered in his little private chapel (much of the group, of course, overflowing outside the doors), what a change! The Archbishop embraced the Bishop of Fatima, and then looking at the statue with the most radiant joy he said:

"We bear the cross, but in the cross there is light, and in the light there is victory—and you have brought us the sign of our victory!"

There are few very tender moments that I remember in my life—like the meeting of the two brothers of St. Maria Goretti at that poor farm outside Naples, like my uncle being embraced by Padre Pio (the Fr. John of the book

The Brother and I) and like Bishop Venancio being kissed
on the top of his head by Patriarch Athenagoras.

But I think this moment, in the chapel of the Archbishop
of Prague, was one of the tenderest and most memorable
of all, if only because of the expressions which were
exchanged between the Bishop of Fatima and the
Archbishop of this first country behind the Iron Curtain
where an image of the Queen of the World was
delivered—to remain permanently as a "National Pilgrim
Virgin."

The common language was Italian, which both Bishops
spoke beautifully, but there was a communication far
deeper and warmer than that of any language.

Archbishop Tomasek told us that not only was there a
very strong devotion to Our Lady of Fatima in his country,
but that he did not believe there was a single Catholic
home in which the Rosary was not recited as Our Lady had
requested, in order to bring about the fulfillment of Her
promises at Fatima!

A few months later Czechoslovakia made a bid for
religious and political freedom—which was answered by
Russia with tanks—an outrage from which the Soviet
Union has never fully recovered in the eyes of world
opinion.

Oddly enough the very last statue of the twenty-four
statues to be delivered on this flight was to the United
States. Of course we had started from Fatima, where the
statues had been blessed the previous May 13 by Pope
Paul VI. Cardinal Carberry, who was then the Bishop of
Columbus, Ohio, had agreed to receive the Pilgrim Virgin
statue for the United States in that city. The municipal
auditorium was filled to overflowing, and Bishop Venancio
spoke beautifully of the wonders and triumphs of that
historic circling of the globe.

On our next trip we made a circle tour of Africa which,
of course, would be an impossibility today. The hammer
and sickle descended like a branding iron on a number of
countries in the Dark Continent only a few years later.
Satan, knowing his time was short, was certainly striving
to maximize his remaining years.

Archbishop Aurelius Sabattani, who had preceded
Archbishop Capovilla (former Secretary of Pope John
XXIII) as Archbishop of Loreto, accompanied us on this
flight. He is now the Vicar General of St. Peter's, and was

closely connected with the Vatican Secretariat of State—
and often it was the Papal Nuncio or Delegate, or representatives of the Papal Nuncio, meeting us at the various
airports. The highlight of the trip was certainly the
reception in Uganda, with crowds lining the road for miles
from the airport into the capital, which had recently been
visited by the Pope. Ethiopia was the only country where
the reception was less than what we had expected,
although the government put on a fantastic show for us
when the plane first landed. In almost every other
country, the crowds and enthusiasm far exceeded anything we had expected.

Thus, gradually, we were building up to the simultaneous coronation of Our Lady's statues around the world on
May 13, 1971, 25th anniversary of the original coronation
of Our Lady at Fatima as *Queen of the World*.

It is important to recall that in his encyclical *Ad Coeli
Reginam* Pius XII had said that in the doctrine of Mary's
Queenship "lies the world's greatest hope for peace."
And instituting the Feast of Mary's Queenship with an
encyclical the Pope proclaimed that throughout the world
a renewal be made, on that day, *of our consecration to the
Immaculate Heart of Mary.*

It is doubtful that this command of the Pope (and His
Holiness used the word "command") was ever obeyed.

In preparation, therefore, for this worldwide event, we
prepared a questionnaire based on the doctrine of Mary's
Queenship and offered a free place on the around-the-
world flight for the person who would score highest in that
questionnaire. It was translated into various languages,
and certainly did a great deal of good in educating persons
to this important doctrine, so relevant to our time.

I was in St. Peter's in 1954 when, over the tomb of St.
Peter, Pius XII placed a symbolic crown on that most
venerable image of Our Lady in the western world, the
Salus Populi Romani, and issued the encyclical. I jumped
within myself, somewhat as the Bishop of Fatima did when
Paul VI mentioned Fatima in Vatican Council II, as Pius
XII said:

"We single out for special mention the message We
broadcast to the people of Portugal on the occasion when
the miraculous image of the Virgin Mary, which is
venerated at Fatima, was crowned with a golden crown,
May 13, 1946. We called that broadcast the Message of

the *Royalty of Mary.*"

Pius XII really *meant* it when he sent a Cardinal Legate to Fatima in 1946 to crown the statue of Our Lady of Fatima as *"Queen of the World.*" Bishop Venancio told me on more than one occasion that one of his most vivid memories in the history of Fatima was the manner in which the Cardinal Legate said to him, when they met in Lisbon:

"The Pope said to me just before I left: *'Remember, Eminence, you are going to crown the Queen of the World.*'"

And now, with statues blessed by the Pope after his visit to Fatima in 1967, and after four years of major trips to every part of the world, we were ready for that worldwide act of recognition of Mary's Queenship in all of the major countries, including several behind the Iron Curtain (Czechoslovakia, Hungary, Poland, Russia).

By now the Soviets were furious. Certainly what had happened in Prague had not eased matters!

Is it any wonder that Pope Paul VI was under such great pressure to withhold any participation in this worldwide event, which the Soviets saw as an attack against world communism?

We may be inclined to wonder that atheists could harbor so much fear of a religious act—but of course we can see the effect of religion in Poland, where faith has given strength to face even the severest suffering rather than tolerate a continued atheistic oppression and denial of God.

The worldwide coronations were a spectacular success and most probably gained time for us beyond our knowing.

The very following year, as already told, we actually took the Pilgrim Virgin statue to Russia, and with 238 pilgrims celebrated Mass before the statue of Our Lady at the foot of the Odessa Steps where the first violent spark of the Soviet Revolution was ignited.

Our reasons for this were not just for the event itself, but to create *news.* I could not understand why, with all of these somewhat spectacular gestures, the secular press continued to ignore the Message of Fatima. It was like some diabolical conspiracy of silence. I felt that we just had to keep trying—just had to keep "doing things" so that we would create the opportunity for the world to get to know that God has sent His Mother in this dark hour of threatening atomic destruction to promise us the conversion of Russia and world peace for just a few very simple acts on our part.

The most recent of these efforts at the time of the writing of this book—and the only other one I will describe in any detail—was the 1978 Queen of the World flight. But I mention it now because Your Excellency will recall that letter *from Poland to the Vatican* protesting the action of Bishop Venancio in urging bishops all around the world to participate in a coronation of Our Lady of Fatima statues!

On the 1978 Peace Flight we had an inkling of what really happened. When we arrived in Warsaw on the Queen of the World flight, on May 5, 1978, it was a Russian officer wearing four stars who met us with armed guards on the tarmac and refused to let the Pilgrim Virgin statue leave the plane. The entire Catholic hierarchy of Poland were meanwhile gathered at the Shrine of Our Lady of Czestochowa where we had been scheduled to go with Our Lady's statue.

When we arrived at the great shrine, Cardinal Wyszynski sent for us and, even though communist guides were present, he told me in a very pointed way: *"Your letters never reached me."*

Peering at me closely to be sure I understood, the Cardinal repeated: *"Your letters never reached me."*

I knew the Cardinal could not be referring to the Queen of the World flight because we had informed His Eminence of this through personal messengers.

So could it have been that the communication from Poland in 1971, which caused me to feel so much grief when the Vatican forwarded it to Bishop Venancio, *was arranged by the Communists in Poland who intercepted the Cardinal's mail?*

Perhaps all this is suitable for reminding us that we are, as Cardinal Tisserant said so long ago and so well, "the Army of the Queen."

The great Cardinal Tisserant, one of the few clergymen in history to be a member of the French Academy and three times the interim head of the Church after he broke the Fisherman's Ring of three deceased Popes, in recommending the spread of the Blue Army throughout the world asked: *"Does not the Queen have need of an Army?"*

FOOTNOTE

1. See Chapter XIII; **Fatima: The Great Sign**; 1980, AMI Press, Washington, N.J.

Below: Monsignor Colgan with portrait of Cardinal Tisserant.

Chapter Twenty-Six

1) Each nation has its own role - 2) Vietnam's Blue Army - 3) Special recognition by the Pope - 4) Buddhist's testimony - 5) Visit of Our Lady reported in Vietnam - 6) Miracle reported in Vietnam - 7) Vietnamese Shrine - 8) Over 100,000 Blue Army martyrs in Vietnam

Below: A Blue Army procession in Saigon, Vietnam, before that city's fall to the Communists.

VIETNAM'S MISSION

"I saw a Lady in the sky bringing peace to Asia."
— Buddhist lady from Cambodia

The Queen of the World flight in 1978 was one of the most exciting events in our history—and says much about the hope for triumph of Our Lady as Queen of the World. The effect in Vietnam alone deserves another book.

The full story of the Blue Army will not *really* close until long after the conversion of Russia, the triumphant return of the Icon of Our Lady of Kazan to Her people, and even the conversion of the Mohammedans, since (as Archbishop Sheen felt) Our Lady had chosen to be known by the name of "Fatima" because of possible future implications for Islam.

But as time passes, and as we ourselves grow older, and hopefully, more understanding (perhaps even "enlightened"), it does seem that certain nations, like specific individuals, are often used by God in very special ways. 1

The more we see of the world, the more we are aware that we are all members of one family. We have our own national characteristics, our own national virtues and national sins. And we know from the revelations of Portugal that we also have our own national Guardian Angels. And we certainly have our own national saints and, regrettably, national renegades.

Someday, perhaps, each nation will write its own history of devotion to Mary, which would eminently include its own record of the growth, strength and ultimate victory of Our Lady's Blue Army.

How much we could write, for example, of Korea! During the Korean War, Father Matthew Strumski, a

Marine Corps Chaplain, wore out a pair of heavy military boots carrying the Pilgrim Virgin up and down the land! And how many ceremonies, how many All-Night Vigils were conducted by the Blue Army at the line between North and South Korea, often with the Pilgrim Virgin statue!

Subsequently, Fr. Anton Trauner got permission from his Bishop to dedicate his full time to establishing a national center of the Blue Army in Korea, and another priest was also released to assist in this work.

What a marvel, in a country which had so few priests that it had to bring in missionaries from other countries!

I must keep restraining myself from recalling the many glorious chapters that have been written in this Apostolate in the past thirty years lest the tale never end!

It seems to me that we must speak of the special "vocation" that seems to have fallen to Vietnam.

The chief organizer of the Blue Army in Vietnam was a Colonel Do Sinh Tu, who had learned about the Apostolate when he was training at Ft. Bragg, here in the United States.

As early as 1964, under the auspices of the Blue Army, thousands attended a Blue Army anniversary Mass in Saigon Basilica and Pope Paul VI sent his benediction to the Blue Army, addressed to the Archbishop of Saigon. The following year, during a lull in the meetings of the Ecumenical Council, the entire Vietnamese hierarchy, accompanied by the Archbishop of Saigon, flew from Rome to Fatima to place at the feet of Our Lady "our hearts, our prayers, our sacrifices."

And it would seem that Our Lady accepted this great national offering.

As mentioned in the previous chapter, Vietnam was responsible for the idea of a "National Pilgrim Virgin"—which also led, not only to the distribution of statues to nations around the world, but to the worldwide, simultaneous act of coronation in which the Pope himself finally participated on May 13, 1971.

Sixty Vietnamese pilgrims had come to Fatima under great hardship to be present on May 13, 1967 and to take their statue back with them.

How can we forget the special audience in Rome on May 24, eleven days later, when the Pope received them at the Vatican and commended them for their faith and prayed with them, through the Queen of Peace, for the peace for which they had already struggled and suffered for more than twenty years!

I remember that when we took the International Pilgrim Virgin to Vietnam the year before the communists overran the south, we were told that among the thousands of persons crowded along the highways greeting the statue there was not one family which had not lost a member in that terrible war.

Before we had come to Vietnam on that occasion, we had stopped in Japan and taken the statue to Hiroshima, where the first atomic bomb had brought instant death to tens of thousands.

Since it is customary in the Orient to give gifts, I acquired a plaque at Hiroshima bearing the famous inscription on a monument placed at Ground Zero. It reads: "Rest in peace. We shall not do this again."

I presented the plaque to Colonel Tu at a meeting in Saigon.

I remember saying that even as we should never use the atomic bomb again, so certainly we should never have a "limited war" again such as had brought so much suffering to this little nation which, like the people of Hiroshima, now offered itself *as a victim on the altar of God in the hope of turning back the terrible scourge of militant atheism* which Our Lady at Fatima had predicted would "spread... errors throughout the world, fomenting further wars."

At this time America had decided to withdraw her troops from Vietnam. There was a lull in the fighting; a strange "peace" had been arranged. China was now concerned with the withdrawal of American troops and the Russian presence, and no one quite knew what was going to happen. But certainly men like Colonel Tu, and the many thousands of all faiths who gathered together on that occasion to pray to God in a united manner for the first time in their 4,000 year history, finally recognized as few nations on earth have ever done *that they were all brothers under one Creator,* and that this dark struggle gradually engulfing the world *was basically between good and evil, between God and anti-God.*

Our stop after Saigon was in Bangkok, where the Blue Army was well established and where it has grown extensively since.

The Cathedral was filled to overflowing. Many people could not get in. One of my staff members was at the entrance of the Cathedral and because of his western appearance was approached by a woman who held a child by the hand and a bouquet of orchids in the other.

"Are you with the group that brought the statue?" she asked.

He said that he was.

4

"I am Buddhist," she said, "from Cambodia. I saw a Lady in the sky bringing peace to Asia and I did not understand what it meant. And then I saw in the newspapers about the statue coming to Saigon. When I saw the pictures of the statue—*it was the Lady I had seen in the sky!* I flew to Saigon to honor Her, but you had already left for Bangkok, so I came here. But I cannot get through the crowds, and I cannot remain. Would you be kind enough, sir, to place these flowers at Her feet?"

There were exactly thirty-three orchids which were then placed at Our Lady's feet, and which remained there until we next arrived at Agra, in India, where Archbishop Athaide, Metropolitan of North Central India, placed the orchids on the altar during Mass and asked all to join in prayers for the suffering people of Asia.

As we reflect on subsequent events in China (object of our next Peace Flight) where Our Lady is said to have appeared on a hill outside Shanghai (U.S. News and World Report, April 27, 1981), the "vision" seen by the Buddhist woman in Cambodia must have a glorious significance. She was "bringing peace to Asia." And "peace" for Mary is only that of which the angels sang over Bethlehem: the peace of Christ.

Because of the strength of the Blue Army in countries like Thailand, South Korea, Vietnam, I had the impression that there were many Catholics in these countries. But they are a very, very small percentage. The vast majority in Asia are pagan. And is it possible that the sincere and devoted members of the Blue Army in that area were being victims for a cause far greater than themselves, far greater even than their individual nations? We tend to think only of the "conversion of Russia" mentioned by Our Lady at Fatima, and forget that She spoke of the "triumph of my Immaculate Heart," and "an era of peace for *mankind*."

Shortly afterwards we received the sad—the terribly sad news following the withdrawal of the Americans: the Communists of the north had suddenly decided to move. They swiftly overran the south, wiping out all resistance before them in a matter of days.

Our Blue Army members, especially those who had been most active, were of course "marked men." Many were martyred.

Among those who suffered was an ex-soldier named Stephen Ho-Ngoc-Anh. Because of our difficulty with Vietnamese names, we will refer to him simply as Stephen.

A shrine had been built just outside Saigon at a place where the Pilgrim Virgin statue had stopped under unusual circumstances. There, he said, the Blessed Virgin appeared to him, cured him (he had been in a wheelchair, and hopelessly crippled after being tortured by the communists), and told him to return to this place, where She would appear to him again. She also gave him a secret to be disclosed on December 28, 1980. (As of the date of this writing, the "secret" Our Lady gave to Stephen has still not been revealed.)

And Our Lady prophesied that by that time great crowds would be thronging to the shrine.[1]

Bishop Venancio and I had been the guests of the Apostolic Delegate to Saigon, the Most Rev. Angelo Palmas, who later became the Apostolic Pro-Nuncio of Canada. Meeting him—not because of his office, but because of his saintliness—was one of those privileges one obtains in the service of Our Lady. This wonderful prelate said the entire fifteen decades of the Rosary daily, despite his many duties, and like Pope John XXIII (who did the same), he frankly attributed to this devotion, after his Mass and Office, the strength and light, not only for his personal life, but for his ecclesiastical duties.

I met the Archbishop at Fatima after we had learned the story of the apparitions and of Stephen's cure. The Archbishop's own secretary had gone to the Fatima Center outside Saigon to study the matter personally and to report back to the Apostolic Delegation.

"It is worthy of belief," the Archbishop told me.

Of course, a few of our Blue Army leaders escaped from Vietnam. Among them was Khong-Trung-Luu, former Secretary-General of the Vietnamese Blue Army. He was constantly working among refugees from Vietnam in the United States and receiving news through them.

Recently, one political prisoner who had escaped from Vietnam, and who had been a Buddhist, told the Vietnamese refugee priests:

"How could I resist embracing the Catholic Faith when I myself witnessed a miracle in the concentration camp?"

He had been in prison together with Stephen who, after his cure, had been preaching the power of Our Lady of Fatima and that She would free the Vietnamese! Predictably, he was arrested and subjected to further torture.

This refugee reported that the communists repeatedly struck Stephen with their fists, so that his face was disfigured in front of other prisoners. They would ask him: "How have you been cured?"

When he answered resolutely: "Our Lady cured me," the soldiers struck him even more fiercely.

It was reported that they moved Stephen from one prison to another, each time making a mockery of him.

And then one day—in the prison where this convert had witnessed what he now told—Stephen said that he had seen Our Lady and that She had said that in ten days, his bloodied and disfigured face would be cured.

Of course the communists thought that this was a way to prove beyond doubt that he was no "seer"—and that there was no Lady from Heaven.

(How similar to the torture of the children of Fatima at Ourem in August, 1917!)

Normally the prisoners were sent into the jungle for hard labor, but on this day, they let them all remain in the prison compound and ordered Stephen to stand on a high platform so that everyone could see his disfigured face, again recently bloodied.

Suddenly, according to this witness, the seer cried out—and all the wounds on his face disappeared!

This same refugee, who now presented himself to become a Catholic, reported that at the same moment, words appeared on a large blackboard in the camp, written by an invisible hand: *"Mesecuu Vietnam"* which means literally, *"Mama will save Vietnam."*

The former Buddhist prisoner said that he himself believed from that moment and began to pray to the heavenly "Mama." And he believes that he heard Her say "I will bring you out of jail."

6

He is now with his family in the United States and studying to be a Catholic.

The former Secretary-General of the Vietnamese Blue Army writes:

"Is it not significant that South Vietnam, after being abandoned by the world in 1975, has been blessed with repeated visitations of the Queen of the World, offering messages of national and universal importance? It was seen that Vietnam is witnessing a triumphant echo of Fatima. The place where the Pilgrim Virgin statue had rested (the truck bearing the statue stopped at that spot and would not move, despite efforts of mechanics, until a priest with the pilgrimage suddenly had the inspiration to promise Our Lady to build a shrine on that spot if She would enable Her statue to continue on its scheduled journey), has now become a radiant and defiant center of hope around which fifty million Vietnamese people have begun to gravitate, waiting for final liberation."

Mr. Luu reports further:

"The sufferings of which we hear in Vietnam today are innumerable and unbelievable. People are literally tortured, physically and spiritually. And I feel that we have been chosen, by Our Lady, to serve Her in a special way as a victim. I was in the army for 17 years and I never saw a Catholic soldier who did not have a rosary around his neck. We were more than 300,000 Catholics in the army, and all were enrolled in the Blue Army. Most of them are now in concentration camps. My own brother was sentenced to death. He said seven Rosaries a day in the camp, and he was martyred on a hill outside because he resisted all efforts by the communists to dissuade him from the practice of his Faith."

Khong-Trung-Luu also reports that in a different apparition Our Lady spoke of Herself as the "general commander" of the Vietnamese Blue Army, to whom She gave Her *pledge* as Her *"instructions"* to Her troops.

He reports Our Lady also to have said: "Everything is happening in compliance with the mystical Will of God. You have Almighty God, full of mercy, and His Most Holy Mother and the great St. Joseph to take pity on you and to protect you. My children, you must adore the Supreme Mind and the holy mystical Will of God...." And over and over was the Message of Fatima repeated.

"Repent, and amend your lives. Pray the Rosary diligently. Be consecrated to My Immaculate Heart."

Is it too early to speak of this recent development of Blue Army history in such detail?

The Blue Army Shrine in Vietnam, at which Stephen was cured, grew out of the incident just previously mentioned (when the float carrying Our Lady's statue had stopped inexplicably.)

7

Fr. Vu Van Bo may have intended to build a small monument there. But the Fatima Center which rose out of that vast area located on the west side of National Highway 13 soon became a leading shrine for the whole of Vietnam. A huge statue of Our Lady of Fatima was erected on the border of the river and a profusion of favors were granted there, especially to non-Catholics!

The former Secretary-General of the Vietnamese Blue Army writes:

"I lived one mile from the Shrine, so I had the privilege of participating in Saturday pilgrimage devotions and of attending Sunday Mass each week, celebrated at the foot of the marvelous and beautifully impressive statue. Every Saturday and Sunday, Fr. Bo had a long list of 'extraordinary graces' to read which were reported daily not only by the faithful, but also by the Buddhist population, including monks who had begun to refer to Our Lady under the familiar title of 'Mother Maria Fatima.'"

Stephen is said to have had his first apparition of Our Lady when we took the Pilgrim Virgin statue to Vietnam in February, 1974. It was actually when he saw the statue that it seemingly came alive with tears streaming from her eyes.

He had been a paratrooper and after being dropped in North Vietnam, he was captured by the communists and severely tortured by the Vietcong in their effort to obtain military information. He drew his consolation and strength from saying the Rosary, using his knuckles instead of beads.

He got back to South Vietnam in an exchange of sick prisoners, completely broken in health, his legs paralyzed. A wheelchair was his only transportation, yet every day he made a five-mile trip to the Fatima Shrine.

When South Vietnam was overrun on April 30, 1975, Stephen was ordered to dig a large and deep ditch in front of the main gate of the hospital in which he was residing.

He had to drive his wheelchair to the spot, and using the strength of his arms, had only partially completed the work when he accidentally fell into the hole and lay there all night. The next morning, the communists found their victim half dead in the ditch. They drove him away.

His condition was now much worse; not only was he unable to walk, but he could not speak.

He wrote on a piece of paper when Our Lady is said to have appeared to him, that he was going to be cured at a given time at the Fatima Shrine. Of course he was not believed, but the cure took place. And then he could speak, and he said that Our Lady would come back on the 14th of each month at 10 o'clock in the morning.

Khong-Trung-Luu believes that Vietnam has given the Church over 100,000 martyrs. Besides this terrible, yet glorious, record of suffering, the country has more than a half a million war orphans, and millions of invalids.

It was seen that having been gradually strengthened in their Faith, the Vietnamese—like the children of Fatima—have been able to respond generously to those first and most important words of Our Lady:

"Will you be willing to accept whatever God will send you, and to offer it up for the conversion of sinners and in reparation for the offenses committed against the Immaculate Heart of Mary?"

Should this not also cause those Americans who fought beside the Vietnamese for so many years, many of them with faith, to reevaluate their role?

Can we expect to see the conversion of Russia, and the turning back of the tide of evil, the crushing of the head of the infernal serpent, without paying a price?

Your Excellency will recall my saying once that to me, one of the most touching events in the history of Fatima, and the spot where I have most poignantly felt the urgency and seriousness of Our Lady's message, was at Valinhos in Fatima, where Our Lady spoke to the three children on August 15, after they had been released from prison, having preferred death in a vat of boiling oil rather than deny Her.

And instead of consoling them, Our Lady said:

"Continue to pray and to make sacrifices. Many souls are lost because there is no one to pray and to make sacrifices for them."

8

Is this not a degree of heroism to which many Blue Army members must feel that they are called?

An army is for battle—and we cannot expect our Queen to have Her victory over Satan and to bring about an era of peace "for mankind" without suffering.

In this regard, one of the earliest bishops to promote the Blue Army in his diocese has recently taken a leadership role in promoting the Message of Fatima among the handicapped and invalid. He is Bishop Constantino Luna, formerly a missionary in China, and then a bishop in Guatemala. Stephen was such a handicapped person, who not only accepted what God had sent to him, but despite all the other sufferings heaped upon him, constantly affirmed his faith, like the children of Fatima. In the face of unspeakable torment, he steadfastly refused to deny God and His Mother!

Oh, that more of us could be like him! Then indeed would Our Lady's Blue Army be an Army worthy of Her!

FOOTNOTES

1. See SOUL Magazine issues of July-August and September-October 1977, January-February 1978, March-April 1979, November-December 1980, and March-April 1981.

Below: Bishop Luna (who succeeded Bishop Venancio in 1981 as International President of the Blue Army), speaking to the handicapped and suffering at the Blue Army Shrine in Washington, N. J.

Below: A part of the crowd that took part in the open-air Mass
behind Saigon Cathedral. At the right front, carrying the statue
of Our Lady, is Col. Do Sinh Tu, president of the Vietnamese
Blue Army. The banners say: "The victorious Mother has shown
the way; love will rebuild our country in peace," and "Mother,
listen to our prayer: stop the war and give peace and joy to all."

Chapter Twenty-Seven

1) World forgetting meaning of sin - 2) Our Lady of Fatima says to "teach catechism" - 3) Today we must *know*—Our Lady of Fatima as Catechist - 4) At Fatima, entire Gospel affirmed - 5) "So that all may believe" - 6) Blue Army Cadets - 7) Father Fox takes youth to Fatima: "Jesus wishes to use you"

Below: Msgr. Colgan and John Haffert look on as Angelo Goretti, older brother of the Saint, signs Blue Army pledge.

CATECHISM AND CADETS

"Continue to teach the children Catechism..."
— *Our Lady of Fatima to Brother Aranguen at*
moment of miraculous cure

The former Secretary-General of the Vietnamese Blue
Army, whose escape to America made it possible for
us to know the ongoing, often heroic suffering of Blue
Army members in his nation, believes that they have been
chosen by God as victims for the sins of Asia, and perhaps
for the sins of the world.

We know that glorious victim souls like Alexandrina[1],
with boundless love and faith, held back the justice of God
from entire nations.

But what about *the legacy of nations*—the legacy of war
passed down from generation to generation as though to
give franchise for Satan's rule over them and over us?

It is we, as well as our predecessors, who made it
possible for Our Lord to say that Satan, the prince of darkness, was the ruler of this world. He had the power to take
Our Lord to the pinnacle of the Temple to show Him all
the nations of the world, and then offered them in return
for being adored.

And finally when the Woman destined to crush the head
of the serpent comes and promises ''an era of peace to
mankind'' through ''the triumph of my Immaculate
Heart,'' who is to make sufficient reparation for the
realization of this triumph?

On that radiant day, when the great era of peace and the
reign of Christ will have dawned upon earth, then we will
have a totally different perspective of history. Nations like
Russia, Poland, Hungary, Korea and Vietnam may shine
like brilliant stars in the crown of the Queen of Peace.

So much of mankind has already been ''taken over'' by

Satan that many people have forgotten the meaning of sin. Even among Catholics, the sense of sin is steadily being lost. Many no longer go to confession, saying, "But I have not committed any sins. I have not hurt anyone. I am living according to my conscience."

But while forgetting sin, the world is becoming more and more aware of war! A first world war, towards the end of which Our Lady came at Fatima, and then a second world war which She had prophesied if men did not listen to Her and finally the threat of atomic war in which Her even more terrible prophecy might be realized: *"Various nations will be annihilated."*

And while the world was forgetting sin but becoming increasingly obsessed with war and the threat of a global holocaust, Our Lady had said quite simply in 1917: "Sin is the *cause* of war!"

I realize, dear Bishop, that in complying with your request to write my recollections of the Blue Army, I would not be expected to analyze the Message of Our Lady of Fatima, even though the Blue Army exists to live and to promote that message.

But I feel it important to stress most strongly that Our Lady also came to Fatima as a Catechist, to reaffirm the basic doctrines of our Faith, especially those which are being undermined or attacked today.

As mentioned earlier, there have been two apparitions of Our Lady of Fatima *since Her appearances from 1917-1929*, both of which have been recognized by the local ecclesiastical authorities as "worthy of belief."

The first was to Stephen Ho-Ngoc-Anh, described in the last chapter, and the other was to a Jesuit catechist in Bogota, Colombia.

His family name was Aranguen, and he was an elderly man teaching catechism in the steaming jungles to the south of Bogota. He developed a cancer of the tongue, and was brought to the city for an operation. Hoping to save the tongue so the Brother would be able to continue his work, the doctors excised only a part of it, but soon the Brother was back with the cancer spreading, and they decided that the entire tongue would have to be excised.

The night before the operation Our Lady reportedly appeared to him, touched and cured him, and then said:

"Continue to teach Catechism, and teach them to say the Rosary. Do not tell this to anyone until you tell the

doctor.''

The next morning when they came to prepare him for the operation, he did not speak but with signs he declined the anesthetic. They insisted, but he emphatically refused the waiting needle.

When the doctor arrived, the anesthetist said in exasperation, "Doctor, he won't let us give the anesthetic."

Thinking that the Brother had decided to let the cancer spread and take his life rather than deprive him of speech, the doctor began to argue about the importance of prolonging his life. And then the Brother spoke.

To the doctor's stupefaction, not only had the cancer disappeared, but the previously excised part of the tongue had been completely and perfectly restored!

There is a plaque in the room of the Jesuit College in Bogota commemorating this.

Br. Aranguen lived on for many more years, singing the praises of Our Lady, the power and importance of Her Rosary, *and teaching catechism to the children.*

It is noteworthy that in the appearance of Our Lady of Fatima in Vietnam, Her very first message was almost identical to the message given to Br. Aranguen: *"The Rosary and Catechism!''*

On August 13, 1980, Frank Sheed, who is perhaps the greatest lay theologian of our time, delivered a lecture at the Shrine of the Immaculate Heart of Mary at the Blue Army's U.S. National Center, in the course of which he repeatedly stressed:

"In earlier times it was perhaps not so necessary to know the reasons for one's faith because life was simpler, and faith alone was often sufficient. But this is no longer true. Now faith is being challenged on every side and ignorance becomes a danger to faith. Now, more than ever, we must *know...''*

One of the best general books on doctrine I have ever read is Frank Sheed's *Map of Life*, and I often chuckle at those words he wrote in the preface and marvel at their wisdom: "If anyone knows less theology than I, it is not enough!"

Many leading churchmen, including Archbishop Sheen, have regarded Our Lady of Fatima as the Woman of the Apocalypse. They see Her in the awesomeness of the Miracle of the Sun—the first miracle in recorded history at a predicted time and place "so that everyone may believe" and they think of Her world-shaking promises, and Her glorious promise of triumph.

3   But when you listen to every word She spoke, and the words spoken by the angels who were sent before Her, you realize that *above everything else, Our Lady of Fatima is a Catechist.*

Even without referring to Lucia's Memoirs, one can easily list the essential doctrines which are affirmed by Her and by the angels.

The greatest emphasis of all, of course, was on the Eucharist. She chose to appear on May 13, which Pope St. Pius X had made, as a result of the teachings of St. Peter Julian Eymard, the "Feast of Our Lady of the Blessed Sacrament." Her first "miracle" occurred that very day when She let rays of light *shine from Her hands* upon the three children, enveloping them and causing them to feel "lost in God," Whom they recognized in that light. And in a transport of love and adoration, they prostrated themselves and cried out:

"O Most Holy Trinity, I adore You! My God, my God, I love You in the Most Blessed Sacrament!"

4   Your Excellency knows that I wrote a book solely about this one aspect of the Fatima Message. (How many books could be written about the other doctrines which Our Lady reaffirmed!)

That one book took seven years to write—not so much because of the research, but in trying to find appropriate, simple words to convey the reality which Our Lady conveyed in that light streaming from Her hands.

The average person cannot expect to have Our Lady appear and envelop him in a heavenly light, and reveal to him *what he is supposed to learn through the normal processes of Catechism!*

The ordinary light from the Immaculate Heart of Mary to each of us is in Her words. That is why Bishop Venancio caused all the words of the angels and of Our Lady, as narrated in the Memoirs of Lucia, to be printed in one small booklet, which he freely allowed to be published throughout the world. The Blue Army of the United States distributed tens of thousands of these booklets. It is recommended that every one of its cells be "armed" with Our Lady's words, as set down by Lucia, *and to read from them at every meeting.*

I do not know, dear Bishop, whether it is an obligation

of members of the Blue Army to teach Catechism. This would be for the teaching authority of the Church to decide. But I do know, beyond any doubt, that it is an essential obligation for members of Our Lady's Blue Army *to teach themselves*, to listen to their Queen! To listen to Her who formed this Army in order to bring about the triumph of Her Immaculate Heart in the world and who "gives Her orders" — as She is reported to have said in Vietnam — *through the pledge, and through all the words She spoke at Fatima*, so that we might understand the formula of holiness which She has proclaimed to us.

I have mentioned only one point of doctrine — the Eucharist — and already paragraphs have spilled out. Without intending to place them in an order of importance, but just as they come to mind, other points of doctrine which Our Lady confirmed at Fatima are:

The doctrine of the Holy Trinity; that Jesus is present Body, Blood, Soul and Divinity in the Blessed Sacrament; that it is fitting to offer Our Lord in the Blessed Sacrament to the Holy Trinity in reparation for the outrages, sacrileges, and indifferences by which He is offended; the need to sanctify our actions; to accept what God will send us; to *repair* for sin; the existence of Purgatory; and that even some persons who seem to have led good lives could be there until the end of the world unless they are relieved by the prayers and sacrifices of souls on earth.

Our Lady gave a special emphasis to the existence of hell, and the fact that *many* souls are lost. At a time when most people think it wrong to speak to children of such things, *Our Lady showed it to them!* And it was so frightening that little Jacinta cried out after it was over:

"O Lucia, if Our Lady had not been there, I would have died of fright!"

Again, in anticipation of the present crisis of Faith, Our Lady reaffirmed the importance of the teaching authority of the Church and the role of the Vicar of Her Son, the Pope. And long before Vatican II — when we never heard of "collegiality" and the importance of the bishops acting *together with the Pope*, Our Lady said that it was God's Will that the ultimate condition for the conversion of Russia should rest upon the decision of the Holy Father together with all the bishops of the world. Imagine! That for which the sacrifices of nations, the prayers and sacrifices of millions, was required — ultimately rested, for the moment of victory, upon the free decision of the Pope together with all the bishops!

Until the time of Fatima, Satan had cloaked himself in silence and was winning perhaps his greatest victories because people no longer believed in him. But at Fatima Our Lady unmasked him—and since then the evidence of Satan has been seen in the world like that of a snake—lying quietly in ambush in the grass and striking at will *until stamped on!*

The world had also forgotten that there were *good angels* and that each of us has one of these luminous beings appointed as our personal guardian, and that even nations have a guardian angel. (The angel who appeared to the children in the summer of 1916 identified himself as "the Guardian Angel of Portugal." As far as we know, up to that time Portugal was the only nation in the world which had a feast day honoring its national Guardian Angel. Subsequently the Blue Army in the United States, at the suggestion of a priest from Portugal who had written a book about the Guardian Angel of that country, and of the importance of angels to mankind, established a monument to the National Guardian Angel of the United States at our Shrine in Washington, N.J.)

And confession! The world was forgetting the seriousness of sin. Churches were filled with people, almost all of whom were going to Communion, but only one or two hours were allotted in a parish each week to hear all the confessions—confessions which were never made!

After all, if there was no sin, if one did all that was necessary by following the guidance of one's conscience, what need was there for confession?

Our Lady made it one of the essential prerequisites for Her great promise of Her special assistance at the hour of death that we go to confession once a month on five consecutive First Saturdays *whether we have sinned or not.*

One could go on and on.... There was *not one* important doctrine of our Faith which Our Lady did not reaffirm in Her apparitions at Fatima—at the same time performing the first miracle in history at a predicted time and place *"so that all may believe."*

On the crucial subject of sin and the importance of confession, I decided to write the book *Sex and the Mysteries.* I felt (as I have dared to say before) that the volume, and my books on the Eucharist (*The World's*

Greatest Secret) and on the Scapular (*Sign of Her Heart*) are the ones I would like to see every Blue Army member read. They are not so much the product of work as an endeavor to seek light from the Immaculate Heart of Mary, like that which shone upon the children during the first apparition, that it might be imparted to all. (Your Excellency remembers that during the writing of *The World's Greatest Secret* I enlisted the prayers of many who had read my previous books, more than 200 of whom offered daily Mass and Communion during the entire last two years that this book was being produced.)

These three books (as I do not seem to tire of repeating!) are a trilogy, even though written at different times and in different ways. They explain *the most important parts* of the Fatima Message: the Scapular and the Rosary to help us to sanctify our daily actions, and thus make reparation to the Sacred Heart of Jesus, beating for us in every tabernacle, and coming to unite with us in each Communion.

Msgr. Colgan and all of us were continually conscious of the imperative need of the Catechism, and of bringing the Apostolate of Fatima to children. We kept reaffirming that Our Lady had appeared to *children*—children who were only six, eight and nine years of age when the angels came to them, and seven, nine and ten years of age when they received the great revelations of Fatima.

6

In the Old Testament when the doctrines of faith were affirmed to mankind, God appeared to the great leader and prophet—Moses.

But in our day, God sends not a prophet, but the Queen of Prophets, His own Mother—and the message is given to children!

We have already spoken of the great work of Fr. Robert J. Fox, who founded the Blue Army Cadets during a national meeting at the Blue Army Center in Detroit, in July of 1975. He had been invited to head a seminar to organize an apostolate for youth under the wing of the adult Blue Army, and all who attended (including myself) were immediately convinced that this was something not only for which we had been longing, but which was finally a practical way of involving young people in the Message of Fatima—which we had never before done successfully.

I offered at once to add eight pages to SOUL Magazine which would be dedicated exclusively to this program and asked Fr. Fox if he would come to a national meeting of all the Blue Army leaders scheduled for that August in Washington, N.J., and which would be attended by our International President, Bishop Venancio.

The Bishop and the attending leaders warmly endorsed the project and helped select the title for the book upon which Fr. Fox had been working: *Catholic Truth for Youth.* Sr. Mary Celeste, A.M.I., was appointed as national coordinator for the Youth Program. She undertook the monumental task of editing that book, which has become the cornerstone of the Cadet Program not only in America but in many other parts of the world.

Next Fr. Fox wrote a 512-page book, *Saints and Heroes Speak; A Prayer Book for Young Catholics;* and *The Marian Catechism* (which sold out its first 10,000 copies in less than six months and has been repeatedly reprinted).

These books fill an enormous gap in Catholic literature for young people, and soon the books were being used in CCD programs and in Catholic schools, often without the realization that they were essentially and originally intended for the Blue Army Cadet Apostolate.

Sr. Mary Celeste, from the national office, next produced a coloring book for the "little ones" to teach the "Catechism" basics of the Fatima Message.

When a slogan for the youth program was being sought, some of the leaders at the National Center decided to go through the actual words spoken by Our Lady of Fatima. When they opened the Memoirs of Lucia they came immediately upon the words of Our Lady to the ten-year-old Lucia: *"Jesus wishes to use you..."*

Fr. Fox recalls that when he himself made a pilgrimage to Fatima in 1974, he found himself repeatedly asking Our Lady at the Capelinha what Lucia had asked: "What do you want of me?"

"There at the place where Our Lady had appeared," Fr. Fox narrates, "I received the conviction to teach the fullness of the Catholic Faith for youth in loyalty to the Magisterium by means of the Message of Fatima."

At a meeting of leaders of the Blue Army from all over the world at Fatima in 1978, Fr. Fox explained the Cadet Apostolate, and it was resolved to include the Youth Apostolate in the international statutes of the Blue Army.

By 1981, over one thousand young people had made a trip from the United States to Fatima for "Youth Retreats" and Cadet Prayer Cells began to mushroom across the United States and throughout the world.

In 1979 Fr. Fox was received in audience by Pope John Paul II and received from the Holy Father a special blessing on the Cadet Program of the Blue Army.

FOOTNOTE

1. Alexandrina Maria da Costa, whose cause for beatification has been entered in Rome, lived at Balazar, Portugal from 1904 to 1955, as a victim for man's sins. Additional information on this amazing Portuguese mystic available from AMI Press, Washington, N.J. 07882 (**The Miracle of Alexandrina**) and from Veritas Publications, Dublin, Ireland (**Alexandrina: The Agony and the Glory**).

Below: Fr. Robert J. Fox, National Cadet Director in the U.S. with the Handmaids of Mary Immaculate. Next to Father at right is Sr. Mary Grace, A.M.I., and at left are Sr. Mary Joseph, A.M.I. and Sr. Mary Celeste, A.M.I.

Chapter *Twenty-Eight*

1) Blue Army now major deterrent to atheism - 2) Communist strategy against the Blue Army - 3) Our answer: More holiness

Bishop Venancio carries the Icon of Kazan: "Are we not soldiers...?"

OUR IMPLACABLE FOE

"I shall place enmities between you and the Woman, your seed and her seed." — *Gen. 3:15*

When the Pilgrim Virgin statue was unveiled in a se-curity van at Warsaw airport on May 4, 1978, to the uncomfortable gaze of Russian officials, one would have thought the cover was being lifted from a hydrogen bomb.

This fear of the statue of Our Lady by the deputies of Russia was not only due to the power of the "Queen of the World" in Poland...but also to the incalculable effect which devotion to Her has in every part of the world, especially under the title of "Our Lady of Fatima" as promoted by Her Blue Army.

The communists have long been fully aware of this mortal threat to their godless ideology. The official voice of world militant atheism, *Science and Religion*, with a circulation of almost half a million copies, sets down important guidelines for the world communist movement. In the issue just preceding the Golden Jubilee of the Soviet Revolution in October, 1967, this magazine analyzed *why* the atheist revolution *had not yet succeeded* worldwide after fifty years. It concluded that there were *three main reasons*:

1) Hitler's attack on Russia in World War II which set back the communists' plans for decades;

2) The Cold War which followed World War II;

3) Fatima, and the Blue Army.

With Nazism and the destruction of World War II long past and with the "thaw" in the Cold War, the only major deterrent remaining to the global triumph of communism is, according to the Russians' own admission, The Blue Army of Our Lady of Fatima.

In 1978, the year the Pilgrim Virgin statue arrived in Poland, Russia spent two *billion* dollars on propaganda in the West. Much of it, we must presume, was channelled into insidious propaganda against Fatima and the Blue Army.

How was it done?

2   Well, suppose the reader were in charge of Soviet propaganda and wanted to destroy the Blue Army in Spain, for instance. How would one spend the millions of dollars allotted to this specific goal in this particular country?

Enormous funds placed at the disposal of the Communist Party in Spain by Moscow *were actually used* to stop the Blue Army by:

1) Well placed agents *to influence the bishops directly;*

2) Pressure for freedom for the Communist Party, as dependent of Russia, as a form of Christian socialism rather than atheist Marxism;

3) Propaganda in the right places to make this convincing;

4) Every major happening to call attention to Fatima countered with something to undermine Fatima.

In 1971 a book appeared in Portugal called *Fatima Unmasked.* If was full of half-truths and outright lies written so convincingly, and with so many details, that anyone who read it and did not know the truth would probably think Fatima the biggest socio-religious fake of all time. This book was translated and widely diffused in Europe. It attacked the Blue Army in particular as a "farce" perpetrated by the Catholic Church and the American CIA.

But the communists must surely realize, from a quarter century of bitter experience, that they cannot defeat the holiness and the powerful effects of that holiness brought about by Our Lady. Hence they resort to subtle innuendo, by raising doubts in the minds of bishops (because they know that Blue Army members are obedient and do nothing without the approval of the bishop of a diocese).

But at the same time *is it not remarkable that the militant atheists are so concerned about the Blue Army,* which is nothing more than *an Apostolate of holiness?*

In an address to the Blue Army leaders at Fatima on August 21, 1978, Fr. Reginald Simonin, O.P., a French Dominican, gave a major address on the scurrilous book mentioned above and said:

"We who believe that the Devil will be overcome by Mary...we who believe in the triumph of Her Immaculate Heart announced at Fatima which will lead to the conversion of Russia and a time of peace for mankind...are neither surprised nor disconcerted to see Fatima and the Blue Army attacked by the enemies of the Church."

The French edition of the book entitled *Fatima: Inquiry into an Imposture*, although skillfully written, is a violent attack against the Blue Army and Fatima. Its appearance coincided with an article *Fatima: The Miracle is a Lie*, published in a leading Spanish periodical. Fr. Simonin saw in this simultaneous publication *the evidence of an internationally directed attack.*

Such a carefully prepared anti-religious offensive is not only directed against Fatima but against the Church. Obviously if the Fatima miracle is false, the Church has either made a grave mistake or has indeed perpetrated a monstrous trick on the believing world.

The French book says "the imposture" is not only that of Fatima, but of all Catholicism...and especially of Pope Pius XII, the "Pope of Fatima," and of Pope Paul VI who went to Fatima in declaration of his belief in Fatima before all the world.

Father Hans Albert Reul, Blue Army leader of Germany, responded to the attacks published in his country by publishing a German edition of *Meet the Witnesses*, a book on the miracle of Fatima as seen through the testimony of eyewitnesses, which had already been published in Portuguese and Spanish after its first printing by the Blue Army in the United States in 1960.

"But what is needed most of all," said the Most Rev. John Venancio, while Bishop of Fatima and International President of the Blue Army, "is a continued growth in the application of Fatima's message of holiness." His Excellency stressed that the wave of evil sweeping over the world cannot be turned back in any other way than by *a counterwave of holiness.*

In a major message to the world about the Blue Army in 1965, Bishop Venancio said that the forces of evil must indeed recognize it as the Queen's Army even though its only weapons are the Rosary and the Scapular, because an army of evil can be overcome only by an army of holiness. And in his most recent address to the Blue Army leaders of the world at Fatima on August 14, 1978, the Bishop said:

"Are we not soldiers? What do I say? We are, in the Church, those responsible for the glorious Blue Army of Our Lady! Let us then behave as such! Let us act as Commanders-in-Chief of this Army which must be led to victory so that, as soon as possible, we may behold the triumph of the Immaculate Heart of Mary...."

Photographed in July, 1981, just before the Blue Army elections in which Bishop Venancio retired and Bishop Luna was elected to succeed him are, left to right:

Rev. Pietro Leoni, S.J., who was a prisoner in Siberia for thirteen years and in 1981 was asked by the International Council of the Blue Army to serve as President of the apostolate in Canada;

The Most Rev. Jerome Hastrich, Bishop of Gallup and President of the Blue Army in the United States;

Most Rev. John Venancio, former Bishop of Fatima and International President of the Blue Army;

Rev. Dr. Andre Richard, of Paris, President of the Blue Army of France.

Below: Blue Army delegates to international meeting leave the
Blue Army International Center for ceremonies in the sanctuary
of Fatima, which begins at fence.

Chapter *Twenty-Nine*

1) Example of disunity in Canada - 2) Greatest unity on
edges of Communist countries - 3) Tribute to U.S. apostles - 4) An apostate - 5) Danger of disobedience -
6) Laity must be formed - 7) Deacons and Blue Army
Cells of Holiness

Below: The Basilica of Fatima today.

AMONG THE APOSTLES

"And one of the twelve was Judas."

I t is axiomatic, and I think recognized by Blue Army
members all over the world, that Satan will not stand
by idly and allow their continued growth without confront-
ing them with fierce, sometimes ferocious, resistance. It is
far easier for him to prevent a Blue Army organization
from developing, with its cells of holiness, than to stop
that march of holiness once it is on its way.

It took thirty years in the United States before we were
able to hold elections of national officers, as mandated by
the international statutes which had been in force almost a
quarter century!

Development of the Apostolate in Canada and England   1
has been even more disappointing.

Apparently the difficulty in Canada was that we had
appointed a man who lived in Ottawa as temporary leader
of the Blue Army. We failed to consider that most
Canadian Catholics lived in Quebec, and many of them
were not ready to cooperate with the "English" capital.

But this was simplistic. The real reasons ran far deeper.

We sent the Pilgrim Virgin statue to Canada, and
instead of uniting the forces of Our Lady's Blue Army
there, it caused another branch to develop.

Poor Canada! We have six thousand Blue Army
crusaders there who get their materials from our U.S.
Center, and I believe that Canada would explode for Our
Lady if Satan were not so effective in playing upon the
threads of pride in a few individual crusaders who present
themselves to become leaders.

When these frictions happen, the bishops become reluctant to "take sides" — and reluctant to have anything to do with an apostolate which lacks the essential marks of unity and charity. This is certainly the view that Satan wants to create, even though this is only on the surface. But there comes a sudden glorious moment when the Heart of Our Lady triumphs among Her own leaders and apostles, and the unity and charity *are* there — and the Army is mustered and once again begins its victorious advance, using the weapons of Rosary and Scapular.

I am sure Your Excellency does not want me to go into the details of the history of the Apostolate in every country. It would take volumes to record the saga of so much toil and sacrifice.

2

As can be imagined, the greatest success of the Apostolate is in countries that are closest to the Iron and Bamboo Curtains — closest to the reality of that which was foretold by Our Lady: "Error will spread from an atheist Russia throughout the entire world, fomenting further wars; the good will be martyred..."

There the reality brings unity.

But in areas where the *terrible reality* of the world situation, and the thrilling reality of Fatima, are not sufficiently felt, an apostolate like the Blue Army is too often a "hobby," a "side attraction" of life, a mode of expression for some who lead an otherwise dull existence. There are too few real saints who don't have to be faced with martyrdom to defend their Faith.

The major apostles of our Apostolate all over the world seem to me to be pretty equally divided between laity and clergy — although of course lay persons are usually the only ones who can devote their full time because most priests are taken up with pastoral obligations as well.

I have already mentioned Abbe Richard in Paris, Fr. Fuhs in Germany, Msgr. Strazzacappa in Italy. These were the *major* leaders of the Apostolate in their countries, although aided by outstanding lay persons like Madame Sevenet in Paris, whose husband was killed in the first world war and whose only son was killed in the second. (I will not be surprised if the French Blue Army builds a monument to her.)

Nuns of course have played a superb role — like Sr. Mary Miranda, here in the U.S., and communities dedicated to the Blue Army, such as the Handmaids of Mary Immaculate and the Sisters of the Immaculate Heart in Italy under the direction of Mother Ludovica.

Among lay persons who have "left all' and worked full time in the Apostolate in America, we should cite Louis Kaczmarek and Alfred Williams, with the Pilgrim Virgin statues of Our Lady, and Martha Loya, whom we have already mentioned, journeying all over the country, and speaking in schools from coast to coast. And there is Toni Cormier, who became my assistant at the National Center, Mary Ortman in Los Angeles, Vivian Maslanka, first head of the Blue Army in the Chicago Archdiocese (the most effective and successful diocesan division in the country) and later the first regional delegate of the Blue Army in the country...*and so many others!*

I hesitate to begin mentioning the priests—for fear of minimizing anyone. Fr. Thomas Gildea, C.SS.R., for example, who was primarily responsible for establishing the Legion of Mary throughout Puerto Rico where it is gloriously flourishing, obtained permission from his superiors to dedicate himself full time to the development of the Blue Army. Fr. John Engler, of the Allentown Diocese, who gave up his parish and took an early retirement to serve as Chaplain of the National Blue Army Center, is another. Fr. Richard Ciurej took a year off from his parish in the Archdiocese of Omaha, and so on. And how many other priests, in addition to their pastoral duties, work for and promote the Blue Army not only in their own areas, but in the media, among youth, overseas, in the mission fields—wherever Our Lady's message can be proclaimed, resulting in such brilliant achievements as those of Fr. Robert Fox, who has added new luster to the Blue Army's name and prestige.

Normally those who dedicate themselves to the Apostolate of Our Lady of Fatima are faithful to that apostolate, and remain steadfast, obedient sons of the Church. Indeed I know of only one exception, of which we have spoken very little through the years because it is difficult to understand—difficult to criticize. When someone leaves, the feeling is that we should follow with charity and love and prayer, trusting for their return.

I speak of Francis Schuckardt, who was one of the most promising organizers of the Apostolate. He gave it his full time, traveling extensively in the western United States.

His spiritual director was known far and wide as a "saint": the Claretian, Fr. Aloysius Ellacuria.

In those days, our only requirement for the endorsement of a "leader" was a letter from a priest saying he knew that person and would be responsible.

It was not until too late that Fr. Ellacuria wrote and told us that Francis was straying—*that he was not being obedient.* We did not know the circumstances. We at once wrote and told him that either he must obey his spiritual director or stop using the name of the Blue Army.

He readily agreed—not to use the Blue Army name.

So we did not denounce him. And we watched with deep sadness when he began to denounce the Church authority and join the extremist reactionaries in the wake of Vatican Council II. Many people, and many bishops, still associated him with the Blue Army because he still referred to the "Fatima Apostolate." The harm caused by his group to our Apostolate throughout the United States, and even beyond, can hardly be measured.

5

Necedah, the place of an unapproved and condemned apparition, has caused us problems—as have similar alleged apparitions in other countries, such as Palma de Troya in Spain and Ladeira in Portugal. For this reason we stress *obedience, obedience, obedience.* Where there is no obedience, Satan is the victor.

It is only through these false apparitions that Satan can get at our really *good* people. Because they are believing, and because they are ready to reach out for whatever seems to confirm their faith, they can be ensnared by Satan and little by little drawn into disobedience. It is a fateful, deadly trap.

The problem is compounded because there are alleged apparitions which have not yet been approved by the Church, and which at the same time are confused with apparitions which *are* condemned.

The Blue Army has adopted a policy that no Blue Army members, as such, can promote *any* apparition which is *not* approved.

This would not mean that they were disobedient, or doing anything wrong if, as individuals, they were to study and indeed promote apparitions which the Church still holds under investigation, such as Garabandal.

On this important point, in his first message to the U.S. Blue Army after becoming its president, Bishop Hastrich said:

"I see the Blue Army as a conservator of the true teachings of the Church today. There are two dangers that I see that have caused difficulty in the past, and we must make it very clear that the Blue Army will have nothing to do with them. There are occasionally some members who fail to distinguish between well-authenticated private revelations and those the Church has condemned. It would be much better if they would not consider themselves members of the Blue Army. They are the ones who diminish the authenticity of the Fatima revelations by equating them with those that have been condemned. There are those, too, who in their great love for the Church, also love her as they knew her many years ago. They do not want her to change, even in the sense of Cardinal Newman's development of doctrine. It does no good to lament the passing of certain forms of worship that are no longer acceptable. This is to close one's eyes to the progress that has been made."

And there is another problem:

For many of our lay apostles there is the problem of "acceptance" because they *are* lay persons.

Since there are not enough priests, we are compelled sometimes to have laymen traveling with the Pilgrim Virgin statues.

As the scarcity of priests continues, the Church has been opening the field of the permanent diaconate more and more and it is my hope that the most dedicated and important leaders of the Blue Army will seek to obtain this special sacrament for their work.

Recently, in order to obviate the need of having a lay person travel with the Pilgrim-Virgin statue and give talks in the various churches, we prepared a basic homily which any priest could read or use as a basis. To our surprise, one pastor after another complained that he had *expected* the one traveling with the statue to give these talks.

As time goes on, there may be fewer and fewer qualified priests who can take time off from pastoral work to travel and explain the Message of Fatima.

In Ponce, Puerto Rico, the head of the Blue Army Apostolate is a professor at the Catholic University and also an ordained deacon. Using the facilities of the Catholic University where he is a professor, he is now publishing a Blue Army magazine for use among Spanish-speaking members of the Apostolate throughout the

Americas. Since his work is concentrated in the Diocese of
Ponce, he could obviously be ordained within that diocese.
And now Ponce is rapidly becoming a propaganda center
of the Blue Army for all of Latin America.

In any event, future leaders of the Apostolate will come
from the "school" of the Blue Army cell program. There
will be catechists imitating their "Catechist Mother"...es-
pecially necessary in mission lands. And we must pray
that the efforts of all to bring Our Lady's message of hope
to the world will be integrated with the teaching authority
of the Church and that, above all, it will never separate
itself from that authority to even the smallest degree.

**Here John Haffert presents to Msgr. Colgan a copy of his book
"SEX AND THE MYSTERIES."**

The witty remark made by Msgr. Colgan on this occasion (the
expression of which is captured in this picture) reflected the
wonderful rapport between this priest and this layman, which
proved to be a major foundation stone in the building of the Blue
Army.

On April 22, 1980, Pope John Paul II chose the Most Rev. John C. Reiss, who for ten years had been the Auxiliary to Bishop Ahr, as the new Bishop of Trenton.

One of the very first invitations accepted by the new Bishop was to speak at the Blue Army Shrine on May 13th, Feast of Our Lady of Fatima and also the new Bishop's birthday.

Shortly before the Bishop was to speak, Pope John Paul was shot during an audience in Rome. Bishop Reiss said to the crowd of pilgrims at the Blue Army Shrine:

Before the events of today, I had actually planned to talk at this Mass on the Feast of Our Lady of Fatima on the present situation in the world. Any newspaper will tell you of the wars, the taking of life, the rejection of God and of human rights, of killing innocent people.

Since so many years have gone by and there seems to be no improvement, we may fall into discouragement. That is always the danger Satan, the power of evil, places before us, to make us feel we are helpless and that the situation is hopeless.

To avoid the triumph of evil, we must continue praying...and ...because of our devotion to Our Lady, we must pray Her Rosary...

We can storm heaven so that this message handed to us by Our Lady, according to the will of Her Son, may again be heard. We must change our lives. We must live differently; we must root out of us evil in all its forms.

We must pray for this, but above all we must continue so that by example we may bring many more voices to that union of prayer so that God will hear the requests of Our Blessed Mother, that She may be our advocate and win for us the peace of Christ.

Chapter Thirty

1) Prophecies of Saint Catherine Laboure and Saint John Bosco - 2) All-Night Vigils - 3) Invitation to China - 4) World Peace Flight - 5) One and one-half million turn out in Rome - 6) Greatest triumph in Poland - 7) Communists grant permission not only for churches but even for seminary! - 8) "Made history"

Below: The author (second from left) serving Padre Pio's Mass. "Russia will be converted," Padre Pio said, "when there is a Blue Army member for every Communist."

FOTO ELIA

OUR LADY'S TRIUMPH

"I will obtain an even greater victory in 19...."
— *Our Lady to St. John Bosco*

It might be well to look again at the rather daring prophecy made by Archbishop Sheen after the celebrations at Fatima in 1951. Although it is a prediction to be taken with extreme reserve, it is worth recalling here, in view of his penetrating acumen.

On his return from Fatima in that year, Bishop Sheen issued a statement through the National Catholic Welfare Conference News Service predicting that the conversion of Russia had already begun, *and that we would see the complete triumph of Our Lady by 1985.*

He added that the White Square of Fatima would then have triumphed over the Red Square, and that Our Lady of the Kremlin would be reviewing *Her troops in Red Square!*

Specific dates are always doubtful in prophecy, but there are other prophecies concerning the promised triumph of Our Lady which give us great heart:

St. Catherine Laboure prophesied that one day Our Lady's statue would be carried around the world—and there was an intimation of a triumph of Our Lady at the time of that event. And was this not fulfilled in our Queen of the World flight in 1978, which had a profound effect in many nations and especially in Poland?

Above all there is the prophecy of St. John Bosco.

Our Lady appeared to him in Turin as the "Help of All Christians" and asked the saint to build a church in Her honor at that spot, stating She would achieve a victory for Christianity even greater than She had obtained at Lepanto in 1571, and this victory would occur in 19...!

1

When the saint built that beautiful basilica in Turin—perhaps one of the most beautiful shrines of Our Lady in the world—he inscribed on the facade the date 1571 on the left, and the date 19-- on the right.

A subsequent superior changed the open date on the right because of the many questions it raised.

Some believe that there have been many signs of the fulfillment of that prophecy already in this century. And in the saint's writings the date "1972" was found, although no significant "great victory" was evident in that particular year.

Perhaps it is needless to speculate about individual dates. *Everything depends on our own free response to the conditions Our Lady has set forth.*

But it is reasonable *to feel close to the great victory* which Our Lady described at Fatima as the triumph of Her Immaculate Heart, marked by the conversion of Russia and followed by "an era of peace for mankind."

Your Excellency knows that back in the early days of the Apostolate, beginning with the March of Pledges in 1946, we were placing great stress on alerting the world to the Message of Fatima and trying to get people to sign a commitment to fulfill the basic conditions of Our Lady for Her triumph.

But in recent years we have striven to live the Fatima Message in even greater depth, thus making up in quality what is lacking in quantity. Our primary emphasis in recent years has been on the cell hours of holiness (an hour of meditated Rosary preferably before the Blessed Sacrament once each week) and the All-Night Vigils.

It is interesting to note that in his "prophecy" made in 1951 Archbishop Sheen referred specifically to Vigils— even though the Vigil Movement had not yet begun! His Excellency had been much impressed by that night of October 12-13 at Fatima in 1951 when tens of thousands of people spent the entire night in prayer. He felt that it was that great act of sacrifice, faith, and adoration which augured the beginning of the conversion of Russia. He said that the triumph of Our Lady by 1985 would be ours...but *it depended* upon how we spent our days..."and our nights."

The late Hon. Henrietta Bower, that great Blue Army apostle who was in a sense the "founder" of the world All-Night Vigil movement, wrote a magnificent book on the history of the Vigils. I hope many, many Blue Army members will read it. It is titled significantly *Challenge to Godlessness.* No one could read this wonderful book without realizing the importance and *power* of the All-Night Vigils.

(Incidentally, the history of the All-Night Vigil movement bears a striking parallel to the history of the Blue Army. Almost every obstacle and every triumph of that movement could be matched by an almost identical experience in our own history.)

What is particularly surprising about the Vigils is that whereas one would almost inevitably expect to find the sacrifice of making them too great, the opposite proves to be true. Wherever a regular Vigil starts, the number usually attending increases from month to month!

With considerable difficulty I launched the All-Night Vigil in New York City some years ago.

I wrote to a few parishes suggesting the idea of the Vigil and stating that we would pay all the expenses, do all the publicity, take all the responsibility and conduct the program.

Only one parish responded: St. John's next to Pennsylvania Station, which Cardinal Spellman had recently decided to close!

As a result of the publicity, about two hundred people attended the first Vigil—and their "Night of Love" before the Blessed Sacrament left an indelible impression.

Five years later the Vigil had spread to other parishes, and St. John's Church was not large enough for Vigil processions to be held! Not only did the Cardinal decide not to close the church, but the parish began to prosper, and the building was extended from 31st to 32nd Street. Even the effect on the priests of the parish was most marked.

The growth of All-Night Vigils of reparation in the Blue Army reached a new peak on the night of June 6-7, 1975, when an estimated *twenty-five thousand* members around the world participated in night-long prayer to mark the tri-centenary of the Great Promise of the Sacred Heart (to St. Margaret Mary) and the Golden Jubilee of the Great Promise of the Immaculate Heart of Mary (to Sr. Lucia).

We had gone to Vietnam in February, 1974, when, as Your Excellency knows, hundreds of thousands of Vietnamese (most of them Buddhists!) turned out to honor Our

Lady. We spoke to them about this "Mother of God," who was not Herself a deity, but who came in the name of God to warn us to stop sinning and to make reparation for sin.

Our next stop was in Bangkok.

3

The Vicar General of the Bangkok Cathedral came to see me with a Chinese gentleman, whom he introduced. To my surprise the man asked: "Why don't you take the Pilgrim Virgin statue to China?"

I answered with some amusement that I was quite sure that the Chinese would not welcome the statue of Our Lady. But very seriously he answered:

"I come to you in the name of Chou-En-Lai. He would welcome a visit of the statue to China."

If it had not been that he was accompanied by the Vicar General of the Archdiocese of Bangkok, I would have thought it a joke. But then I realized that China was in serious confrontation with Russia. And what, perhaps, had impressed the Chinese was that so many hundreds of thousands of people were turning out to honor Our Lady of Fatima—and that She had spoken of the conversion of only one nation: *Russia.*

So we began then to think of taking the statue to China, the only major nation which the Pilgrim Virgin had not yet visited.

As we planned the itinerary for the flight, we included Korea, of course, where Our Lady is so loved. And we decided to take the Pilgrim Virgin statue once again to the 69th Parallel between North and South Korea for an All-Night Vigil.

Then, unexpectedly, Chou-En-Lai died. The political situation in China abruptly changed. All our communication with that vast country ceased. The flight now seemed rather irrelevant.

Meanwhile we had been receiving enthusiastic letters from Korea—especially from Fr. Joseph Slaby, and Fr. Anton Trauner, a German priest who had been laboring for many years in Korea and who was our greatest apostle in that country. They reported extensive preparations had already been made for the visit of Our Lady's statue throughout the country.

The thought began to occur to me that perhaps we should not cancel the flight, if only because of Korea. But the difficulties of arranging the flight had increased. The cost of jet fuel had soared, and the best price I could obtain for chartering a plane around the world was one million dollars! It seemed out of the question....

But the decision to cancel plans for the flight had scarcely entered my mind when two things happened in immediate sequence.

First I received a call from Captain Frank Schaeffer, an Eastern Airlines Captain in Florida who was a Blue Army member. He said he had a possible solution to the arrangement of a world flight and asked if I could come down to see him.

The next day I was in Minneapolis to participate in an All-Night Vigil, and at the entrance to the church I met Fr. Joseph Slaby from Korea!

"Father," I exclaimed in astonishment, "What are you doing here? I just sent a letter to you the other day to your address in Korea!"

He explained that it was a last minute decision. There were some orphans to be brought to the United States and because he had not seen his family for some time, he was given the privilege of accompanying the orphans, and he had flown up to Minneapolis, where his family lived. By chance he saw a poster in the Cathedral advertising the All-Night Vigil, so he had come along.

We found ourselves praying during that night for the world flight.

After sleeping only a couple of hours, I took a plane to Florida and that same First Saturday I met with Captain Schaeffer and he bowled me over with his suggestion:

"John, why don't you *buy* a 707? And then after the flight you can sell it again and I think the flight will cost little more than its operation."

There is no need to go into all the details, Excellency, which would fill pages. Suffice it to say that I was now convinced that this world flight was something Our Lady Herself wanted. It was God's Will. And I would do whatever was in my power to see it come to fruition.

By the time I had the plane (which fortunately I acquired on a purchase-lease arrangement, rather than an outright purchase, entirely without touching any funds of the Blue Army), the world flight was arranged. The plane was named "Queen of the World" and we would take the original Pilgrim Virgin statue—the one that was first blessed and sent forth from Fatima on May 13, 1947 and which had never before made a circuit of the globe. (The previous flight had been made with the second statue, the one that had been traveling in America.)

While the publicity in the American newspapers was scanty, the impact on many of the nations we visited was enormous. A book would be needed to tell all, but there are three or four highlights which should most certainly be included in this story. But first, let me be permitted a little "aside"—to acknowledge the great Providence of God, the loving providing of dear St. Joseph and the reassertion experienced throughout the years of our apostolic endeavors, that Our Lady is never outdone in generosity:

I had expected to use at least $100,000 of my own money (from family inheritance) to subsidize this flight.

Just before we took off, an elderly lady sent a check for $5.00 with a simple note: "I am 81 years of age and cannot participate in the flight, but I am sending $5.00 to help pay for the gas in Our Lady's plane."

I was so touched by this—not so much by the money, but by the generous prayer-act behind it, that I published that little note in SOUL Magazine suggesting that perhaps some others might want to make an offering of "gas" for Our Lady's plane. And I sent a letter to this effect to my Christmas list.

I did not know the results until the end of that epic flight. *People sent in $140,000 more* than was needed to cover the excess costs of the flight. (Of course, it was well needed by the Blue Army!)

I have already briefly referred to the dramatic reception that awaited us in Poland; but perhaps the *most* momentous experience on that flight happened between Egypt and Israel.

The President of Egypt had recently made a historic flight from Cairo to Jerusalem to open peace negotiations. So we petitioned both Egypt and Israel for permission to make a direct flight (never before made by any civilian plane) between the two countries as an expression of the world's aspirations and prayers for peace. Our own White House frowned on us and said that they did not encourage civilians to interfere in "diplomatic" matters!

First the telegram came from Israel, granting permission if the President of Egypt would also grant it.

The day before we were scheduled to leave Cairo, President Sadat of Egypt gave permission.

But suddenly we found there was no way to let Israel

know! There was no communication between the two countries! The only possible communication—which President Sadat himself had used—was through the American Embassy.

An Associated Press reporter gave me the private address of the Ambassador, and on the very morning of the flight itself, the communication was completed and *the Queen of the World made the first civilian flight in history between Egypt and Israel,* carrying the statue of the Queen of the World—*and it was Passover Day!*

Oh, what a glorious memory we have of Our Lady's welcome in Jerusalem! The saintly Patriarch had arranged a major reception for the Pilgrim Virgin statue, and had issued a pastoral letter for the month of May to all the Catholics of the Holy Land—explaining in detail how this was *"Our Lady's land"*—and Jerusalem *"Our Lady's city."* She had died in Jerusalem, She had been presented as a child in the Temple, She had presented Her own Child in the Temple, and twelve years later found Him there.

But I must restrain the joy of detailed memories which must be more of a joy for us who experienced them than of interest to others.

The Patriarch had wanted the Pilgrim Virgin statue to remain in Jerusalem for May 1, the opening of Our Lady's month, but I had wanted the statue to arrive in Rome on that day, which was May Day, because of the tremendous power of communism in Italy—which had extended to the point of now having *the Eternal City governed by a communist mayor!* 5

The first reception of the Pilgrim Virgin statue in Rome was at the Shrine of Our Lady of Divine Love—which is a title of Our Lady as the spouse of the Holy Spirit.

The shrine is about nine miles from the center of Rome where there had been a fortress in ancient times, on the wall of which was a fresco of "Our Lady of Divine Love." The fortress had been destroyed through the centuries by invading barbarians and wars, but that one wall, with the fresco of Our Lady, had remained intact. Shepherds used to go and pray before the image, and then when there was a threat of Rome being bombed in the second world war, Pope Pius XII encouraged copies of Our Lady of Divine Love to be placed all over Rome and expressed the hope that even as She had preserved Her image on the outskirts of Rome through all these centuries of previous invasions,

She would now preserve Rome itself.

So Cardinal Poletti, the Pope's Vicar for Rome, had arranged that the Pilgrim Virgin statue should first be taken to that shrine, since Rome was now menaced by a different enemy—*one which had already penetrated deeply into the city and which threatened not only Rome and Italy, but the entire world*—as Our Lady Herself had foretold at Fatima.

The statue was flown from the airport, where the Queen of the World plane landed, to a spot near the center of the old city. From there *it was carried in an All-Night Vigil March* the nine miles to the Shrine of Our Lady of Divine Love, where Cardinal Poletti would arrive next morning for the first ceremonies.

Our group of 183 from the Queen of the World plane joined the crowds traveling to the Shrine of Divine Love.

We never arrived.

There was a complete road blockage four miles before the Shrine! Police cars with screaming sirens, and guards armed with machine guns to protect Cardinal Poletti, sped past us and had to run on the shoulder of the road to get the Pope's Vicar of Rome to the place where the Pilgrim Virgin was enshrined.

The Rome newspapers estimated the total crowd which turned out on those two days at well over one million. It was the largest religious demonstration witnessed in Rome in my lifetime, not excluding the coronation of Popes, the Holy Years, the Marian Year, and even the memorable procession of the *Salus Populi Romani*, the most venerated image in the Western Church, which His Holiness (Pope Pius XII) then crowned. At that time he also issued the encyclical *Ad Coeli Reginam*, proclaiming Our Lady Queen of the World (while at the same time making reference to Her "miraculous image at Fatima" which he had crowned in 1946).

The same image was now in Rome on May Day, when the Communist International in *all the capitals of Europe* was staging huge demonstrations of solidarity *with the world atheist revolution!*

When the Pilgrim Virgin statue was conveyed to St. John Lateran, the cathedral of Rome and "first of all churches" of the world, the crowds were so dense that not a single vehicle could pass. At night the statue was taken in procession from St. John Lateran to St. Mary Major, up the Via Merulana, and past the church of St. Alphonsus in which the original picture of Our Lady of Perpetual Help is venerated. The "procession" was so dense that the entire mile of that wide avenue was packed tight with people from one end to the other.

All of this contributed mightily towards what was about to happen in Poland.

As I mentioned previously to Your Excellency, Vatican Radio sent for me and asked me to give a brief summary of the World Peace Flight and to explain the Blue Army. This was broadcast on Vatican Radio to all countries of Europe—and of course was heard by thousands in Poland who regularly tuned in to Vatican Radio for the news.

On the way to Poland we stopped in Vienna because I wanted to take the Pilgrim Virgin statue secretly to Budapest. We had no problem because our stay in Vienna was not publicized. Everyone would have thought that we were going from Rome direct to Warsaw.

We did not get the rights to overfly Czechoslovakia, but our captain never said a word. I did not realize what a chance we were taking until I happened to enter the cockpit and I saw Captain Schaeffer (the Eastern Airlines captain who had suggested the purchase of the plane, and who had taken time out to be co-pilot) and Captain Grue, the senior captain, looking anxiously in various directions. Already the mountains between Czechoslovakia and Poland were in view as Captain Grue said: "Well, no fighter planes yet!"

But the power of Russia was waiting for us at Warsaw Airport. **6**

Everything looked normal as the big jet taxied to a halt. The buses rolled out to where the plane was, the hydraulic steps were moved into position near the front door of the plane—but not quite all the way!

After about ten minutes, I went up to ask Captain Grue if he understood why the steps were not put in place. He was looking somewhat worried—and puzzled.

"They want to talk to the one in charge," he said.

"Well, I suppose that's me," I replied. "How do I talk to them?"

The answer was soon given. An unusual red van raced across the tarmac and stopped beneath the plane. An officer with four stars on his tunic climbed out of the vehicle, and from ample radio equipment in the van

Captain Grue was getting the instructions. The door of the plane was to be opened, and I—and no one else—was to come down.

Indeed there was little chance for anyone else to leave the plane because I was still on the top step when it moved back away from the door and I seemed to be descending directly from the air rather than from the plane.

But perhaps I'm going into too much detail. The upshot of it all was that they would let the group land, *but the Pilgrim Virgin statue had to remain on the plane.*

I took a vote of the group. We all agreed that it was better for the group to visit Poland as planned, representing Our Lady, even though we were unable to take Her statue with us.

As our buses pulled away from the plane, we saw armed guards taking a position around it—and they were there night and day during all the time we were in Poland!

This is all very reminiscent of what happened on Poland's millennium, when Pope Paul VI had been invited to Poland—but the Russians would not give him a visa. Henrietta Bower led an All-Night Vigil group from England, and I led a group from America. We met on the Czech-Polish frontier on that occasion and had an All-Night Vigil there. I sometimes wonder how greatly the power of that Vigil contributed to what was now about to happen in Poland...

When the Russians had prevented the Pope from coming to the millennial celebration at Czestochowa, the Poles had placed an empty chair where the Pope would have sat, draped with the papal colors. Now, at the suggestion of one of the priests traveling with us (Fr. Matthew Strumski), a wire outline of the Pilgrim Virgin was made and painted white, and this *empty* figure was carried to all the places that Our Lady's statue would have visited! The word spread like wildfire all through Poland that the visit of Our Lady, which had been announced over Vatican Radio, was not to take place...*that the Russians had forbidden Her image to enter the country!*

At Czestochowa, where the future John Paul II had been waiting with all the bishops of Poland, Cardinal Wyszynski said to us:

"You from the free world may be surprised at this, but we are not always free to do what we would like to do."

Oh, how I wish I had a recording, preferably even a

sound film, of that meeting that we had with Cardinal Wyszynski at the Shrine of Our Lady of Czestochowa! How warm he was to the black pilgrims with us, saying that the Black Madonna had apparently also brought "Her daughters" to visit Her.

After our plane left, we discovered that there was *a spiritual revolt throughout Poland* which extended even to the members of the armed forces.[1] Its intensity was such that the Communist Prime Minister was compelled to visit the Cardinal and confess:

"It was all a misunderstanding. We have nothing against the visit of a statue to our country. Tell them to bring the statue back."

But the Cardinal wanted something far more important 7 than just the return of Our Lady's statue. For a quarter century the Communists had prevented the building of any churches in Poland. They had restored some damaged churches, but had persistently refused to allow the twenty-four churches destroyed by the war in Warsaw to be rebuilt.

In the "bargaining" which ensued, the Cardinal agreed to ask the Blue Army to bring the Pilgrim Virgin statue back and Gierek, the Communist Premier, *agreed to the building of eight new churches in Warsaw!*

The first one was substantially completed by the following year. Twenty-five thousand dollars of the extra money given for the Queen of the World flight was sent to help with its construction. And the completed church was, of course, dedicated to the Queen of the World!

On August 22, 1979, Feast of the Queenship of Mary, *we returned to Poland with the Pilgrim Virgin statue,* to be present while Cardinal Wyszynski blessed that new church in honor of Our Lady Queen of the World—the first church he had been able to dedicate in Warsaw in a quarter century!

We were detained for eight hours at the frontier, but going without sleep, we arrived just as the trumpets were sounding and the Cardinal was beginning the blessing. And the Pilgrim Virgin statue was carried in and placed beside that wire outline which had been carried throughout Poland just one year before.

But there is another touching incident which I think Your Excellency would like to hear.

Cardinal Wyszynski had not only wanted new churches,

but even more, *he had wanted the building of a seminary.* Indeed he had longed for this so much that he made known to everyone that his greatest desire was *to live long enough to see a seminary restored in Warsaw.*

Some twenty years earlier, a house had been opened to be used as a seminary, *and a statue of Our Lady of Fatima was placed in a provisional chapel.* The seminarians were instructed to pray to Our Lady of Fatima every day that the government would give permission for a proper seminary to be built.

Now on this golden day, the Feast of the Queenship of Mary, *a priest arrived while we were at dinner after the dedication of the church, with the breathtaking news that shortly before the arrival of the Pilgrim Virgin statue at the new Church of Our Lady Queen of the World, official documents had come from the government authorizing the building of the seminary!*

Shortly after the first trip of the Pilgrim Virgin statue to Poland, a new Pope came out of that country—with the symbol of Mary below the cross as his coat of arms! And after that came the surge of freedom in Poland, under the auspices of "the Queen of Poland." To us who could only watch and marvel, it seemed like the first thrilling glimpse of Our Lady's coming triumph.

I "diverted" to tell you about our return to Poland in 1979, but to conclude news about the 1978 Peace Flight:

8   The Queen of the World plane made history again when we left Warsaw and flew to Berlin—the first flight (except for a hijack) from behind the Iron Curtain into the free city of Berlin. And this, too, was on a most historic day: the anniversary of the Berlin agreement.

From Berlin we flew directly to Lourdes, and the Rector of the Sanctuary was waiting at the airport to greet Our Lady's image. Simultaneously a large group, under the presidency of the Cardinal Archbishop of Paris, participated in ceremonies honoring the Queen of the World in Paris. And while the statue remained in Lourdes, there was a repetition of the miracle of the doves.

The flight concluded at Fatima—where it all began in 1917! There the Pilgrim Virgin statue, which had left Fatima in May 1947, was carried in the candlelight procession of the great vigil of the 12th-13th, the same kind of vigil which had inspired Archbishop Sheen to exclaim in 1951 that by 1985 the White Square of Fatima would have triumphed over the Red Square in which Our Lady of the Kremlin would then be reviewing Her troops!

Had not the Queen of the World truly used Her Blue Army *to manifest Her power* to bring peace to the world?

FOOTNOTE

1. See Chapter XIII, p. 127-129; **Fatima: The Great Sign** for a published summary of this great "triumph" of Our Lady as Queen of the World.

Below: The statue of Our Lady arrives on the special "Queen of the World" flight at Rome airport on May 1, 1978.

Chapter Thirty-One

1) These recollections span 45 years - 2) Three reasons for optimism - 3) Light in China - 4) Events seem to move slowly - 5) Satan works incessantly - 6) We must beware of pride and position

Above: Most Rev. George W. Ahr, seventh Bishop of Trenton, speaking to Blue Army leaders in Washington, N.J.

TO THE READER AGAIN

"In the end, my Immaculate Heart will triumph."
— *Our Lady of Fatima, July 13, 1917*

This book-long "letter" to the Most Rev. George W. Ahr, who had been our bishop for thirty years, was written in 1981...just a quarter century after an historic meeting in Fatima chaired by Msgr. Colgan.

Cardinal Tisserant presided, and assisting were the Most Rev. Jose Correia da Silva, first Bishop of Fatima, and his auxiliary and successor, the Most Rev. John Venancio. Also present was Msgr. Jean Rupe, Auxiliary Bishop of Paris and subsequently Bishop of Monaco.

At that meeting the Blue Army was "born" as an official, international Apostolate of Fatima. Statutes drawn up by Rev. Dr. Lourenco, a canon lawyer of the Diocese of Leiria-Fatima, were adopted and taken by Cardinal Tisserant to Rome where they were given *ad experimentum* approval.

Even as I completed these pages I was preparing to go to Fatima for the "silver jubilee" of this event when again leaders of the Apostolate from the four corners of the world would be assembled at our international center to review the statutes, to hold election of international officers, and to plan the future.

In this "letter" I was recalling events which span forty-two years of apostolate, hoping to recall especially the action of Divine Providence and experiences which might contain lessons for the future.

Some important problems which arose over the years have been given little more than passing notice. Some accomplishments...such as the CRISIS television series, international seminars held in our centers in Fatima and

1

Pontevedra, various peace flights such as the one around Africa, and many other major events...have also been mentioned only in brief.

What seems most important...and what I think Bishop Ahr had in mind when he asked me to record these remembrances...is to attribute to Our Lady the raising up of an army in response to Her Fatima warnings and promises, and that this victorious army (with victory assured by Our Lady Herself) must experience many setbacks (often sudden and from most unexpected sources), and even many defeats (and one could point to some dioceses, even some nations, where this is painfully evident).

2   At the same time the previous pages are intended to reveal three reasons for optimism:

First, *the promise of Our Lady:* "In the end, my Immaculate Heart will triumph...Russia will be converted, and an era of peace will be conceded to mankind." (And to this great promise is added the comfort of the prophecy of St. John Bosco that leads us to believe that this victory will begin before the end of 1999.)

Second, the Blue Army is active on so many fronts that even *if one action fails, another succeeds.*

Third, frequent intervention of Our Lady Herself... through the Church, and even through miracles.

We have mentioned two reported apparitions of Our Lady of Fatima...in Bogota and Saigon. We have not spoken much of it, but there is also the phenomenon of tears flowing from the eyes of the Pilgrim Virgin and many similar phenomena reported in my book *Explosion of the Supernatural.*

The reason why we do not speak much of such matters is because much time is required to evaluate them. Their impact *is primarily on those who are directly involved,* with a consequent almost overwhelming reassurance of Our Lady's power.

3   Even as this book was being completed we were learning of the light which was seen by millions shining over the closed Shrine of Our Lady of Fatima outside of Shanghai. In mid-August of 1980 it shone for three nights over the Shrine where the statue of Our Lady of Fatima had been reported to have shed tears for three days in 1953, just before the Communists closed the Shrine and put many to death or in prison for their faith.

During those three days in 1980 the word spread through all of China and the thousands who gathered at the Shrine *came from every Province* of that vast nation of a billion souls.[1] We are now planning a peace flight to China which may be "history" by the time you are reading this book.

My most vivid memory of all the past forty-two years, and which I have scarcely mentioned, was near the Cambodian border in February, 1974, in a veritable sea of humanity which had gathered around the Pilgrim Virgin statue (which had been reported to have shed tears) *in united prayer*. Most of them were non-Christians!

Oh, what a wonderful day is coming!

Before her death, Jacinta reminded Lucia:

"Do not be afraid to tell everyone about devotion to the Immaculate Heart of Mary...and that God has entrusted the peace of the world to Her..."

Pope Pius XII *commanded* an annual renewal of consecration to the Immaculate Heart of Mary on the Feast of Her Queenship, and said that in the doctrine of Mary's Queenship *"lies the world's greatest hope for peace."*

What a role the Army of the Queen...and not only the Blue Army but *all* Her regiments...must play at this moment of world history!

As I look back over the past half a century, I must say that events have moved more slowly than anticipated... but now they seem to move more rapidly. Perhaps it is because of the All-Night Vigils. Perhaps it is because more and more persons—even outside the Church—are being touched by that light which at Fatima streamed from the Immaculate Heart of Mary causing the three children to feel "lost in God." And being lost in God, the world will not be lost. 4

We have mentioned in these pages the enemies we *know*. But before we close it is important to say something about the enemy we don't know: Satan. 5

He is manifesting himself more than ever in the wave of crime and pornography over the world. He is like a serpent who in previous ages was hidden in the grass and struck out with his poison unexpectedly and lethally. But now he is like a serpent who is being crushed beneath a heel...and all the grass thrashes about as though given life by his powerful presence.

This we do not fear. This confirms to us all that Our Lady said...and impels us to respond to Her requests with greater earnestness and fervor.

But what may take us unawares is the work of Satan upon ourselves, and upon those working at our very side.

6 In my opinion the explanation is primarily Satan's "entrance" by the doors of money, pride (feelings injured in persons who have not received expected recognition), and in just the ordinary weakness of human nature.

Thomas Merton remarked in his magnificent book *Seven Storey Mountain* that when he entered the Trappists he began to see for the first time *the individuals* in the community rather than seeing the net "formal liturgical anonymity which clothes the body of men obscurely in the very personality of Christ Himself."

And he says that he had the grace to realize that *one of the most important aspects* of his vocation was the willingness to accept life in the community in which "everybody is more or less imperfect."

And if this was true in the Trappists, how much more should it not be true in an apostolate in the world?

From what he had experienced in the Trappists, Thomas Merton was able to make this rather amazing statement: "People even lose their vocations because they find out that a man can spend forty, fifty or sixty years in a monastery and still have a bad temper."

Frank Sheed, in his extraordinary book *The Church and I*, tells of the time when he was giving a talk on the Immaculate Conception at a meeting of the Catholic Evidence Guild in London. Seated behind him was the president of the Guild, and during the talk the secretary came and was whispering to the president about something while Mr. Sheed was speaking. Little by little the whispers were becoming louder and louder, and finally Frank Sheed heard the secretary saying to the president:

"Do you call me, a daily Communicant, a liar!?"

"They're the worst!" the president snorted.

And smiling within himself, Frank said that he went on giving his talk about the Immaculate Conception.

How human!

How much to be expected!

And, with all my heart I assert that if this could happen among totally dedicated, unselfish, Eucharistic men, how much more we must expect it *in the Apostolate to which is attached the solemn promise of Our Lady* that Her Immaculate Heart is *now* going to triumph in the world!

We have instances in the history of the Blue Army where the Apostolate has literally had its hands tied behind its back in an entire nation because of conflicts between different persons who claimed to be leaders of the Apostolate in that country!

A priest in Canada, who had been bitterly calumniated after he had undertaken the task of carrying the Pilgrim Virgin through the dioceses of Canada and of bringing unity to the Blue Army there, reminds us of the incredible persecution which St. John of the Cross experienced in his own community and of St. Anthony Mary Claret, the great model of devotion to the Immaculate Heart (who experienced a miraculous inward presence of the Blessed Sacrament for the last 16 years of his life) had slanderous reports published against his character and good works. And his reply to these calumnies was:

"I see what they say of me. I can only comment that it is a reminder of the patrimony left to us by Jesus Christ. This is the pay the world accords. We do well to recall the words of Isaiah: 'In silence and in hope is your strength.'"

He also recalled that St. Philip Neri said: "If a man finds it very hard to forgive injuries, let him look at a crucifix, and think that Christ shed all of His blood for him, and not only forgave His enemies, but He even prayed to His heavenly Father to forgive them also."

And St. Thomas of Villanova said: "Dismiss all anger, and look a little into yourself. Remember that he of whom you are speaking is your brother."

But above all, we must remember the words of Our Lord Himself to St. Peter told in the Gospel of St. Matthew: "Lord, when my brother wrongs me, how often must I forgive him? Seven times?" "No," Jesus replied, "not seven times; I say, seventy times seven times." (18:21-22)

The future? It is bright with Our Lady's own promise!

The present? It requires *personal holiness,* and an awareness that we are engaged in a mortal battle between Satan and Our Lady...his seed and Hers.

Archbishop Sheen liked often to recall that Our Lord said that "this is Satan's hour," and to add, "Satan will have his hour...but Our Lady will have Her day."

---

1. **U.S. News and World Report,** April 27, 1981 issue.

Chapter Thirty-Two

1) What are the Signs of Victory? - 2) Great Sign: Icon of Kazan - 3) The "Miracle"' of Red Square - 4) "Rediscovery" of Original Icon - 5) 1950: Turning Point - 6) Reconciliation Service - 7) Sign of Hope?

Below: Blue Army pilgrimage with Pilgrim Virgin statue arrives in Prague, Czechoslovakia. It was the delivery of this Pilgrim Virgin statue in October, 1967, which caused Cardinal Tomasek, Archbishop of Prague, to say: "You have brought us the sign of our hope."

SIGNS OF VICTORY

_____

"Russia will be converted..."
— *Our Lady of Fatima*

As we look back over the years of this Apostolate, what might be singled out as the greatest sign of God's approval upon it? Would it be the sheer achievement of some twenty-five million signed pledges—some twenty-five million personal commitments to fulfill the essential conditions of Our Lady for the conversion of Russia and world peace? Or might it be just the fact that this Apostolate has *survived* all these years, and continues to grow towards the success of its goal, namely the fulfillment of the prophecy of Our Lady, despite the implacable resistance of Satan and his iron control of the terrifying power of militant atheism directed and financed from Moscow?

To a holy Russian like Fr. Karl Patzelt, S.J., the greatest sign of God's approval upon the Blue Army is the fact that He has entrusted to it the precious miraculous Icon of Our Lady of Kazan, Liberatrix and Protectress of Russia.

But to the eminent Spanish authority on Fatima, Fr. Joaquin Alonso, the greatest sign of God's approval is that He has entrusted to the Blue Army the actual convent of the apparitions (which Fr. Alonso calls the "Pentecost of Fatima") in Pontevedra.

For others there are "permanent" signs: the Blue Army's new world center of devotion to the Immaculate Heart in Pontevedra; the 120-room International Center behind the Basilica at Fatima; and the National Center and Shrine of the Immaculate Heart of Mary in Washington, New Jersey.

Another very significant sign has been the development of the All-Night Vigil movement around the world. Is this not one of the greatest movements of holiness in the Church today?

What a glory it is for The Blue Army of Our Lady of Fatima to have been a prime organizer of this Vigil movement around the world—a movement which has been warmly endorsed by the Supreme Pontiffs, and which is extending the spiritual power of the cloistered communities of the world into parish churches, into all levels of the Church.

How could one ever forget the historic Vigil made by tens of thousands during the Eucharistic Congress in Philadelphia—the All-Night Vigil which was conducted by the Blue Army?

Perhaps some readers may have perceived very different signs of Heaven's approval of this Apostolate, such as the fact that Lucia herself drew up the pledge, that the first Bishop of Fatima authorized its promotion and the establishment of the International Center of the Blue Army at Fatima, and that the second Bishop of Fatima became its active promoter and International President.

But certainly no less important a sign, and one which I can appreciate in a special and personal way, has been the participation of the wonderful Bishop to whom most of these pages are addressed.

There is also the great sign of the intervention of Rome, in the person of the most important Cardinal of the Church, Eugene Cardinal Tisserant, Dean of the Sacred College. He became in reality the first "Cardinal Protector" of the Apostolate.

Still other readers might consider the greatest sign to be Padre Pio's endorsement of the Blue Army as the "ideal apostolate" of our time, and that the venerable stigmatist consented to be the Spiritual Father of all those who would live up to their Blue Army Pledge.

For me personally there are other signs—perhaps not objectively as important as the above, but in some instances even more important subjectively, such as a remarkable sign received in Warsaw concerning the Felicians, and the foundation of the Handmaids of Mary Immaculate to serve the centers of this Apostolate to which God has entrusted the fulfillment of the Message of Fatima—the most important message of the 20th century.

The worldwide coronation of statues of Our Lady of Fatima by bishops in fifty different countries, in which Pope Paul VI finally participated with a message on both radio and television, was also very significant. It probably did much to speed the greatest sign of all: the Collegial Consecration of Russia to the Immaculate Heart of Mary.

But this book...and at least three other books I have written (*Russia Will Be Converted, The Brother and I,* and *Explosion of the Supernatural*)...list many, many other signs of the coming victory.

However, when all is said and done, I would tend to agree with Fr. Patzelt *that the greatest sign of all is the Icon of Kazan.* 2

Russia, from which in just fifty years the power of militant atheism was marshalled over two-thirds of the world, did not even begin to emerge as a nation until after the fall of Constantinople in 1453. It was well after the discovery of America that Russia had her first Czar, in 1547. Soon after that the newly-emerging nation was plunged into the worst and darkest period of her history. For eight years robber bands roamed the country, armies from Poland and Sweden fought for control, each with the intention of putting their own kings on the throne of Moscow.

At this time, in the city of Kazan, which until recently had been the capital of the Mongolian Empire, Our Lady appeared to an eight-year-old girl and told her of a sacred picture which had been hidden and lost during the time of the Mongolian and Mohammedan rule in Kazan. No one believed the little girl until after two more apparitions of Our Lady. Then to the amazement of everyone, the Icon was found beneath the ruins of a burned-out building, in perfect preservation.

There was an obvious "presence" to this sacred image (which is now in the custody of the Blue Army). Miracles occurred, including the giving of sight to two men who had been born blind.

The Icon was taken to a church in Kazan whose pastor was Blessed Ermogen, later Patriarch of Moscow. He had an apparition of one of the greatest saints in the history of Russia, St. Sergei. The saint told Blessed Ermogen that this sacred image of Our Lady of Kazan would be the rallying point of the people, and that it would be the means of saving and establishing the Russian nation.

This indeed happened—in just a few years!

The Swedish king agreed to withdraw in return for receiving the Gulf of Finland, and the Polish king withdrew upon receiving firm boundaries, including a section which had in the previous fifty years been considered part of Russia.

From that time on the miraculous image of Our Lady of Kazan was known as "the Liberatrix and Protectress of Holy Mother Russia." It was used in all the crises of Russian history up to and including the invasion of Napoleon—whose defeat was directly attributed by the Russian people to Our Lady of Kazan.

It can be said that as the sacred image of Our Lady emerged from beneath the ruins of a burned-out building in Kazan, *the soul of Russia emerged with it.* The Russian nation (which had its first Czar only fifty years before) was "born."

One of the bitter and long-remembered dark periods of the subsequent history of Russia was the war with Poland in 1667.

The Poles invoked *Our Lady of Czestochowa*, and the Russians invoked *Our Lady of Kazan!*

Oh, how the motherly heart of Our Lady must have been truly pierced with thorns on this sad occasion!

The conflict was deeply embittered because by now the schism between the Western (Latin) Church and the Eastern (Byzantine or Russian) Church had intensified to the point of bitter hatreds. But in this war, Russia gained Smolensk, Kiev, and the Eastern Ukraine. *And* (we sometimes forget how *recent* this was!) *only thirty years later,* under Peter the Great, *the great Russian Empire began to form.*

From the time of the peace with Poland and Sweden in 1613, the Icon of Kazan was taken to Moscow and enshrined in a special Basilica opposite the Kremlin, now known throughout the world as "Red Square." When Peter the Great built a new capital to the north, on the sea, he decided to build for the Icon of Kazan a most magnificent church, modeled in style after St. Peter's Basilica in Rome.

The new capital of Petrograd was called "the Venice of the North." It was truly a glorious city, and its Cathedral of Our Lady of Kazan was indeed a fitting setting for the "Liberatrix and Protectress of Russia."

However there was a national reaction against the Icon being removed from its old cathedral in Moscow, so the Czar had a beautiful copy made for the new capital and left the Icon in its original church on Red Square.

In 1917, when the Communists took over Russia, they almost immediately focused their attention on the Icon of Kazan as an expression of the "soul" of the Russian people.

The great Cathedral of Our Lady of Kazan in Petrograd (now Leningrad) was made into an atheist museum and *the official center of militant atheism in the world.*

The Basilica of Our Lady of Kazan on Red Square was destroyed by battering rams while the Reds announced that *they would thus prove that God did not exist*—because they destroyed the Church of the "Liberatrix and Protectress of Holy Mother Russia" and there was no God, and no "Protectress," to prevent the destructive blows of their battering rams!

But on the other side of Europe, at the very time that the atheists were taking control in Russia, *Our Lady was appearing to three little shepherds.* And the only country She mentioned besides the country in which She was appearing was *Russia!*

She foretold the spread of militant atheism from Russia throughout the entire world, fomenting further wars, and even the annihilation of nations, due to the sins of men. But She said that "in the end my Immaculate Heart will triumph. *Russia will be converted....*"

The youngest of the three children was seven years of age, and the other two children were nine and ten. And the child to whom Our Lady had appeared to reveal Her sacred image in Kazan just over three hundred years before was eight years old.

To the amazement of everyone, when the Communists tried to build another structure where they had destroyed the Church of Our Lady of Kazan in Moscow, accidents occurred over and over. This happened so much that finally the workmen refused to build on that spot. It was therefore turned into a small park, simply covered with green grass. It is the only "open" spot circling Red Square—only a few hundred feet from Lenin's tomb!

Some call it "the green miracle of Red Square."

No one knows how the precious, original Icon upon which was centered the Russian nation's devotion to Our

Lady "escaped" from its cathedral and from Russia. It turned up in an auction of precious objects in Poland after the first world war, and finally ended up in 1950 on the wall of a castle in England. It was discovered there by a Russian countess who, recognizing the original Icon beyond any doubt because of the configuration of diamonds and rubies given by Catherine the Great and Ivan the Terrible, fell on her knees before it.

4   The Icon was then taken to Windsor Castle, and the Metropolitan Leonty, in exile in Paris, came to England to see if it might possibly be truly the "original."

When the old Metropolitan beheld the Icon, he clasped it, falling onto his knees, and exclaming with joy that this was the Icon with which he had celebrated the Holy Liturgy in Moscow—but which he had never dreamed of ever seeing again.

Orthodox Christians of the western world then began to raise money to "redeem the Icon"—but twice thieves absconded with the funds and the Icon was about to be put up for general auction when the Blue Army stepped in and made the commitment to redeem it for the people of Russia.

I told in an earlier chapter how the Icon was carried at Fatima by Bishop Venancio and Bishop Katkoff to the Chapel of the Apparitions, where it was placed at the very spot of Our Lady's appearance to the children, together with the original miraculous statue of Our Lady of Fatima which Pius XII had crowned "Queen of the World."

5   It was in 1950 that we "got the idea" of building a world center for our Apostolate at Fatima with *two* chapels, one Latin and one *Byzantine*. As I try to recall the motives, I can only remember that I thought of *symbolizing* in this way the unity and peace promised by Our Lady, which we believed would be the fruit of the Blue Army's worldwide effort.

I did not know, of course, that this same *Holy Year* (in which the *Assumption of Our Lady* was proclaimed a Dogma) was also the year in which the Icon of Kazan *would be "discovered"* intact in the West...while (also in the same year) *the Pilgrim Virgin statue was taken to Moscow*. Only now, more than thirty years later, the powerful effect of these simultaneous events seems to show upon the horizon like the rising sun of Our Lady's triumph in the world.

Meanwhile the beautiful building at Fatima, with the Latin and Byzantine chapels, was completed. Today that Byzantine chapel of the Blue Army's world center lifts its onion-shaped dome into the sky of Fatima, highest point after the great Fatima Basilica itself. And in that beautiful chapel there is now a side oratory reserved exclusively to hold and to honor the Icon of Kazan (here at the very place where Our Lady promised the conversion of Russia) until that historic and holy image returns to the Russian people.

On Pentecost Sunday in 1981 a special Byzantine service was held at the Shrine of the Immaculate Heart of Mary at the U.S. National Center of the Blue Army in Washington, N.J., in which the Icon of Kazan was touched to a copy which will remain permanently enshrined there. The Most Rev. Thomas V. Dolinay, Auxiliary Bishop of the Byzantine Eparchy of Passaic, and the Most Rev. Constantino Luna, a Latin Bishop then associated with the Shrine, jointly held the Icon of Kazan in the blessing ceremony.

I had been invited to speak that day on the story of the Icon. Afterwards an Orthodox of Russian descent approached me and said with deep emotion:

"I was here today almost by accident. I felt proud being Russian, and proud of my faith!"

He was a doctor associated with a large pharmaceutical firm not many miles away, and apparently had seen a reference to the Icon of Kazan being honored in ceremonies at our Shrine and wondered what it could mean.

The obvious joy and pride which radiated from this learned man gave us some inkling of what it will be like when the precious Icon of Kazan returns to "Her" people. He offered to return to our Latin Shrine for the Byzantine Day in 1982, and to provide on that occasion an Orthodox choir...an offering which Bishop Dolinay readily and gladly accepted.

Already we could see the "instant healing" between East and West in the presence of the *Theotokos*...the Heavenly Mother. 6

It was just five years before this (in July, 1976), when the ground was broken for our Shrine in Washington, N.J., that the same original Icon of Kazan was taken to the Shrine of Our Lady of Czestochowa in Doylestown, Pa., and there Bishop Venancio of Fatima and the Most Rev. Nicholas T. Elko, former Byzantine Bishop of Pittsburgh

and now Latin Rite Auxiliary Archbishop of the
Archdiocese of Cincinnati and former Vice President of the
Blue Army in the U.S., carried the Icon to be touched to
the famous copy of the Icon of Czestochowa in a *"reconciliation ceremony"*—a ceremony which could not have
taken place in Poland at the Shrine of Czestochowa under
the Communist government there, and could therefore
only have taken place in the free world, in a "sister
shrine," conducted by the same Pauline Fathers who are
in Czestochowa itself.

Oh, how mysterious are the ways of Divine Providence!

It is primarily through the Blue Army that Our Lady's
children have responded to Her Fatima Message.
Therefore is it not fitting that She should have entrusted
Her Russian Icon to this "Army," and have also had it
perform the "reconciliation ceremony" as a spiritual
symbol of the wiping out of the scandal of 1667, when Her
Heart was pierced by the thorns of Her conflicting
children?

This seems indeed a wonderful augury of the fulfillment
of the great promise made at Fatima in 1917—*when
enough persons* are in Her Blue Army: *"...my Immaculate
Heart will triumph; Russia will be converted and an era of
peace will be conceded to mankind."*

And now...we have saved the best to the last: The
epilogue which follows is the description of the Blue
Army, and a message to its members, written by the Most
Rev. John Venancio, D.D., while he was Bishop of Leiria-
Fatima. It is followed by a brief message which this great
Bishop gave to the international leaders of the Blue Army
at Fatima when His Excellency felt forced to resign
because of ill health.

Since it was written by "the Bishop of Our Lady of
Fatima" we may consider it as a message to every disciple
of Our Lady from Herself...our Mother and Queen,
"victorious (as the Bishop reminds us) in all of God's
battles"....

7

Below are pictured some of the major leaders of the Blue Army in 1968.

First row, seated left to right: Rev. Andre Richard, D.D., Blue Army President of Europe; the Bishop of Fatima, International President; Msgr. John Mowatt, Byzantine Director; Rev. Messias Coelho, major promoter in Portugal.

Second row, left to right: Madame Dauprat-Sevenet, Secretary of Europe; three Oblates serving at the International Center; Maria Moura do Carmo, Secretary of Portugal; and Maria de Freitas, International Secretary (just behind Fr. Messias).

Back row: John Haffert, International Lay Delegate and Camille Berg, then business manager of the International Center, which came to be known as "Domus Pacis." Later an International Secretariat was opened in Switzerland.

Appendices

1) Blue Army's Important Task - 2) Asks Nothing New - 3) For All the World - 4) Why the Blue Army? - 5) Should be Accepted by All Marian Movements - 6) Obedience - 7) Children - 8) Urgency - 9) Pledge of Victory

Below: Bishop Venancio with Bishop Ahr at the Blue Army's U.S. National Center on the occasion of the blessing of the "Holy House, U.S.A.".

BISHOP OF FATIMA
EXPLAINS BLUE ARMY

*Address of Bishop Venancio explaining the
Blue Army, September-October 1964 issue of*
Voice of Fatima

Notwithstanding the excellent organization *of the Apostolate* of the Church which operates under various well-
known titles in many lands, there is no doubt that much
remains still to be done and there are still millions of
believers who have never heard of this organized Apostolate. For instance, the great number of children, old
people, invalids, millions of parents, for example,
absorbed exclusively from morning to night in household
chores, the care of their children or their work in the fields
or the factory, without either time or possibility for the
intense organized work of the Apostolate.

To mobilize these reserve forces and bring them to
conscientious service of the Church, to collaborate with
other movements, to give new life to the various forms of
apostolic activity: that is or can be the great and important task of the Blue Army of Our Lady of Fatima. All the
above-mentioned believe that, in spite of their physical or
psychological incapacity, they can serve the active Apostolate of the Church in the strict sense of the word, seeing
that they are fully capable of responding to the requests
made by the Queen of the Rosary. They can pray, they can
sacrifice themselves, they can expiate, they can live and
work according to the desires of the Immaculate Heart of
Mary, thus contributing to the fulfillment of the essential
part of the spirit of the message, the great work to which
we are all called—the interior renovation of the Church,
the victory over atheistic communism and securing for the
world a true and lasting peace.

Pope Pius XI said in his encyclical on Atheistic
Communism:

320

"Nevertheless We cannot deny that there is still much to be done in the way of spiritual renovation. Even in Catholic countries there are still too many who are Catholics hardly more than in name. There are too many who fulfill more or less faithfully the more essential obligations of the religion they boast of professing, but have no desire of knowing it better, of deepening their inward conviction, and still less of bringing into conformity with the external gloss the inner splendor of a right and unsullied conscience, that recognizes and performs all its duties under the eye of God. We know how much Our Divine Savior detested this empty pharasaic show—He Who wished that all should adore the Father "in spirit and in truth." The Catholic who does not live really and sincerely according to the Faith he professes will not long be master of himself in these days when the winds of strife and persecution blow so fiercely, but will be swept away defenseless in this new deluge which threatens the world. And thus, while he is preparing his own ruin, he is exposing to ridicule the very name of Christian."

2   Another factor that contributes to the popularity of the Blue Army is the fact that it asks for nothing new in practice. The old devotional practices of the Church carried out with greater fervor of spirit will suffice.

Allow me just one parenthesis here: Those who preach the Message of Fatima are censured at times, in some places, for announcing a doctrine of pain and thus causing unnecessary perplexity among believers. We must take note first of all that there exists a salutary pain which can be a great grace. In the Old Testament we read of how God threatened His people with chastisement and at times unleashed it upon them and allowed them to fall when the chosen people were in danger of deviating from the Law. These threats and punishments caused the people to reconsider their life and move away from the danger. "Thy own wickedness shall reprove thee, and thy apostasy shall rebuke thee," says the prophet Jeremiah to the people of his time (Jer. 2:19). St. Paul confirms this way of thinking when he writes, "My son, neglect not the discipline of the Lord, for whom the Lord loves He chastises...now all discipline seems for the present to be a matter not for joy but for grief; but afterwards it yields the most peaceful fruit of justice to those who have been exercised by it" (Heb. 12:5-6, 11). And in his Second

Epistle to the Corinthians, Paul rejoices that he has saddened them for the good of their souls (2 Cor. 7:8ff). Every threat of chastisement and even the chastisement itself is a call from the infinite love of God to sinful humanity. As Our Lady said at Fatima on July 13, 1917: "If men do not listen to my words Russia will spread her errors...promoting further wars and persecutions... The good will be martyred; the Holy Father will suffer much and various nations will be annihilated."

To say this is not to set up among men a psychosis of pain but to call us to listen to the counsel that comes from the loving heart of Mary that *men may know they can be saved.*

Truly, neither did Christ preach a doctrine of pain but in His redeeming love for men He wished that they *would ponder the gravity of His decision* when He affirmed "but except you do penance you shall all likewise perish." (Lk. 13:5) Neither the Message of Fatima nor the message of the Gospel can be called a doctrine of pain. *The message is one of hope and of joy* so that according to the wise plan of God, there will be achieved that of which Our Lady was thinking when She said, "In the end my Immaculate Heart will triumph."

The task of The Blue Army of Our Lady of Fatima 3 consists in making known to the whole world the Message of Fatima, by all the means at its disposal so that men of all nations will realize it in their personal lives. In a word this message asks for nothing more than that which the Church recommends to her children with pressing urgency. The Apostolate of The Blue Army of Our Lady of Fatima does not address itself to an elite class. Its practices are contained in those *duties of the Christian which are rooted in the Gospel.*

Again to quote Pope Pius XI's encyclical on Atheistic Communism:

"As in all the stormy periods of the history of the Church, the fundamental remedy today lies in a sincere renewal of private and public life according to the principles of the Gospel by all those who belong to the Fold of Christ, that they may be in truth the salt of the earth to preserve human society from total corruption."

Still, if anyone asks, "Why the Blue Army? Why this 4 special form of propaganda for things which the Church daily asks from the consciences of each one?" we ask in return "Why did the Mother of God come especially to Fatima to ask for this?"

Why? Because humanity so often turns a deaf ear to the voice of the Church, God sends His Immaculate Mother *to remind men in an extraordinary way of these obligations* which the Church preaches sometimes in vain.

In this way God reminds men of the Church which He Himself instituted among us as a propagator and defender of the Truth.

No more than Fatima has the Blue Army any private objective of its own: it is simply at the service of the Church. The reason of its existence is to try by means of the message and the apparitions to give to the Church new hearers of her word and proselytes especially in those places where she is not listened to and at times despised.

As the Message of Fatima *is addressed to all men without exception,* independently of the fact that they already belong or do not belong to an ecclesiastical organization, so the Blue Army is open to all.

5   To already belong to any Marian Association does not justify a refusal to join the Blue Army. Practically speaking this is not a movement apart from others but rather an appeal to all to establish in the life of the individual and in the life of society a Christian foundation built on the message of Mary.

There is no doubt but that each organization and movement has its own specific end, its own method, but all are directed towards the same final end. In harmony with the Message of Fatima the Blue Army seeks with this special motive to bring the individual in these organizations to work with double application. If, in a last analysis, all the members of all Catholic associations, spurred on by the Message of Fatima, pray more than they ever did before, do penance for the sins of the world and consecrate themselves to the Immaculate Heart of Mary, it follows logically that each and every form of the Apostolate of the laity, animated by this spiritual renewal, will be of inestimable profit not only in the personal sanctification of the individual associated but also in the accumulated work of the entire Apostolate. To each member will be given that broad Catholic outlook which must always be the *sine qua non* (indispensable condition) of spiritual fecundity.

It would be a lamentable error to see in the Blue Army nothing more than a tributary stream to other Marian movements. Not at all. These Marian movements should be the first to seek to accept, understand and realize the Message of the Queen of Heaven. They should form the vanguard of the Army of "the Conquerer of all the battles of God," who in Fatima called us all to fight against the powers of darkness, comforting us with the promise that Her Immaculate Heart would triumph in the end.

Those who join The Blue Army of Our Lady of Fatima have one sole obligation—to make every effort in all seriousness to fulfill the obligation which they sign. (There is no question of being obliged under sin.)

Only when one is thoroughly acquainted with the content and completely possessed with the spirit of the message may one proceed to the further obligation of doing all in one's power to secure that the greatest possible number of one's friends and acquaintances be ready to fulfill the conditions laid down by Our Lady for the realization of Her promises.

Needless to say, neither the organization of collaborators nor the active Apostolate of the movement may be attempted in any place *without the express permission of the ecclesiastical authority.* Any Catholic animated with the Marian spirit knows that an apostolate alienated from ecclesiastical authority, or in opposition to it, is a silly illusion.

6

Without the seal of obedience there can be no authentic apostolate.

As we all know, in order that Unity (of Eastern and Western Christianity) be realized in a lasting way, *the West must prepare for and proceed to an authentic spiritual renovation.* We must decide once and for all to return to the Cross of Christ. It was at the foot of the Cross that Mary became our Mother. So the Message of Fatima is the splendid offer and the strong incentive to this renovation.

"The conversion of the West," says Archbishop Fulton J. Sheen, "is the anterior condition for the conversion of the East." To this all Christians of the world are called, *even little children.* In fact Christ Himself called, embraced and blessed the little children and Mary in Her apparitions spoke again and again to children and called them to Her service. In some countries the movement provides formulas of dedication especially for children, adapted to their mentality, and from time to time they receive their own circular letters. The prayer of a child pierces the clouds. At this hour of the world's history when we hear such expressions as "Mothers who have no time," "increasing critical conditions for children and young people," *the little ones are surely in great danger.* However, "their angels in heaven always see the face of my Father who is in heaven" (Mt. 18:10). *Does God will to save this generation by children?* "But the foolish things of the world hath God chosen, that He may confound the wise; and the weak things of the world hath God chosen, that He may confound the strong" (I Cor. 1:27-28). Our Lord also said to the grown-ups "Amen, I say to you, unless you are converted, and become as little children, you shall not enter the kingdom of heaven." (Mt. 18:3)

The Blue Army of Our Lady of Fatima calls to each and all, great and small, rich and poor, cultured and ignorant. In truth *"our wrestling is not against flesh and blood,* but against principalities and powers, against the rulers of the world of this darkness, against the spirits of wickedness in the high places" (Eph. 6:12). In this combat every man of good will is engaged. And peace belongs to those who are united in the fight.

To strengthen ever more and more "the peace of Christ in the kingdom of Christ," being the first and greatest intention of its Apostolate, The Blue Army of Our Lady of Fatima takes as its motto those words of Pius XI in his encyclical "Divini Redemptoris" of March 19, 1937:

"When our country is attacked, all that is not strictly necessary for and immediately directed towards the common defense, takes second place. So now it is our duty to desist from work, however good and beautiful it may be, *confronted as we are with the vital necessity of saving the very foundations of our Faith and Christian culture."*

I am sure that we all agree that we have arrived at a very definite crossroads in the history of the world. The future is in the balance. Today more than ever before that verse of Scripture is verified, "They arise, the kings of the earth, princes plot against the Lord and His anointed" (Ps. 2:2). The powers of darkness in an apocalyptic effort advance in their united strength *to try to blot out the name of God from the entire world.*

It is into this scene, so full of foreboding, that Our Lady comes, appearing in the Cova da Iria to bring us Her celestial message.

The Blue Army is born in the light of Fatima that the message may be made known to the whole world.

Again let us listen to the words of Pope Pius XI in the encyclical on Atheistic Communism:

"When the Apostles asked the Savior why they had been unable to drive the evil spirit from a demoniac, Our Lord answered: "This kind is not cast out but by prayer and fasting." So, too, the evil which today torments humanity can be conquered only by a world-wide holy crusade of prayer and penance... Let them implore also the powerful intercession of the Immaculate Virgin who, having crushed the head of the serpent of old, remains the sure protectress and invincible Help of Christians."

The Church is essentially an Army, in pacific march to the Fatherland of Heaven—an army in which every one of us is enlisted.

9

The Blue Army is to remind us that every single one of us is needed, that victory may be ours; that there is a common front where each has his place, from the least fervent to the most zealous and exacting member of Catholic Action and all Apostolic Movements.

It comes to remind us and convince us in a practical way that, with Mary the Mother of God and our Mother, the Holy Church once again will triumph and in her and with her will triumph Christ, Our Lord.

The Blue Army of Our Lady would alert us now to the great supernatural realities—eternal life, redemption, reparation, penance, prayer, faithful discharge of our daily duty and the perfect fulfillment of the Law of God—these will be the powerful contribution to the carrying out of the Message of Fatima—the conversion of the communistic world, the construction of that long-desired peace and the triumph of the Immaculate Heart of Mary.

- II -
ADDRESS
TO BLUE ARMY LEADERS

---

1) Leadership Responsibilities - 2) Dawn of New Times

At a meeting of the international leaders of the Blue Army at Fatima in 1978, Bishop Venancio felt forced to resign as International President because of ill health. On this occasion His Excellency delivered the following statement:

Let us beg Our Lord and Savior that this meeting of Mary's children, who have come from all the world (to the Blue Army's International Center at Fatima) may be truly successful in such manner that each may humbly recognize how to leave one post or to occupy another if the glory of God and the service of the Church, of the Most Blessed Virgin, and the salvation of souls, demand it. May each of us recall the words of Jesus: "The Son of Man did not come to be served but to serve." To serve God is to reign according to the words of the Liturgy.

This house of our meeting, the International Center of Our Lady's Blue Army has been "prophetically" named Domus Pacis, *House of Peace. And we know that peace is a gift of heaven which we beg of God each day in the Eucharistic Liturgy. This is true. Let us not forget it.*

But we must also remember that not all peace comes from God. Christ Himself made this distinction. There is a peace given by Christ. That is the true peace. And there is another peace, a false peace, given by the world, by human accommodation..

May each of us on reflection have the courage to take decisions not according to personal interest, or guided by human points of view, but although ever conscious of charity and justice, may we choose only what is for the greater glory of God.

1

327

Are we not soldiers?

What do I say?

We are, *in the Church,* those responsible for the glorious Blue Army of Our Lady of Fatima...its "condottieri" *(leaders).*

Let us then behave as such! Let us act as commanders-in-chief of this army which must be led to victory in such a way that, as soon as possible, we can see the triumph of the Immaculate Heart of Mary and the definitive victory of the Lamb of God. "We have become a spectacle for God before angels and before men." (1 Cor. 4:9)

I hear some among you murmuring perhaps in your hearts: "But after all, who are we and what is our power?"

You are right.

We are indeed only poor instruments in the Hand of God! It is He Who conducts the history of the world and its destiny.

Let us then also be docile instruments (faithful to Grace) and God will triumph!

It seems that very dense waves of darkness have fallen upon the world and envelop us. This is true. And we do not know when it will all end...

*But if one looks well and knows how to read the signs of the times, there can be no doubt that already breaking through are the rays of the dawn...*the dawn of new times...

It is therefore in a climate of confidence, of hope, of faith, and of charity, that I invite you to work together without, on the one hand, losing sight of Christian prudence, and on the other of Christian strength, being leaders of valiant heart.

We thank Our Lady for a wonderful beginning and look forward to the promised triumph of Her Immaculate Heart.

2

Below: Leaders of the Blue Army in meeting at Fatima in July, 1968. Bishop Venancio is center, front row, and next to him (right) is Canon Jose Galamba de Oliveira, who for over 25 years was a member of the International Council.

- III -

DEATH BATTLE
OF THE DOVES

It happened in 1954, when the first Blue Army pilgrimage was going to Fatima for the laying of the cornerstone of the Blue Army's International Center.

Those 125 pilgrims heard this amazing story and so did many others on the ship, including two Cardinals, seventeen Bishops, sixty priests and as many nuns. Fr. John Loya wrote this account for SOUL Magazine in 1963:

I was the only Byzantine priest among the 125 persons going to Fatima. All of us in the group had conspicuous badges which read: BLUE ARMY PILGRIMAGE.

Two nuns from Detroit approached me and asked if I would request the pilgrims to pray for a Sister who was very ill in Detroit, and told me this extraordinary story:

Before the two nuns had left Detroit they had visited the Sister who was seriously ill and she told them: "When you are going to Europe you may meet the Blue Army. If you do, ask them to pray for me."

The Sisters had never heard of the Blue Army (which still was comparatively new in 1954) and they were very surprised to see this large pilgrimage on the ship going to Fatima for the laying of the cornerstone of their International Center. So they approached me and asked prayers for the sick Sister back home. And then they told me the rest of the story, which was still more amazing:

"I dreamed," the very ill Sister said, "that a blue dove was flying east to meet a white dove which was flying west. They were supposed to meet over the Black Sea. Suddenly a black dove with red breast appeared as though trying to prevent the meeting. The blue dove attacked it.

A fierce fight ensued, and finally the black dove fell to the sea. It was on the surface for some time. Then the blue dove descended with forceful speed and pierced its red breast. Immediately the black dove sank beneath the waves.''

Then from her sick bed, the Sister said that she dreamed that a Blue Army was going east and a Red Army was coming west. They met in terrible battle. It often seemed as though the Red Army would win. "But after a very long battle the Blue Army was victorious.''

Almost ten years have passed since these two nuns approached me on the ship and told me their story. At that time I was myself very "new" in the Blue Army.

But in the past decade, since the day I was present among the thousands at Fatima when the aged Bishop of Fatima blessed the cornerstone of the Blue Army International Center, I have seen much of the great battle that has ensued as the Blue Army expanded through the world to recruit millions from among Our Lady's children who would be willing to fulfill Her conditions for the conversion of Russia.

I have seen the battle come and go. I have seen the Blue Army itself, although backed by the Bishop of Fatima as THE Fatima Apostolate of the world, often brought to what seemed the edge of ruin. I have seen the suffering and sacrifice of many of its members. I and my own family have become so involved that much, if not most of our time (not spent in pastoral duties) is spent in promotion of the Blue Army.

Perhaps the meaning of that extraordinary dream... which revealed the existence of the Blue Army to two nuns who had never heard of it before...is now evident:

The white dove could represent Our Blessed Mother, the Immaculate Virgin. The black dove with red breast might be Satan and Communism. And if enough of Our Lady's children would join the Blue Army (as Padre Pio has positively said), then Our Lady would be enabled to convert Russia.

In reality the Blue Army is not fighting Communism. It is struggling to get Our Lady's children *to join with Her*. It is struggling to awaken the world to the Message of Fatima and to get enough persons to fulfill Our Lady's conditions for the Promise She Herself made: "If my requests are heard, Russia will be converted.''

The devil fights with all force to prevent the Blue Army from reaching its quota...from meeting with Our Lady over the heart of Russia (the Black Sea).

But little by little the number of those who sign the Blue Army Pledge increases. Now, in 1963, on August 28, just ten years after the Sister's dream and ten years after the laying of that cornerstone at Fatima, the Dean of the Sacred College of Cardinals (Cardinal Tisserant) will fly from Rome to dedicate the Russian Chapel in the newly-completed International Center of the Blue Army at Fatima. A few weeks later the second session of the Ecumenical Council will open, in an atmosphere of East-West unity which ten years ago seemed improbable.

Satan and the Blue Army have been, and continue to be, in mortal combat. We do not need visions to know this. It is a fact which we know both from our faith and from our experience.

Does the Blue Army have to make one last, tremendous effort? Will it seem that Russia is converted when the forces of Satan may suddenly decide to "play possum" and float on the surface?

Whatever the future holds, again we do not need to guess or conjecture. We have Our Lady's own promise: "In the end, my Immaculate Heart will triumph."

For many years I enjoyed wonderful physical health. Then suddenly I was stricken with a very painful ailment. I suddenly realized that this pain was something more I could give. I deserved it for my own sins and failings, but knew, too, that this could be my contribution to the battle.

And many, many, many other souls have had a similar experience.

This is something the average person doesn't know. Even if you, personally, have had a great cross in your life recently and — like the children of Fatima — had the grace to offer it up, you don't know how many others of Our Lady's children have had the same.

The leaders of the Blue Army (Msgr. Colgan and John Haffert) have suffered so much, physically and morally, that I sometimes wondered how they stood up under it. They have told me they have letters from many of their best members of the Blue Army with similar accounts.

Could this not be that final dive against the red breast of the Satanic dove, which has been floating on the surface of "co-existence?"

If not, then the final death-stroke against atheistic communism will nevertheless, I feel sure, be something similar.

But it will come. And each of us who has been touched by the Message of Fatima—each of us who has been privileged to become a member of Our Lady's Blue Army—should take courage and welcome with open arms any suffering which the good God may deem to send us. We are locked in a terrible battle. And even though victory may be assured to us, the battle rages now.

Fr. John Loya was pastor of St. Nicholas of Myra Church in Yonkers, N.Y. He was appointed the first national Byzantine chaplain of the Blue Army in the United States in 1955. He died on February 12, 1970, seven years after writing the above account.

Below: In his first audience with Blue Army leaders, Pope Paul VI is presented with a special plaque from all Blue Army members on the occasion of the dedication of the Blue Army Chapel for Russia at Fatima on August 28, 1963. As Fr. John Loya, Byzantine Chaplain for the Blue Army in the U.S. makes the presentation, John Haffert (behind Fr. Loya) and Msgr. Colgan (above Fr. Loya) look on. On this occasion, Pope Paul VI said: "I bless you and all your members. I pray for you. Please pray for me."

TRAGICOMEDY IN FOUR ACTS

(Translated by Fr. Karl Patzelt, S.J., from article in October, 1967 issue of Science and Religion, *official propaganda magazine of the Communist Party of the Soviet Union, recognizing The Blue Army of Our Lady of Fatima as one of three principal deterrents to the success of the world atheist revolution.)*

The anti-Soviet crusade of the end of the twenties and the beginning of the thirties...anti-Comintern hysteria on the eve of the Second World War...the modern "democratic" anti-communistic apologetics of the "free world"... all these widely known phenomena have been constantly exposed and are being exposed in the pages of our press, the presses of socialistic countries, and in the western progressive publications. However, there are few who know that anti-communism, the idea of a crusade against the motherland of the October revolution, besides all the rest, are mixed into wonder working yeasts. And this is no accident. As emphasized in the theses of the report of the Central Committee of the Communist Party of the Soviet Union, "Fifty Years of the Great October Socialist Revolution", "imperialist ideology longs to inculcate individualism into the masses, taking them from politics, from solving basic social problems. It works upon lively prejudices and the vestiges of the past in people's minds."

A clear example of such speculation on religious prejudices is the tumult arising from the international Catholic reaction to the "last appearance of the Blessed

Virgin Mary to the people,'' which took place, if we are to believe the "seers,'' on the 13th day of every month from May to October, 1917, (the first coincidence!) near the Portuguese hamlet of Fatima.

True, at first this was, in general, a completely ordinary "miracle'' of which the history of Catholicism is rich (Lourdes, the visions of the first Jesuit, Ignatius Loyola, etc.) At Fatima, the Madonna floated to three young shepherds on a white cloud, and as happens in such cases, asked for penance, daily prayers and a collection of money for the building of a chapel in her honor at the place of the apparitions. This was the first version of the "Fatima miracle,'' appearing in the clerical and anti-clerical Portuguese press a few weeks before the great October Socialist revolution in our country.

But now, on one sixth of the globe the authority of exploiters is overthrown, interior and international counter-revolution is crushed, which is supported by the reactionary clergy of the whole world. A deep economic, social and cultural transformation is being achieved. Tens of millions of people are being liberated from the captivity of religious prejudices, are actively involved in the building up of a new and happy earthly life. The sermons from the pulpit no longer help. Means that are more forcefully active are needed.

Thus the idea was born, the dust of the middle ages having been hastily shaken from it, of a crusade against the atheistic Soviets, proclaimed by the "Holy Father'' Pius XI at the height of the world wide economic crises of 1929 to 1933, which gave rise to revolutionary circumstances. However, the idea of the return of the bolshevik apostates to the bosom of the Church by fire and sword evidently did not become popular.

And here the "thousand-year-old'' Reich comes to the fore, having overloaded itself with the "missionary'' burden....

It is the eve of the Second World War: Munich. All international counter-revolutionaries are holding their breath, are in anticipation: here it is, the long-awaited unification of the western world, now the sword of chastisement will be released on the heads of the Soviet unfortunates... it would not be bad on this occasion to bless the soldiers of the cross, for this heroic act for the glory of the faith. Yet here is the trouble: the people are spoiled, with one service of thanksgiving you do not go to hell...not these days...where are the days when not only adults, but children flocked to win back the tomb of the Lord from the infidels... Now we must think of something more clever...

Here (one more coincidence!) begins the second act of the Fatima farce. In 1939, Lucy dos Santos, the only one of the three shepherds still living, who for 32 years now, at the insistence of her bishop, has been Sr. Maria of the Carmelite Monastery, gave him the shocking news of the "secret in two parts," the last revelation of the Virgin Mary, supposedly heard by her, a 10-year-old shepherdess, on October 13, 1917. Lucy dos Santos, however, only disclosed the first half of the revelation of the Virgin Mary.

"To prevent a new war," the Holy Virgin revealed, "I will come to request the consecration of Russia to my Immaculate Heart, and for prayers of expiation. If my word is not heard, if offenses against God are not stopped, Russia will spread her errors throughout the world, bringing war and persecution of the Church....But in the end my Immaculate Heart will triumph, Russia will be converted to the true faith and a time of peace will reign upon earth."

The publication of this "revelation" came after three years, in 1942 (the third coincidence!) when the international counter-revolution, already delayed, was celebrating in thanksgiving over the close victory over the atheistic bolsheviks... Everyone knows how this fared. As is mentioned in the theses of the Central Committee of the Communist Party of the Soviet Union..."the outcome of the great war for the fatherland of the Soviet Union shows most convincingly, that there is no power in the world which can cut short socialism, which can bring the people to their knees, the people true to the concept of Marx-Leninism, loyal to the socialistic homeland, and solid around the Lenin Party. This outcome is an ominous warning for the imperialistic aggressors and is a stern and unforgettable lesson of history."

So nothing came of the crusade, although "Our Lady of Fatima" blessed it. This idea, as well as the idea of the war, was eventually compromised in the eyes of all people of good will, including masses of believers. On the other hand, the most popular idea in modern times is the dream of peace and the effort to attain it.

But here begins the third act of our tragicomedy. In 1946 the "hot" war ended and the cold war began. Then *Abbot Colgan*, director of the Washington Catholic Institute "Ave Maria" and *John Haffert* founded a formally religious, but actually political anti-soviet organization under the pretentious title of the "Blue Army of the Virgin Mary."

However, differing from the crusade sermons of their predecessors in anti-sovietism, the fathers of the new "missionary" army count not on a "holy" war but on "the renewal of the world" — on the cold war. In the program of the new organization this task is set: "to attain the spiritual renewal of the modern world, by means of a total rejection of the materialistic and worldly spirit" and "in this way to deal defeat to atheistic communism," realizing thus the "promise of the Virgin Mary of the conversion of Russia to the true faith."

The seed left upon the rich soil of religious fanaticism, by anti-soviet strategy, of a peaceful offensive, germinated abundantly. Now the "Blue Army" in the countries of the "free world" numbers 20 million "soldiers of the Virgin Mary" in their ranks, 7 million of them in the United States.

Three days and three nights under the burning noon-day sun, the icy night wind from the mountains and the heavy showers, hundreds of thousands of pilgrims, the majority made up of needy poor from the Latin countries, pushed, pressed and crawled miles along the dirty asphalt, staining it with their blood, just to hear the "holy" word of the Pope and kiss the "holy" stones of the basilica and the statue of "Our Lady of Fatima." Dozens of doctors and ambulances on duty around the clock were not able to rescue all the bleeding people who had fainted.

An immense asphalt field, covered with blood and dirt, more than 10 thousand wounded, such is the result of the terrible "march" organized by the "Fatima Crusaders" in May of this year.

But the nightmarish tragicomedy does not end with this. The second part of the mythical secret, which the Blessed Virgin "entrusted" to Lucy Mary has not been revealed, but has been given to the last two Roman Popes.

The publication of the "second secret" apparently, is postponed for "a dark day." The quality of the unknown and the anticipation only heightens religious feeling. The future will show what turning point in history the Fathers of the Church will consider suitable for the next summons to the spirit of "Our Lady of Fatima."

By the efforts of the fanatics of the "Blue Army," the statue of "Our Lady of Fatima" in the original and in innumerable copies has been taken in pilgrimage throughout the world for 20 years, inspiring participants of every kind of anti-soviet, anti-communistic and neo-colonial provocation to works which are far from peaceful. The Korean war of 1950-53, the counter-revolutionary revolt in Hungary of 1956, the "dirty" war of many years against the people of Vietnam, the intervention against Cuba, the punitive campaign of the Portuguese fascists against the people of Angola and Mozambique are far from a full enumeration of the bloody enterprises which the Fatima crusaders encouraged and fought for.

But toward the end of the '50's and the beginning of the '60's the stake of the international counter-revolution on the cold war was finally and irrevocably defeated. It could not be otherwise. The fiasco of the cold war was predetermined by the unprecedented growth of the power of the October Revolution, the victory of its idea in a number of countries in Europe, Asia and America, the inculcation of a peaceful system of socialism, and the downfall of the imperialistic colonial system.

And here (notice the coincidence), ends the third and begins the fourth act of the Fatima mystery.

As has already been said, the Carmelite Sister Maria (in the world, Lucy dos Santos) in 1939 disclosed the secret to her bishop, and in 1942 he published only the "first part of the secret," which has already been quoted. In 1960 the favored nun finally informed the now deceased Pope John XXIII of the second part of the "revelation" of the Virgin Mary. He passed the secret on to the present Pontiff of the Catholic Church, Paul VI. However both considered it impossible to make it public.

In any case, from the Pontificate of John XXIII, coincident with the political fiasco of the cold war, in influential Catholic circles a certain shift to realism was noticed, a change of attitude from that which had been in progress for the last half century. In his final words for the closing session of the Vatican Council, on December 8, 1965, Pope Paul VI, summing up his work, put in the forefront the task of adaptation to this change (in Italian: "aggiornamento'') but along with this he emphasized the necessity of continuing the fight against "Godless atheism.'' Of course, in comparison with the words of his predecessors, Pius XI and Pius XII, the preachers of crusades against the soviet countries, such wording represents a certain deviation from the bug-bear of anti-communism, which set their teeth on edge, but it certainly was no renunciation by the Fathers of the Church of the realization of the program of "Our Lady of Fatima.''

To a large extent the propagation of the illusion about the abandonment of the Vatican from traditional anti-sovietism, from support of reactionaries and fascists in the whole world, was accomplished by the recent encyclical of Paul VI, "Populum Progressio,'' published on March 28 of this year. (See the article of M. Andreyev, "Meeting with Modernism,'' in "Science and Religion,'' No. 6, 1967.) The message of the Pope evoked the symphathetic response of progressive forces, especially in developing nations. However, the recent visit of the Author of the encyclical to Portugal for the solemnities on the occasion of the 50th anniversary of the "Apparitions of Our Lady of Fatima'' forced them to doubt seriously the sincerity of the "new course'' proclaimed by Paul VI.

Moreover, if the latest encyclical struck at anyone it would first of all be at the Portuguese mohicans of colonialism, tormentors of the people of Angola and Mozambique. But this did not prevent the "Holy Father'' from ascending to the tribune next to the basilica of Our Lady of Fatima and in the presence of a crowd of millions of pilgrims, to shake hands with the bloody dictator guests, and a half-dozen overthrown monarchs and pretenders to non-existent thrones.

True, in his speech to the gathered nobles, princes of the Church, journalists and a whole army of pilgrims, the head of the Catholic Church tried ashamedly to disassociate himself from the clearly anti-soviet nature of the Fatima myth and did not speak of a "crusade'' but of the "miracle of peace.'' Nonetheless, the participation of Paul VI in the "Fatima Jubilee'' was perceptibly extremely disapproved of by people all over the world, and even by some Catholic circles, especially in developing countries (for example: the declaration of the bishop of Mozambique).

But the reader would be interested to learn the concrete

circumstances of this propaganda-religious presentation, unprecedented in scale.

The idyllic village pasture, on which a half-century ago Lucy dos Santos's sheep grazed, and those of her two companions, who soon died of Spanish flu, is now asphalt from one end of the valley to the other, and can hold a whole army of pilgrims. In the place of the humble little chapel, erected after the first world war in honor of the "apparitions of the Blessed Virgin" now towers a huge basilica with adjoining sheltered tribunes for honored guests (one of these, by the way, almost collapsed on May 13, under the weight of hundreds of correspondents).

AMI PRESS BOOK LIST

B1	*Sex and the Mysteries
B1a	Sex and the Mysteries, paperback
B2	*Sign of Her Heart (Scapular)
B2a	Sign of Her Heart, paperback
B4	Catholic Truth for Youth
B7	*"There is Nothing More"
B7a	"There is Nothing More", paperback
B8	What Happened at Pontmain?
B9	Fatima and the Seven Sorrows
B12	I Knew Blessed Maximilian
B14	Blue is for Triumph
B24	The Scapular of Carmel
B26	*The Brother and I
B26a	The Brother and I, paperback
B29	Our Lady of the Eucharist
B30	She Promises Peace
B31	*Jacinta, Flower of Fatima
B33	In Garments All Red
B36	The Problem of Teenage Purity
B37	*A Heart for All (Russia's Conversion)
B40	*The World's Greatest Secret
B40a	The World's Greatest Secret, paperback
B43	*Am I Not Here? (Guadalupe)
B48	The Sorrowful and Immaculate Heart of Mary
B49	Meet the Witnesses
B53	The City of God (4 volumes)
B53a	The City of God (1 volume abridgement)
B57	The Angels: God-Given Companions and Servants
B62	Most Beautiful Story: Our Lady of Fatima Coloring Book
B64	Night of Love (All-Night Vigil guide)
B65	A City on a Mountain (Padre Pio)
B67	Ten Sermons on Mother of God w/Addendum
B101	The Passion of Our Lord
B102	Fatima: The Great Sign
B109	The Spirit and the Bride Say, "Come!"
B110	Dear Bishop! (Memoirs of author concerning Blue Army)

(Books marked with an * are hardcovers.)

All the books listed above and other titles are available from the Blue Army supply shop. Request ordering and price information by writing to:

The Blue Army
Mountain View Road
Washington, N.J. 07882